THE KNIGHTS OF BUSHIDO

THE KNIGHTS OF BUSHIDO

*A History of Japanese War Crimes
During World War II*

Lord Russell of Liverpool

Skyhorse Publishing

Skyhorse Publishing books may be purchased in bulk at special discounts for sales promotion, corporate gifts, fund-raising, or educational purposes. Special editions can also be created to specifications. For details, contact the Special Sales Department, Skyhorse Publishing, 307 West 36th Street, 11th Floor, New York, NY 10018 or info@skyhorsepublishing.com.

Skyhorse® and Skyhorse Publishing® are registered trademarks of Skyhorse Publishing, Inc.®, a Delaware corporation.

Visit our website at www.skyhorsepublishing.com

Library of Congress Cataloging-in-Publication Data

Russell of Liverpool, Edward Frederick Langley Russell, Baron, 1895-1981.
 The knights of Bushido : a history of Japanese war crimes during World War II / Lord Russell of Liverpool.
       p. cm.
 Subtitle of the previous edition: A short history of Japanese war crimes.
 Includes index.
 ISBN 978-1-60239-145-1 (alk. paper)
 1. World War, 1939-1945–Atrocities–Asia. 2. Sino-Japanese War, 1937-1945–Atrocities. 3. War crimes–Japan. 4. Japan–Armed Forces–History. I. Title.

D804.J3R8 2008
940.54'050952–dc22

                                    2007052801

10 9 8 7 6 5 4 3

Printed in the United States of America

PREFACE

EVER since my short history of Nazi war crimes, *The Scourge of The Swastika*, was published I have been approached by many people to write a companion volume on Japanese war crimes.

This book is the result of those requests.

Like its predecessor, it has been compiled from evidence given and documents produced at various war crimes trials, and from affidavits and statements made by eyewitnesses of such crimes to war crime investigation commissions set up after the War by the Allies to bring the criminals to justice.

I regret that it has been necessary to include so much that is unpleasant, but it would have been impossible to have done otherwise without, at the same time, failing to achieve the whole aim of the book, namely to give a concise but comprehensive account of Japanese war crimes. Nevertheless, for every revolting incident which has been described, a hundred have been omitted.

ACKNOWLEDGMENTS

I SHOULD like to express my thanks to the following:

To the Rt. Hon. Antony Head, CBE, MC, MP, formerly Secretary of State for War, for arranging for me to have access to the proceedings of Japanese war crime trials:

To Sir Frederick Gentle, QC, Judge Advocate General of the Forces, and his Registrar, for placing these proceedings at my disposal.

To Sir Arthur Comyns Carr, QC, Mr. C. S. A. Dobson, Librarian to the House of Lords, and his Assistants, and Mr. A. D. Wilson, Librarian to the Foreign Office, for providing me with copies of the shorthand transcript of the proceedings of the International Military Tribunal, Far East.

To the Director of the Imperial War Museum for placing a number of photographs at my disposal.

To Leo Rawlings, for allowing me to reproduce some of the graphic paintings he produced while a prisoner of war in Japanese hands.

To the Editor, *Picture Post*, for access to his files; and to the following, who have placed at my disposal the proceedings of war crime trials, diaries, reports and other documents: Major-General E. C. O. Morphy, Major-General F. N. Tottenham, Colonel L. R. S. MacFarlane, OBE, MD, Colonel C. W. Maisey, OBE, Lieutenant-Colonel M. B. Allsebrook, DSO, MC, Lieutenant-Colonel H. S. Flower, OBE, Wing Commander C. Pitts, Major E. N. Hebden, Major R. Lucas, Major B. Peacock, Squadron Leader M. C. Mainprice. Mesdames Carvell, Deacon, and Wemyss and Messrs. I. T. A. Atkins, MBE, K. A. Attiwill, MC, G. Gordon Barnes, P. Bartram, L. Beswick, J. B. Charlton, H. R. Cheeseman, CMG, A. Chettle, E. J. Coffey, L. G. Coleman, C. E. Collinge, CBE, R. T. Cooke, G. Craig, E.

ACKNOWLEDGEMENTS

Davies, F. G. Davis, J. P. Fisher, F. Alistair Forbes, MB, ch.B, J. A. Foster, F. W. Fox, R. L. N. Harward, K. E. W. Hislop, N. D. Kerr, H E. Kingdon, R. A. Lever, L. S. Millsom, A. J. Neville, R. Plummer, P. E. F. Routhey, J. C. Sharp, A. H. Taylor, V. G. Underwood, Frederick W. Ward, R. J. M. Watson, Graham Williams, J. H. Woodbridge, A. R. H. Wooster.

CONTENTS

ILLUSTRATIONS

Between pages 144 and 145

ILLUSTRATIONS

Javanese labourers bayoneted by the retreating Japanese
(*U.S. Army Photograph*)

Cave No. 3 in Tuba, Benguet, Philippines (*U.S. Army Photograph*)

Mr. A. Raven, at seventy the oldest prisoner in Stanley Gaol, Hong Kong (*Admiralty Photograph*)

General Hideki Tojo (*Exclusive News Agency*)

The seven accused at the 'Chinese Massacre Trial'

Prisoner of war Christmas card

xii

NEW INTRODUCTION

WHEN I was a schoolboy in 1950s Glasgow, the manager of the Western Baths, where I swam, was a taciturn chap called Jamieson. We often wondered why he was so sour, and someone said that he had been a prisoner of the Japanese during the war; they had knocked out his teeth, but he himself never talked about it. There were, as this classic book shows, tens of thousands of such men.

In 1942, 90,000 British Indian and Australian soldiers had surrendered at Singapore, after their commander, Sir A. E. Percival, had been outwitted (the authorities had not expected a Japanese attack from the land; many Japanese even arrived by bicycle). There were thousands of others, taken when a nearly defenceless Hong Kong fell, and when the Japanese swept into the Dutch East Indies and the American-run Philippines. A horrible few years followed. The men—even generals and former governors—were humiliated, beaten, starved. They were even forced to work on Japanese military projects (Canadians worked in the shipyards, and, at the very end, even in the mines) and on the notorious killer-railway projects through the jungles of South-East Asia.

No doubt there were some romantic episodes of collaboration, as in *The Bridge over the River Kwai*, but such episodes seem to have been few and far between, as the men's memories of Japanese captivity are hellish. Another old ex-prisoner in my boyhood years just said that when they all heard that The Bomb had been dropped, they cheered: it was retribution for what so many tens of thousands had suffered under the Japanese occupation of South-East Asia, Indonesia, and a large part of China. Even now, bitter old men note, in rage, the prosperity of post-war Japan.

Lord Russell of Liverpool's book *The Knights of Bushido* became a classic on the subject in the late 1950s, and followed an earlier classic, *The Scourge of the Swastika*, on the misdeeds of the Nazis. The stories in this book are horrible—starvation, torture, disease, cannibalism. The well-chosen illustrations, and especially the drawings executed by Leo Rawlings, show it all.

At least the Germans' treatment of prisoners of war was, in the main, correct, in the sense that the Geneva Convention was observed (this did not apply with the Soviet Union). In 1929, when the Convention was re-enacted, Japan did not ratify it. The military, then rising in power, refused to follow up on what the diplomats had prepared (Lord Russell does not point this out). Why? Probably because they expected every man to fight to the death; maybe they also did not wish to be bound by tiresome international obligations once they invaded China, as they did two years later. Their problem was, of course, that if they treated Chinese prisoners with proper humanity, they might lose control: as the atrocities committed during their invasion, particularly at Nanking, showed, the Geneva Convention would have got in the way.

When war broke out with the United States and Great Britain late in 1941, the Japanese indicated rather vaguely that they would behave in accordance with the spirit of the Convention. Notoriously, they did not, and some three thousand war criminals were put on trial (a very lengthy process because of the difficulties of proper interpretation between languages as different as Japanese and English). Many were sentenced to death, others to terms of imprisonment. A few were released, as it could be shown that they had behaved humanely, warned prisoners of an impending execution, or otherwise done what they could to help. But the general impression is of a talented people, led by maniacs, who knew perfectly well that the war would end in disaster but who were determined to keep their honour intact to the final gruesome, suicidal point. Even at the very end, when it came to recognition of common sense, and surrender, the Emperor's very vocabulary—given the peculiarities the language—did not embrace such a phrase as 'we have been defeated': he could only say that the war had not necessarily turned out to Japan's advantage.

The post-war years, at any rate after the ravages of the later 1940s, certainly did turn out towards Japan's advantage, and the country made an astounding recovery. In reputation, she is back to where she stood in, say, 1925—he vastly admired puller-up-of-self-by-bootstraps which attracted such attention, especially in 1904, when she defeated a Great Power, Russia, in a full-scale modern war (she was the first non-European power to achieve this). The Anglo-Saxon world in particular was interested in the reasons for this extraordinary success, and Japanese education was much studied.

It is as well to put Japan's, as Germany's, success in perspective: for in 1945 much of the Old World was simply wiped out. Both countries learned, and learned well, from a new start. How far this was necessary, is shown in Lord Russell's pages— a gruesome story, well documented and well told.

Norman Stone, 2002

THE KNIGHTS OF BUSHIDO

AFTER having been subjected to all the standard forms of torture they were taken, one at a time, marched blindfold for a considerable distance and then halted. The victim then heard voices and marching feet, the sound of a squad halting and loading their rifles as a firing party would.

A Japanese officer approached the American pilot and said, 'We are the Knights of Bushido, of the Order of the Rising Sun. We do not execute at sunset, but at sunrise.'

The pilot was then marched back to his cell, and told that unless he talked before dawn he would be executed.

(Extract from evidence
given before the
International Military
Tribunal for the Far East)

CHAPTER I

FROM MUKDEN TO PEARL HARBOUR

THE object of this introductory chapter is to trace briefly the struggle for political power in Japan during the ten years immediately preceding the attack on Pearl Harbour, to outline the development of Japanese foreign policy, describe the preparations made for an aggressive war and the roles which some of Japan's 'major war criminals' played in these events.

During those fateful years, step by step, the Army gained the ascendancy. Though it met with temporary setbacks from time to time, it was able eventually to ride roughshod over both Cabinet and Diet whiie even the Emperor's advisers could not restrain the military faction.

It is ironical that two admirable principles of Japanese conduct dating, according to Japanese historians, from the time of the foundation of the Empire of Japan over 2600 years ago, should have been responsible for the militaristic expansionist policy of Japan in the twentieth century, but so it would appear. These are the principles of 'Hakko Ichiu' and 'Kodo'. The former meant simply, making the world one big family. The second meant that the first could be obtained solely through loyalty to the Emperor.

These two estimable concepts, harmless in themselves, have been exploited and misused, again and again, in recent times by those who most urged, in Japan, a policy of territorial expansion. Those who made military aggression the national policy of Japan turned it into a moral issue by invoking the names of Hakko Ichiu and Kodo.

Hakko Ichiu was the moral goal, and loyalty to the Emperor was the road which led to it.

Dr Okawa, who was one of the major war criminals originally brought before the Tokyo Tribunal, but was later

B

declared unfit to stand his trial because of insanity, published a book in 1924 on the very same subject. His argument was that as Japan had been the first State in existence it was her Divine Mission to rule the world, and during the years immediately following the publication of this book he frequently lectured to students at Japanese Military and Staff Colleges on the importance of having a nationalist spirit with a capital 'N'.

The Sino-Japanese War of 1931–45 cannot be understood without some knowledge of the events which occurred in Japan prior to its outbreak culminating in the infamous 'Mukden Incident'.[1]

By certain treaties and other agreements Japan had assumed an important and unusual position in Manchuria.

She governed the Leased Territory with practically full rights of sovereignty. Through the South Manchurian Railway she administered the railway areas including several towns and large sections of such populous cities as Mukden and Changchun; and in these areas she controlled the police, taxation, education and public utilities. She maintained armed forces in many parts of the country; the Kwantung Army in the Leased Territory, Railway Guards in the railway areas and Consular Police throughout the various districts.

This very brief summary of the long list of Japan's rights in Manchuria shows clearly the exceptional character of the political, economic and legal relations created between her and China in Manchuria.

There is probably nowhere in the world an exact parallel to this situation, no example of a country enjoying in the territory of a neighbouring State such extensive administrative privileges. A situation of this kind could conceivably be maintained, without leading to incessant complications and disputes, if it were freely desired or accepted by both sides, and if it were the sign and embodiment of a well considered policy of close collaboration in the economic and political spheres. But, in the

[1] But see Chapter II: 'The China Incident', where it is explained that although there was armed conflict in 1931, a state of war did not exist between the two countries.

[2]

absence of such conditions, it could only lead to friction and conflict.[1]

There was, however, no such freely desired acceptance on both sides and Japan, no longer satisfied with the extensive rights which she already possessed, sought an enlargement of them which could only be acquired by military conquest.

This became known as the 'Positive Policy' towards China, and a number of political Societies, like the Black Dragon, and political writers like Dr Okawa, worked unceasingly for Japanese expansion. In his writings, Okawa maintained that the sole existence of the League of Nations was to 'preserve the status quo and further the domination of the world by the Anglo-Saxons . . . a war between East and West was inevitable. . . . Japan would strive to fulfil her predestined role of champion of Asia'.[2]

The 'Positive Policy', nevertheless, had its ups and downs, and when the Cabinet of Prime Minister Tanaka fell in 1929 the new Government resumed the 'Friendship Policy' which the new Foreign Minister, Baron Shidehara, always a thorn in the side of the military faction, had consistently favoured. This was based on goodwill and friendship in all dealings with China.

It was at this juncture that the Army and its political supporters decided to consolidate their position. Lieutenant-Colonel Hashimoto, who had recently returned from a three-year tour of duty as military attaché in Istanbul, had definite ideas on 'how to reform Japan'.[3]

He called a meeting at the Tokyo Army Club of newly graduated officers from the Staff College and with them founded the 'Sakura-Kai', or Cherry Society, whose aim was to bring about national reorganization, by armed force if necessary, in order amongst other things to effect a settlement of the 'Manchurian problem'.

[1] Extract from *Report* of the Lytton Commission.
[2] *Asia, Europe and Japan*, 1925.
[3] *The Road to the Reconstruction of the World.*

[3]

Manchuria, the members of the Society maintained, was Japan's life-line. It should be under absolute Japanese control and become a land founded on the 'Kingly Way'.

This 'Kingly Way' was the concept of Kodo and was thus described by Hashimoto in one of his books:[1]

> It is necessary to have politics, economics, culture, national defence and everything else, all focused on one being, the Emperor, and the whole force of the nation concentrated and displayed from a single point . . . reorganized according to the principle of oneness in the Imperial Way. This system is the strongest and the grandest of all . . . there is no nation that can compare with our national blood solidarity[2] which makes possible a unification like ours with the Emperor in the centre.

After Manchuria had been set up in its 'Kingly Way' Japan could then assume leadership of the Asian peoples.

Two months after the formation of the Cherry Society the Japanese Prime Minister, Hamaguchi, was assassinated, though it took him nine months to succumb from his wounds, but this did not further the designs of Hashimoto and his friends as Foreign Secretary Shidehara became Prime Minister in Hamaguchi's place, and Shidehara had been a long standing opponent of the policy of warlike aggression.

But more trouble was not far off. A plot hatched by Okawa and Hashimoto to bring about the fall of the Government and the creation of a military Cabinet under martial law, only failed because Ugaki, the War Minister, who had been selected by the conspirators as the new Prime Minister, would have nothing to do with the projected *coup d'état*. Consequently, the 'March Incident', as it was called, came to naught, but the struggle between the Government and the Army was not to end there.

Nevertheless, the incident hastened the Government's fall; and another took its place under a new Prime Minister, Wakatsuki, but as Shidehara remained in the post of

[1] *The Inevitability of Renovation.*
[2] Strangely reminiscent of Hitler.

Foreign Secretary the military faction could make little headway.

The new Cabinet pursued a policy of retrenchment while Okawa and Hashimoto continued to whip up resistance to it, and to advocate the occupation of Manchuria by force. The Black Dragon Society held mass meetings, there was a crescendo of propaganda, and it was then that the idea of the 'Mukden Incident' was conceived.

Meanwhile, a conference between Shigemitzu[1] and the Finance Minister of the Republic of China had been arranged to open in Mukden on 20th September 1931 in an attempt to settle 'all outstanding differences between Japan and Marshal Chang Hsueh-Liang'. But it was destined never to assemble for on the night of 18th September the 'Mukden Incident' took place.

At about 9 p.m. a Chinese officer named Lin, belonging to the 7th Chinese Brigade and stationed in Mukden Barracks, reported to his superiors that a train consisting of four coaches, but drawn by an unusual looking engine, had stopped on the railway line opposite the barracks. At precisely 10 p.m. a loud explosion was heard, followed by rifle fire. According to the Japanese version, which was proved later to be wholly untrue, a patrol was engaged on night operations on the railway track when an explosion occurred about two hundred yards behind them. On investigating, the patrol leader found that a portion of the track had been blown away. The patrol was then fired upon simultaneously from both flanks.

About 11.30 p.m. that same night, after receiving considerable reinforcements, the Japanese attacked the barracks, which were in complete quiet and blazing with electric light, employing artillery in the assault as well as machine-gun and rifle fire. Most of the Chinese soldiers got away but the Japanese claimed casualties of 320 Chinese killed and twenty captured and wounded. At the same time another Japanese

[1] See Chapter XV, page 297.

[5]

regiment attacked the walled city of Mukden, where no resistance was offered and the only casualties incurred were in a brush with the police of whom about seventy-five were killed.

At 7.30 a.m. on the following morning (19th September) the arsenal and aerodrome were captured. In this assault use was made of heavy guns which the senior staff officer at Mukden, Colonel Itagaki, later admitted had been secretly installed in the Japanese infantry compound a week before the 'Incident'.

Meanwhile, the Japanese Consul-General had been informed by telephone that an explosion had taken place on the South Manchurian Railway and that the presence of a member of the Consular Staff was required immediately at Special Service Headquarters. Arriving there, the representative, named Morishima, found Colonel Itagaki and Major Hanaya already present. Itagaki told Morishima that the Chinese had blown up the permanent way and that orders had been issued that appropriate military action should be taken. Morishima pressed for calm thinking and moderation. He was sure that the whole affair could be amicably settled.

Was the Consul-General, the colonel asked, questioning the right of the military commander to take what action he thought fit? Morishima said 'No', but remained obdurate; he was certain that the matter could be satisfactorily adjusted through the normal diplomatic channels.

At this point in the conference Major Hanaya, who had hitherto taken no part in the conversation, could contain himself no longer. Drawing his sword, the gallant major made a threatening pass at this tiresome civilian, who was doing his best to upset the whole applecart, and shouted that he would kill anyone who tried to interfere. The conference then ended.

During the night ceaseless attempts were made by Marshal Chang Hsueh-Liang's headquarters to get the Japanese Consul-General to persuade the Army to call off their attacks, but with no avail.

As no impression could be made on Colonel Itagaki, the Consul-General himself, on the morning of 19th September, cabled the Japanese Foreign Minister, Baron Shidehara, in the following terms:

> In view of the fact that it was proposed several times from the Chinese side that this matter be settled in a peaceful way I phoned staff officer Itagaki and said that since Japan and China had not yet formally entered into a state of war and, moreover, as China had declared that she would act absolutely upon the principle of non-resistance, it was necessary for us at this time to endeavour to prevent the aggravation of the 'incident' unnecessarily and I urged that the matter be handled through diplomatic channels, but the above mentioned staff officer replied that since the matter concerned the prestige of the State and the Army it was the Army's intention to see it through thoroughly.

The Government, however, took no action.

There is overwhelming evidence that the Mukden Incident was carefully planned by officers of the Army General Staff, officers of the Kwantung Army, members of the Cherry Society and others, with the object of affording a pretext for the occupation of Manchuria by that Army, and the setting up of a new State as a satellite of Japan. Although designed on a grander scale, it was similar to 'Operation Himmler' which was carried out by the SS nine years later at the radio station of Gleiwitz on the German-Polish frontier. The object of that exercise was to make it appear that a raid had been made on the station by the Poles.[1]

Several of those who were tried by the Tokyo Tribunal as major war criminals were implicated, and many of them have since admitted participation. Their defence was that the Japanese operations were in the nature of a reprisal, that the Chinese Army in superior force had made a surprise attack on the Japanese troops at Mukden, and that the latter had

---

[1] *The Scourge of the Swastika*, Chapter I.

then counter-attacked, routed the Chinese and captured the city.

In fact, the Japanese troops were never attacked on that night. The Chinese were taken completely by surprise. When their barracks were attacked the Chinese were all inside, unarmed, and the building was brilliantly lit up by electricity. There was virtually no resistance.

There is also ample evidence that the existence of this plot was quite well known in Japan, and known to the Japanese Consul-General in Mukden as early as 8th September. This well meaning official had received information that within a week 'a big incident would break out and that units of the Kwantung Army from Fushan would move to Mukden on the night of 18th September and carry out night exercises'.

Putting two and two together, the Consul-General got in touch with the Japanese War Minister Minami[1] who agreed to send a general, named Tatekawa, to Manchuria in order to 'stop the plot'. As General Tatekawa was himself one of the chief conspirators it was unlikely that he would take any effective action to circumvent his own plans. He arrived in Mukden at 1 p.m. on D day. He was met, in the absence on duty of the Army Commander General Honjo, by Colonel Itagaki and was taken straight to the Shinyokan Inn where they dined together. The general said that he was very tired after his trip, and declined to talk 'shop'.

After dinner Itagaki departed, and left the general behind, promising to call for him in the morning. According to his own story General Tatekawa had no intention whatsoever of calling off the plans which were to be put into operation that night, and had allowed himself to be decoyed to the inn. 'There,' he said later, 'I was entertained by Geisha girls while listening to the sound of firing in the distance. I retired later and slept soundly until called in the morning.'

So much for the 'Mukden Incident' which very shortly became the 'Manchurian Incident'.

[1] See Chapter XV, page 295.

The Army Commander returned to Mukden on 19th September and declared his intention of waging a 'punitive war'. Three days later China lodged a protest with the League of Nations, but on the Council receiving an assurance from the Japanese representative that all Japanese troops were in the course of being withdrawn to the 'railway zone' it adjourned for three weeks.

The assurance thus given by the Japanese Government was not at all popular with the Army, and the extremists began plotting again to overthrow the party system of government by a military *coup d'état*, and set up a new Government which would pursue a militarist policy.

The conspiracy, which later became known as the 'October Incident', was planned by Hashimoto and his fellow members of the Cherry Society. Unknown to themselves, however, they harboured among them a traitor who informed the police, and the War Minister had the leaders arrested.

The plot, therefore, came to nothing, but military operations continued in Manchuria in defiance of Cabinet policy and in less than two months the Prime Minister, realizing that his Cabinet had no hold over the Army, resigned. He and his Cabinet had tried hard to limit, if not to suppress, the 'Manchurian Incident' but they found that they were no match for the Army.

As the Tokyo Tribunal stated in its judgment, 'the Army had achieved its goal of a war of conquest in Manchuria and had shown itself more powerful than the Japanese Cabinet.'

The next Government, with Inukai at its head, fared no better. The new Prime Minister even opened up negotiations with Generalissimo Chiang Kai-Shek but they had to be abandoned when their existence came to the knowledge of Mori, the leader of a powerful pro-military faction within the Prime Minister's own political party.

By this time a new bid was being made by Okawa and Hashimoto to get rid of democratic government in Japan, this time for good. Neither of them made any secret of their aims. 'Democratic government is incompatible with the prin-

ciples upon which the Empire was founded,' wrote Hashimoto, and a new society was formed by Okawa 'to develop
nationalism, to inspire the Japanese to the leadership of East
Asia, and to crush the existing political parties'.

In May 1932 the Prime Minister made a speech in which
he condemned fascism and defended democracy. Seven days
later he was dead, murdered in his official residence by a
party of naval officers. Assassination was fast becoming an
occupational hazard for Japanese Prime Ministers.

So at last the Army got its way. The new coalition
Government, which was formed after the Prime Minister's
assassination, decided that Manchukuo should be developed
economically and industrially, but under Japanese domination.

Meanwhile, the Council of the League of Nations, after
their three weeks adjournment, discussed the Japanese
operations in Manchuria, and appointed a Commission under
the Earl of Lytton to investigate them.

The Lytton Commission duly reported, and the League
of Nations expressed strong disapproval of Japanese action.
This resulted in Japan leaving the League and preparations
for war against the Soviet Union were set on foot.

The decision to withdraw from the League of Nations was
of great significance. It will be remembered that Okawa had
said that the League was purely the instrument of Anglo-
Saxon supremacy.[1] Now the Japanese would be able to fulfil
their sublime mission, to be the lords and masters of Eastern
Asia.

Hakko Ichiu and Kodo came into their own again. The
path to follow was 'the way of the Emperor' and anyone who
stood in the Emperor's way was the enemy of the Army, for
the Army was the Emperor's.

Thus spoke Araki[2] in 1933 when he was War Minister,
and similar words were soon to be uttered by another leader

[1] See page 3.
[2] Tried at Tokyo by the International Military Tribunal (IMT) for the
Far East. See Chapter XV.

in another country. The doctrine of the Herrenvolk, or 'Master Race', was also 'made in Germany'.

Manchuria was to be only the beginning, the whole Chinese Empire was to become subservient to Japan. Then, in quick succession, would follow French Indo-China, Malaya, the Dutch East Indies and the Philippines. India would have got rid of British rule a little earlier than she did, but would have acquired the Japanese in its place, not a very beneficial exchange. Finally Australia and New Zealand would be annexed.

That was the long and the short of it. Now that Japan had left the League the way seemed more clear. At any rate there were fewer obstacles.

During the next two or three years preparations continued apace under a cloak of deception. While Hirota, the new Foreign Secretary, was denying that Japan's policy had any aggressive intentions, the Army went on with its plans for offensive action, and those who tried to hinder it were dealt with in the usual way. Ministers, generals or admirals who were suspected of not being wholeheartedly behind the Army's policy were driven from office by blackmail, or still more effectually removed by assassination.

In 1936 there was an insurrection by a number of young Japanese officers and over a thousand men. They seized all the Government buildings, assassinated two ministers and attempted to murder the Prime Minister.

Now the grip began to tighten. As in Hitler's Germany, when he was taking steps to hold the Third Reich in the 'hollow of his hand', censorship began to rear its ugly head. The freedom of the Press was virtually stifled, newspapers became little more than organs of Government propaganda, and the police were given far reaching powers for the control of any individual expression of opinion.

In the same year an important statement of national policy was made by the Cabinet. It expressed unequivocally the aims of Japanese foreign policy and it has been described,[1]

[1] See Proceedings of the IMT, Far East, 4th November 1948, page 48,560.

without exaggeration, as the 'cornerstone in the whole edifice of Japanese preparations for war'. This policy could only be brought to a successful conclusion by a complete organization and mobilization. The entire nation would have to be put on a war footing and no secret was made of the fact that, in terms of naval strength, they were thinking of a fleet powerful enough to secure command of the Western Pacific and, in terms of military strength, an army formidable enough to defeat any forces which the Soviet Union could deploy on its Eastern frontiers. Furthermore, all the industrial and financial resources of the country were to be mobilized for 'The Day'. Shipbuilding was subsidized, and by the end of 1936 Japan had the most up-to-date merchant fleet of its size in the whole world.

During these years a growing dissatisfaction with the restrictions imposed by the London Treaty was noticeable in Japan and was duly reported to his Government by the United States Ambassador. In 1934 the Japanese Government decided to terminate the Washington Treaty by the end of the year.

Twelve months later at the London Conference, which was attended by representatives from all five signatories to the Washington Treaty, a proposition was made by the United States delegation that there should be an all-round reduction of naval armaments. Japan would not agree, her delegation formally withdrew from the conference, and the way lay clear for the expansion of the Japanese Navy. Now the ships would be forthcoming, but to have command of the Western Pacific naval bases was also essential.

After World War I Japan had received, under the terms of the Treaty of Versailles, a mandate from the League of Nations for three groups of islands in the Pacific Ocean, the Marianas, the Marshalls and the Carolines.

The mandatory power was, in accordance with the terms of the League Covenant, under an obligation to prevent the establishment of military fortifications and naval bases on the islands.

For a number of years, however, in breach of their undertaking, the Japanese had been secretly erecting military and naval installations and fortifications there. By 1935 a naval air base was well under construction on the island of Saipan in the Marianas and only two hundred miles from the American island of Guam.

To maintain this secrecy restrictions on foreign travel to any of these island groups had been in force since 1933, and by the end of 1935 the restrictions had been greatly intensified. Another measure taken for security reasons was the appointment of serving naval officers to be administrative officials in the islands.

Nor were warlike preparations neglected in the fields of education and propaganda. Hashimoto, now retired from the Army and a colonel on the Reserve List, became the free-lance Goebbels of Japan and founded yet another Society. Once again Kodo and Hakko Ichiu were the guiding themes, and the twin aims of the Society, called the Greater Japan Young Men's Society, were totalitarianism and world domination. The young men of Japan were to be the framework upon which these aspirations could be built.

At the same time Hashimoto was preparing the Japanese civilian for war, and all his writings and speeches harped on the same subject, that the Japanese were a Master Race whose mission was 'to end the tyrannical rule and oppression of the white race', that the British Navy was one of the chief obstacles to the attainment of this objective, and that the answer to it was an invincible Air Force.

Hand in hand with this campaign by Hashimoto went the suppression of freedom of speech and the dissemination of propaganda. Laws were passed concerning every form of public expression.

There had always been a limited freedom of the Press in Japan. Now everything was subjected to censorship, the material for speeches, the manuscripts of plays, books and articles. These laws were strictly enforced by the police, and offenders were fined or imprisoned, and a special security

[13]

constabulary called the 'High Police' spied on all those opposing or suspected of opposing the Government in power.

In addition to all this the Army maintained a vigilance committee of its own. An author or a publisher who had incurred the displeasure of the military faction would be visited by members of this committee and left in no doubt of the unpleasant consequences which would befall him unless he saw the error of his ways.

The Army was gradually gaining the ascendancy and the opposition growing less. There was still some life, however, in the Seiyukai Party, who criticized the Government of Hirota for pandering to the Army and never ceased to warn the Japanese nation that if the soldiers were allowed to dominate the political scene, the Government would be constitutional in name only and the country would be run by a tyrannical cabal of army officers.

The Army itself fully realized what was at stake and took up the challenge when, two days later, the Hirota Cabinet fell. General Ugaki was offered the Imperial Mandate to form a new Cabinet but the Army, by preventing any general officer from accepting the appointment of War Minister, forced Ugaki to decline the offer. The Mandate was then given to General Hayashi who was *persona grata* with the military faction.

This attempt of the Seiyukai Party to stop the rot was the last serious one ever made. It had failed, but it had clearly shown that no Cabinet could remain in office without the Army's goodwill.

All these warlike preparations were not made solely for the conquest of China. War with the Soviet Union had for long been regarded in Japan as inevitable, and by 1937 it was realized that her aims might eventually bring her into conflict with the Western powers.

By the middle of 1937 Japan was irrevocably committed to the conquest of China,[1] but no one then realized the drain on Japanese strength which that campaign was to be. General

[1] Another 'Incident', called this time 'The China Incident'. See Chapter II.

Tojo who, at its outbreak, was Chief of Staff of the Kwantung Army, assumed that it would be a minor affair, an appetizer before the main dish which was to be a trial of strength with Russia. What they thought would be a 'blitzkrieg' lasted almost eight years.

An attempt was made before the year was out to obtain German intervention to bring the fighting in China to an end, but Germany's disapproval of Japan's action in China was still strong, and the war might have come to an end by way of a compromise peace in December 1935 had the Japanese Cabinet really wished it.

By this time even the Japanese General Staff had given up all hope of a quick victory. Negotiations were opened, but they were broken off, and in January 1938 the German Ambassador, being now convinced that Japan would win the war, urged his Cabinet to withdraw their opposition and accept the *fait accompli*. At the same time Japan offered Germany some promise of economic participation in the new China of the future under Japanese domination.

On 20th February 1938 Hitler announced German recognition of the State of Manchukuo and expressed a desire for a Japanese victory in China. This began a period of closer and more friendly relations between Germany and Japan which culminated years later in the Triple Alliance.

For a time the Japanese tried to have the best of both worlds, and pursued a policy of great duplicity. In return for Germany's recognition of the new state of affairs in China, Japan promised that whenever possible German interests in that country would be preferred to those of any other power, but such preference could not be given if it 'should threaten to cut off entirely the future participation of Great Britain and the United States in the economic development of China'.[1]

Notwithstanding this, relations between Japan and the Western powers gradually and persistently worsened. Attacks upon British and American citizens and property in China

[1] Evidence given before the IMT, Far East, Tokyo, 1947-8.

[15]

were frequent, and in 1937 an unprovoked attack was made on their naval forces in the Yangtse River. The continuation of these attacks, despite protests, during the first six months of 1938 led to the United States placing an embargo on the export to Japan of aircraft and all other war material.

From this time onwards Japan's relations with Germany became more and more significant. Although neither country had much in common with the other, Hitler's Germany, like Japan, was engaged in preparations for a war of aggression. Both had designs on the Soviet Union, as the Anti-Comintern Pact of 1936 testified. Japan wanted something more, a military alliance. Much preliminary groundwork had been done, since Hitler had come to power, by Colonel Oshima, the Japanese military attaché in Berlin.

By early 1938 it did appear that the Japanese Government had succeeded in convincing Hitler that Japan would emerge victorious from the 'China Incident', which is surprising having regard to the fact that some Japanese themselves were beginning to have doubts about it. But before the year ended serious misgivings had arisen in the Third Reich.

Nevertheless, a proposal for a general military alliance had been made in the spring by von Ribbentrop. This had been engineered entirely by the Japanese General Staff and the first draft of such an agreement had been drawn up between the German Foreign Secretary and Oshima, the Japanese military attaché, without the knowledge of his own Ambassador Togo.

A month later Oshima was appointed Ambassador in place of Togo. Thus the Army scored yet one more point in the game of soldiers versus politicians which had been going on in Japan for the past ten years, for this new appointment placed a soldier, who had the complete confidence of the Army, in a position hitherto always filled by a professional diplomat. It also marked one more step forward in the Army's preparation for war.

But there were even better things to come. Oshima, now

returned to Germany with enhanced status and enlarged prestige, settled down to the task of persuading the Germans that Japan really desired a tripartite military alliance with Germany and Italy. A suitable representative was needed to do the same thing in Italy. The Army was lucky again, for almost simultaneously with the appointment of Oshima, Shiratori became Japanese Ambassador in Rome. He had long been associated with the military faction. When he had been Chief of the Foreign Ministry's Information Department, five years earlier, he had shown himself to be a steadfast supporter of the Army's policy of conquest and expansion. He had been in the forefront of those who had called for Japan's withdrawal from the League of Nations, he was steeped in the Kodo tradition.

The stage was now set for the wooing of Germany to begin in earnest. On the day after the Munich agreement was concluded, the Japanese Minister of War sent a message to Hitler congratulating him on his handling of the Sudeten question in Czechoslovakia; 'may Germany's national fortunes continue to rise,' he wrote, 'and the friendship of the German and Japanese Armies, united on the Anti-Comintern front, be strengthened more than ever.'

Simultaneously the terms and scope of the Tripartite Alliance began to be discussed in detail. It became clear that Germany was thinking in terms of a military alliance directed, at least in part, against the Western powers. At that time her appreciation of the international situation was as follows. War with the Soviet Union was inevitable, Hungary and Czechoslovakia were potential allies, and Roumania would remain neutral. It would not be possible to drive a wedge between France and England, and if it came to war between those countries and Germany, the USA would probably give them financial but not military aid.

Meanwhile the relations between the Western powers and Japan had been gradually worsening, for in China attacks were still being made on British and American subjects and their property. The Governments of both countries made diplomatic protests, but without any satisfactory results. The military members of the Cabinet were more than ever anxious to strengthen Axis relations, but the others still wanted the new alliance to forestall rather than to precipitate war with the West.

When Hiranuma formed a new Cabinet in January 1939 his War Minister Itagaki openly supported the Oshima-Shiratori idea of a general military alliance against both the Soviet Union and the Western powers. That was what Germany also desired. The Emperor, however, wanted the Treaty to be directed solely against the Soviet Union, and certain members of the Cabinet held the same view.

This division of opinion led to a prolonged struggle which continued for several months until the downfall of the Government just before the outbreak of World War II. The protagonists on either side were Arita, the Foreign Secretary, and Itagaki, the War Minister.

While these wrangles were proceeding Hitler and Mussolini had reached agreement regarding a war in Europe when they met in Rome on 16th April 1939. They would proceed with their warlike preparations, and when a suitable opportunity should arise they would start a war against Great Britain and France.

As Japan was still holding back, von Ribbentrop warned the Japanese Ambassador that unless they decided, and decided quickly, to join a General Tripartite Alliance, Germany might feel obliged to come to some arrangement on her own with Soviet Russia.

The situation had become critical and the Japanese Prime Minister, short-circuiting his Ambassadors in Berlin and Rome, made a direct approach to Hitler and Mussolini to try and come to a compromise arrangement. It met with no success, however, and the deadlock continued.

The Army was out for a full alliance and Hashimoto, not unexpectedly, supported its views with some virulent anti-British propaganda. His constant theme was that Great Britain was Japan's foremost enemy. She was the chief opponent of Japanese aims in China, and the war there would never be ended until all those powers who supported Chiang Kai-Shek had been destroyed. He even advocated an attack on Great Britain, for with her departure from the international scene the Soviet Union would be left isolated. 'Japan,' Hashimoto wrote, must 'attack England; it would be easy to defeat the British', Hong Kong should be captured and the concessions at Shanghai and Tientsin should be seized. By means of a military alliance with Germany and Italy all these aims could be achieved, for the interests of the Axis powers and Japan were identical.

Throughout April, May and June the fight went on. Prime Minister, War Minister, and Army, versus the Emperor, his Foreign Secretary and Navy. Emperor Hirohito had been consistently opposed to a policy which might lead Japan into a state of war in the event of a European conflict. How could the Government overcome this obstacle? Itagaki, the Minister for War, falsely represented to the Emperor that at last the Foreign Minister had changed his mind about a Tripartite Alliance with Germany and Italy and had come into line with the Army. The plan failed, however, for the Emperor found out that he had been deceived and severely rebuked his Minister for War.

The military faction could make no progress with their precious alliance so long as Emperor, Foreign Minister and Navy remained opposed to it. Nor had the Army's activities in China and on the Manchukuo border lessened the Cabinet's difficulties. Units of the Kwantung Army had attacked the Soviet forces stationed on the Manchukuo frontier, and the action developed into a campaign of considerable magnitude which ended, in September 1939, with the defeat of the Japanese forces engaged.

Meanwhile it had become evident early in August that war in Europe was not far distant, and War Minister Itagaki doubled his efforts to bring the Cabinet round to the idea of an offensive and defensive alliance with the Axis, an alliance without any reservations.

[19]

It was at this critical moment that a crushing blow fell. On 23rd August 1939, the Berlin-Moscow Pact was signed. The policy of the Japanese Cabinet had become completely discredited in one night. The nation to which Japan had looked as an ally against the USSR had ranged herself on the side of the potential enemy.

The Cabinet fell, and the way was left open for the pursuit of a policy of co-existence with the Western powers, a policy which the Emperor favoured but the Army feared.

The Emperor, indeed, took such steps as he was able in order to ensure that such a policy would be adopted. He summoned General Abe to form a Cabinet and said who was his choice for War Minister. He also told the Prime Minister that the Cabinet must pursue a foreign policy of co-operation with Great Britain and the United States.

Under Admiral Nomura, who had become responsible for foreign affairs, no attempt was made to reopen negotiations with Germany and Italy and some steps were taken to improve Japan's relations with the Western powers. The plans for a Japanese invasion of South-East Asia were not proceeded with, and an indemnity was paid by Japan for a bombing incident in French Indo-China, which had taken place during the last weeks of the previous Prime Minister's period of office.

Notwithstanding this new orientation of policy, the military faction continued to work for complete solidarity with the Axis powers. The German-Soviet Pact had, without doubt, come as a great blow to both Japanese Government and people, and Hiranuma's Cabinet had made a protest concerning it to Germany.

Oshima the Japanese Ambassador in Berlin, however, who enjoyed the complete confidence of Hitler and the Wehrmacht, did not deliver it until after the completion of the German invasion of Poland, remarking as he did so, that he was sure that von Ribbentrop would accept the document 'unofficially and for his own information'.

In Rome also, the Japanese Ambassador, Shiratori, made

it quite clear that he recognized the German-Russian Non-Aggression Pact for what it was, a device on the part of Germany to avoid the ever-dreaded war on two fronts.

The joint efforts of Oshima and Shiratori did not fall on barren ground. Von Ribbentrop told the former that 'Japan's fate was, as ever, linked with Germany's. Should Germany be defeated, a coalition of the Western powers would prevent further Japanese expansion and would take away Japan's position in China: but should Japan maintain and enhance her relationship with Germany, Japan's position would ultimately be secured by German victories. The idea of close co-operation between the three Axis powers was not in the least dead. The three countries having an understanding with the USSR would, in accordance with the world situation, direct their activities directly against Great Britain'.[1]

Von Ribbentrop was seeking to encourage Japan to go south, to give up her anti-Russian aspirations and to penetrate deeply into South-East Asia where glittering prizes awaited her; the naval and air base of Hong Kong, oil from the Netherlands East Indies, tin and rubber from Malaya, and wool from Australasia.

Moreover, the aim of the new Cabinet's foreign policy, namely the re-establishment of friendly relations with the Western powers, had never had any real prospect of success for the following reason. No Japanese Government which renounced the aim of establishing Japan's 'new order' in China could expect to remain in power for long, and as General Abe's Government, unwilling to commit hara-kari, had not renounced it, it was bound to remain a perpetual obstacle to friendly co-existence between Great Britain, France and the United States.

In December 1939 the United States lodged fresh complaints concerning damage done to their property by the Japanese forces, and added a further list to the moral embargo which had already been placed on the export of new

---

[1] Judgment of the IMT, Far East, pages 48,878-9.

materials to Japan. Three weeks later the Netherlands Government gave notice of their intention to abrogate the arbitration treaty between Holland and Japan.

These two events caused the fall of General Abe's Cabinet, and with it went the foreign policy of maintaining friendly relations with the Western powers.

The new Cabinet under Prime Minister Yonai, for the first few months of its life, maintained the policy of non-intervention in the European War.

It received support from the Army which wanted to bring the war in China to a successful conclusion and was anxious not to intervene in Europe until Japan's own position had been consolidated.

It was never pretended in Japan, however, that this was anything more than a policy of expediency which would preserve Japan's complete freedom of action for the future. Meanwhile plans for a move southward were secretly prepared and developed.

The Sino-Japanese War, however, showed no signs of coming to an end, and as the alarm and despondency at the trend of events grew in Japan, so did pro-German sympathies. As one German victory succeeded another, members of several parties in the Diet called for a strengthening of ties with Germany and Italy.

Germany's special envoy, Herr Stahmer, who had just returned from a visit to Tokyo, was able to give von Ribbentrop a very encouraging report about the state of public sentiment in Japan. 'German successes,' he said, 'had created a deep impression in Japan and had diminished the importance of Great Britain in the Far East. Within the Army and within the people of Japan, anti-British sentiment was markedly stronger . . . the tension between Japan, on the one hand, and the United States and Great Britain, on the other, was bound to continue undiminished even if it did not increase.'

Nevertheless, the report ended with a word of warning, 'until the China problem has been settled, and urgent measures of domestic relief have been taken, Japan will be unable to change her policy'.

Yet there were some resolute members of the Japanese Government who, resisting the ever increasing public demand for closer ties with Germany, still strove to avoid complete disruption of friendly relations with Great Britain and the United States, and no one worked harder or more consistently to this end than the Japanese Ambassador in London, Shigemitzu.[1]

Even after Hitler's victory in the Low Countries and in France, Shigemitzu still maintained in his reports home that the issue of the European War was still in doubt, and that Great Britain was firmly resolved to continue the fight. He urged abandonment of the plans for a southward advance by Japanese forces under cover of German victories in Europe, and argued that whatever the outcome of the war, Japan's position would be strengthened if a settlement in China were brought about by conciliation.

The days of the Japanese Government under Yonai, however, were numbered, for the pro-German faction were preparing to bring about its fall and assassinate the Prime Minister and certain other Ministers, known to be in opposition to collaboration with Germany, but the plot was discovered and the conspirators arrested.

It was now July 1940 and Sato, Japan's new special envoy to Germany, had arrived in Berlin where he lost no time in endeavouring to persuade von Ribbentrop that by strengthening Japan's position in the Far East Germany would be strengthening her own in Europe. Germany was invited, therefore, to declare her policy regarding Japanese aspirations in French Indo-China and the Netherlands East Indies.

Germany, being now confident of victory in Europe, no longer attached much importance to an alliance with Japan and von Ribbentrop cautiously refrained from making any such declaration, saying that he was unaware what were Japan's objectives in the Far East. This diplomatic rebuff

[1] See Chapter XV.

[23]

undermined still further the position of the Yonai Cabinet, and before the end of the month it had resigned.

The Army, and the military faction in the Government, had been working for this for some months. On 1st June 1940 Kido, who was the vice-president designate of a new political party to be headed by Prince Konoye, had been offered and had accepted the position of Lord Keeper of the Privy Seal. The tenure of this office was independent of changes in the Government, and the duty of its occupant was to act as permanent adviser to the Emperor on all matters of State. Behind the scenes, from the date of his appointment until 16th July, when the Yonai Cabinet resigned, Kido had been consistently working for those who were trying to overthrow it, and he was 'in the know', from the very beginning, of the Army's plan to bring Konoye into power.

The foreign policy of the new Cabinet envisaged a rapprochement with Germany and Italy, a successful settlement of the war in Indo-China and full national mobilization. Konoye and Kido were resolved that by suppressing all political groups opposed to its policy the Cabinet would become the Government of a totalitarian State. At long last the leaders of the military faction would become the undisputed rulers of Japan.

A great historic moment had arrived in Japanese history. Great Britain, France and the Netherlands had, it seemed, been defeated. Japan would, therefore, seize all British, French, Dutch and Portuguese possessions in East and South-East Asia and the Pacific. These ambitious objectives included Hong Kong, French Indo-China, Thailand, Malaya, the Netherlands East Indies, the Philippines, New Guinea, all territory lying between Eastern India and Burma on the one hand, and Australia and New Zealand on the other.

It was not Japan's intention to intervene in Europe, but to assist Germany in conquering Great Britain by every means short of a declaration of war, by undermining her position in the Far East and aiding and abetting nationalism in India and Burma. At the same time the possibility of intervention by the United States in the European War would be reduced by Japan's actions which would constitute a threat to that country in the Far East.

The new Foreign Minister lost no time in putting this idea to the German Ambassador in Tokyo, simultaneously with an approach to the German Foreign Ministry in Berlin made by Ambassador Kurusu. It appeared to the Germans that it could be in their interest to collaborate with Japan upon some such terms, and Herr Stahmer was once again sent as special envoy to Tokyo.

While Stahmer was still on his way, there was an important meeting between Prime Minister Konoye, Matsuoka the Foreign Minister, the War Minister Tojo, and the Minister for the Navy. This conference was to decide the tactics to be followed in the coming talks with Germany.

Five days later Matsuoka and Stahmer met and the negotiations began. Stahmer said that Germany was no less eager than Japan to conclude the proposed Tripartite Alliance.

> Germany desires to end the European War quickly, and does not at present require Japan's military assistance, but she would be glad if Japan would restrain and prevent the United States from entering the war. . . . Germany and Italy themselves would do everything possible to restrain the United States and would supply Japan with such war equipment as they could reasonably spare. . . . Germany recognized and respected Japan's political leadership in East Asia and would assist in bringing about a rapprochement between her and the Soviet Union.[1]

Stahmer then unfolded Germany's grandiose scheme of aggression in which she regarded Japan as an ally. 'The present war,' he said, 'may end quickly, but the great struggle will go on, in one form or another, for decades . . . the war in Europe is destined in the end to develop into a struggle against the whole Anglo-Saxon World.'

[1] Proceedings of the IMT, Far East, pages 48,994–5.

[25]

Germany was anxious that Japan should join the Axis quickly 'before the war with Great Britain was ended'. Had the Nazis been able to look into the future they would have seen that there was no need for such haste.

On 27th September 1940 the Tripartite Alliance was concluded. In an Imperial Rescript it was hailed as 'an instrument of peace' which would enable each nation 'to have its proper place in the world'. But the Lord Keeper of the Privy Seal understood its full significance, for he told the Emperor that if it was concluded a supreme effort would have to be made to end the war in China, for sooner or later Japan would have to reckon with Great Britain and America, and would be involved in war with France, the Netherlands and all the countries of the British Commonwealth.

At the trial of the Japanese 'major war criminals' in Tokyo the defence contended that the alliance, as the Imperial Rescript had stated, was 'an instrument of peace'.

Dealing with this contention in its judgment the Tribunal used these words:

> The decisions of the leaders of Japan which followed the downfall of the Yonai Cabinet, are of outstanding importance ... they show that the conspirators were determined to extend the domination of Japan over a huge area and population and to use force, if necessary, to accomplish their aims. They show by plain admission that their purpose in entering into the Tripartite Pact was to secure support for the accomplishment of these illegal aims. They show that notwithstanding the seemingly defensive terms of the Pact which were designed for publication, the obligations of the parties to support one another were expected to come into force if one of the parties became engaged in war whether defensive or aggressive. They wholly refute the contention of the defence that the purpose of the Tripartite Pact was to promote the cause of peace.[1]

Although there was no mention in the Tripartite Pact itself that it was directed against the USSR, the Japanese Army

[1] Proceedings of the IMT, Far East, page 49,006.

had no doubt of it when the alliance was concluded. The Foreign Minister himself left the matter in no doubt. Addressing a meeting of the Japanese Privy Council Investigation Committee, on the day before the Pact was signed, he said, 'Although there exists a non-aggression treaty, Japan will aid Germany in the event of a Soviet-German war and Germany will assist Japan in the event of a Russo-Japanese war.'

Before nine months had passed Germany invaded Russia, whereupon Japan, in complete disregard of a Neutrality Pact into which she had entered in April 1941, managed to give aid to Germany while refraining from open warfare with the USSR.

Japan had been approached by the Soviet Union as early as 1931 to enter into a Neutrality Pact, but had refused to do so. By 1941 the international situation had considerably changed and Germany and Italy were practically Japan's only friends. She was, therefore, only too willing to enter into a pact which the USSR then proposed, and it was concluded on 13th April 1941, barely more than two months before Hitler's invasion of Russia on 22nd June 1941.

In signing the Pact Japan acted with great perfidy, for she can have been in no doubt of Germany's impending attack on the Russians. The Japanese Ambassador in Berlin had been informed only two months before by von Ribbentrop that many new divisions had been formed during the winter of 1940–41, and had also been told of the prospects of a 'German-Russian conflict which would result in a gigantic German victory and signify the end of the Soviet Regime'.[1]

Nor was that all. Less than three weeks before the conclusion of the Neutrality Pact, during a conversation with Matsuoka in Berlin, von Ribbentrop had said, 'the German armies in the East are available at any time. Should Russia one day take up an attitude which could be interpreted as a threat against Germany, the Führer would dash Russia to pieces. One is positive in Germany that such a campaign

[1] Extract from a report by Oshima, produced at the trial of major war criminals in Tokyo.

[27]

would end in a complete victory for German arms and the absolute destruction of the Russian Army and the Russian State. The Führer is convinced that in case of an advance against the Soviet Union, Russia, a few months later, would cease to exist as a power.'[1]

Matsuoka, before he left Berlin, assured Hitler that in the event of a war between Germany and Russia, 'Japan would be a loyal ally who would devote herself entirely, and not just in a lukewarm way, to the joint effort'. He then took the train to Moscow where, a fortnight later, he signed the Neutrality Pact, and on his return to Tokyo he told the German Ambassador that no Japanese Government would ever be able to keep Japan neutral in the event of a Russo-German conflict. 'Japan would be driven,' he said, 'by force of necessity, to attack Russia at Germany's side, and no neutrality pact could change this.'

From the first moment of the invasion of Russia it became clear that it was regarded by Japan as a convenient opportunity for the seizure of Soviet territories in the Far East. At the outset there was even some apprehension in Japan that she might be too late with her military preparations for attack.

The Germans themselves were anxious that their ally should enter the war at the earliest possible moment. In a telegram addressed to the German Ambassador in Tokyo, von Ribbentrop stressed the importance of an early participation, for 'the natural goal must be to bring about the meeting of Germany and Japan on the Trans-Siberian railway before winter sets in . . . with the collapse of Russia the position of the tripartite powers[2] in the world will be so gigantic that the question of the absolute annihilation of the British Isles will be only a question of time'.

As the initial rapid German advance through Russia began to slow down towards the end of the summer, the impetuosity of the Japanese Government gave way to caution. The German Ambassador in Tokyo reported that 'in view of the

[1] Grossmacht.
[2] i.e. Germany, Italy and Japan.

resistance put up by the Russian Army against an army such as the German, the Japanese General Staff does not believe itself capable of achieving a decisive success against Russia before winter sets in . . . the tenacity displayed by the Soviet Union against Germany indicates that not even by a Japanese attack in August or September could the route via Siberia be opened this year'.

The Japanese, nevertheless, had not given up any thoughts of aggrandisement at the expense of what they called their 'mortal enemy'. Vladivostok, they maintained, was a perpetual threat on their flank, and at an appropriate stage in the Russo-German war an occasion would doubtless arise for removing that danger.

But this 'sooner or later' attitude was not congenial to Hitler, who hoped that Japan 'would arrive at a decision to attack Vladivostok at the very earliest moment, provided she was strong enough to conduct such an operation without having to free other forces which would weaken her position against England and America, for example, in Burma . . . otherwise it would be better if she maintained neutral relations with the Soviet Union since, in any event, Russia must maintain troops in Eastern Siberia in anticipation of a Japanese-Russian conflict'.

Although Japan still held back from attacking Russia itself she did give other military assistance. By concentrating a large army in Manchuria, and carrying out other extensive military preparations she pinned down many Soviet divisions on Russia's eastern frontiers which would otherwise have been thrown into the battle now furiously raging in western Russia.

Japan also supplied Germany with military intelligence regarding the Soviet forces, and interfered extensively with Soviet shipping. Russian ships at anchor off Hong Kong were shelled, others were sunk by Japanese aircraft, and many more unlawfully captured by the Japanese Navy and taken to Japanese ports where they were often detained for prolonged periods.

All these measures were taken to assist Germany in her war against Russia in complete defiance of Japan's obligations under Article II of the Neutrality Pact which provided, 'in case one of the contracting parties becomes the object of military action from the part of one or several other powers, the other contracting party *will maintain neutrality during the whole period of the conflict*'.[1]

Immediately after the conclusion of the Tripartite Pact a 'Tentative Plan for the Southern Regions' was prepared by the Japanese Foreign Office.[2] Its primary objectives were to seize and occupy Singapore, Malaya and the Dutch East Indies without becoming involved in war with Russia or America. Should war break out between Japan and the United States, further objectives would include the Philippines, Guam and other American possessions in the Pacific.

To secure public support for this aggressive policy Hashimoto launched a campaign of extensive propaganda. 'Rise up resolutely,' he adjured his fellow countrymen, 'for the time approaches. Instigate at once a powerful national movement using every kind of method . . . and begin a sweeping campaign against sympathizers of England and America.'

'Now is the time,' he wrote, 'to attack Great Britain while she is engaged in war with Germany and Italy in order to eliminate her opposition to the establishment of our "New Order" in Asia and the Pacific region.'

Extensive preparation for war with the United States, Great Britain and other Western powers followed, and by the beginning of 1941 the alarm had already been sounded in America. 'Never before,' President Roosevelt told Congress, 'has American security been so seriously threatened.'

The one great obstacle to the Japanese conquest of the whole Pacific area was the United States Pacific Fleet based on Pearl Harbour in Hawaii. A plan was, accordingly, drawn up and submitted to the Commander of the Japanese Combined Fleets for the destruction of the fleet while at anchor in

[1] Author's italics.
[2] See Chapter XIII, page 242.

[30]

Pearl Harbour. A surprise air attack was to be made by a special task force and was to be carried out *while the two countries were still at peace*. Were the attack successful, it was most likely that Japan would be able to occupy all her objectives in the Pacific and Indian Oceans before the United States could recover sufficiently from the blow to mount a counter-attack.

Meanwhile, in February 1941, Nomura, the new Japanese Ambassador to America, had arrived in Washington. His instructions were to make the President and Secretary of State Cordell Hull understand 'that Japan had been forced to sign the Tripartite Pact because of American and British interference with the organization of the Co-Prosperity Sphere,[1] and that it would be better if the United States would cease interfering with Japan's aims in East Asia and would co-operate with her in return for an opportunity to participate in the benefits which would thereby accrue'.[2]

By this time Japan had decided to make an attack on Singapore in order to deprive the United States of friendly bases in the Pacific in the event of her entering the European war; and the preparations for this operation were expected to be completed by May 1941.

Early in March 1941 Nomura was interviewed by Cordell Hull. The Japanese Ambassador said that it was inconceivable that their two countries should become involved in hostilities which would be disastrous for both of them. The Secretary of State concurred, but asked how could the United States be expected to sit back and take no notice while Germany, Italy and Japan set out to conquer the rest of the world.

During the same month of March, Matsuoka met the American Ambassador in Moscow and assured him emphatically that in *no circumstances* would Japan attack Singapore or any American, British or Dutch possession as she had no territorial ambitions. A few days later, on his arrival in

---

[1] The Co-Prosperity Sphere was the new name for what had previously been called the 'New Order in East Asia'.
[2] Proceedings of the IMT, Far East, page 49,479.

Berlin, Matsuoka told Hitler of his conversations in Moscow with the United States Ambassador and explained that his denials of his Government's intentions were in order to mislead the British and Americans until the day when Japan would suddenly attack Singapore.

At this point relations between Germany and Japan were becoming a little strained. Certain conditions had been laid down by Cordell Hull as a preliminary to opening up negotiations between Japan and the United States.

They were as follows:

(1) Respect for the territorial integrity and sovereignty of all nations.
(2) Non-interference in the internal affairs of other countries.
(3) Equality of commercial opportunity.
(4) Non-disturbance of the status quo in the Pacific, except by peaceful means.

Japan had decided to open talks with America when von Ribbentrop got to hear of it. He expressed his surprise to Ambassador Oshima and accused the Japanese Cabinet of having abandoned its plans to attack Singapore. Japan, von Ribbentrop insisted, should refuse to negotiate upon the Cordell Hull conditions unless the United States would agree to remain neutral. Furthermore, he demanded, Singapore should be attacked without delay. Oshima took a serious view of the situation and urged his Government not to disregard what was, in his opinion, the justifiable resentment of the German leaders.

On 28th May 1941 negotiations between Cordell Hull and Nomura began. Hardly had they got under way when Chunking was bombed by more than one hundred Japanese planes and American property was destroyed. The Secretary of State then told the Japanese Ambassador that his Government felt that before continuing the talks they 'must await some clearer indication than had yet been given that the Japanese Government intended to pursue a course of peace'.[1]

[1] Proceedings of the IMT, Far East, page 49,496.

It was a pious hope, for the Japanese Navy were already training for the proposed attack on Pearl Harbour. Practice in dive bombing and refuelling at sea was being carried out, and the development of a shallow water torpedo was in its final stages.

At the same time, discussions were taking place with von Ribbentrop which were to lead to the acquisition by Japan of more naval bases in French Indo-China, which were later used in the attacks on Singapore and the Netherlands East Indies. An ultimatum was eventually handed to the Vichy Government, and the German Foreign Secretary was asked to *advise* the French to accept. Vichy was in no position to refuse the Japanese demands, and on 24th February 1941, forty thousand Japanese troops sailed for southern French Indo-China to occupy it and construct air bases near Saigon and naval bases at Saigon and Camranh Bay.

During the months of June, July, and August almost continuous diplomatic discussions were taking place between the United States and Japan, but the minimum Japanese demands were such that the negotiations could not have been expected to reach a satisfactory conclusion.

Nor, indeed, were they intended to succeed. They were nothing but a cover for the final preparations then being made for the attacks on Singapore and Pearl Harbour, and to gain time while the Japanese forces were taking up their war stations in French Indo-China and Thailand.

There was, as yet, to be no attack on the Soviet Union. The Japanese policy *vis-à-vis* the Russo-German war was to remain neutral whilst making secret preparations to attack the USSR at a time when, as Tojo put it, 'she will be ready to fall to the ground like a ripe persimmon'.

The training for the attack on Pearl Harbour, and the practice landings along the coast of China in preparation for the combined operations in Malaya, had by now been completed, and in September 1941 the final 'War Games' had been held at the Naval War College in Tokyo. At these exercises without troops high ranking officers of both the services worked out the details of the carrier attack on Pearl Harbour, and drew up a schedule of operations for the occupation of Malaya, Burma, the Netherlands East Indies, the Philippines and the Solomon and Central Pacific Islands. No detail was overlooked. The Japanese Consulate-General in Hawaii became a nest of spies, and arrangements were made for information about the American fleet in Hawaian waters to be transmitted to Tokyo by a special secret code.

Munitions production was stepped up, a new plan for the mobilization of all workers was put into operation, and the Cabinet Printing Office printed large quantities of occupation currency notes in pesos, dollars and guilders for use in the Philippines, Malaya and the Netherlands East Indies.

The time for the irrevocable and final decision to go to war was fast approaching. The Army, led by Tojo, was convinced that there was nothing to be gained by continuing the talks with America. The Navy, however, thought differently. Prince Konoye agreed with the latter view, and tried to persuade his War Minister to abandon all plans for a southward advance, and to make a concentrated and determined effort to bring the China War to a successful conclusion.

He made no impression on Tojo, however, and eventually resigned for he felt unable, as he wrote in his letter of resignation, 'to accept the responsibility for plunging the nation again into a titanic war the outcome of which could not be forecast'.

Prince Konoye was succeeded in the office of Prime Minister by Tojo, who was promoted to General on 18th October 1941, and allowed to remain on the active list although Prime Minister, in order that he might still retain the post of War Minister.

With Tojo in the saddle, holding the offices of Prime Minister, Minister for War and Minister of Munitions, and still remaining on the active list as a General, all political obstacles to the Army's plans for war were removed.

The final plans were completed by 1st November 1941 and

[34]

the last smoke-screen diplomatic negotiations with the United States were about to begin. Two alternative proposals were drawn up, known respectively as 'A' and 'B'. Proposal 'A' was to be presented to Cordell Hull first, and Proposal 'B' was only to be handed over if no agreement could be reached on Proposal 'A'. The contents of neither of these documents are of great importance for it was never expected that they would be acceptable to the United States Government.

Be that as it may, Proposal 'A' was presented to the Secretary of State by Ambassador Nomura on 7th December, two days after the final draft of the Combined Fleet Operation Order had been approved by the Japanese Chiefs of Staff. This order covered the proposed attacks on Singapore, the Netherlands East Indies, the Philippines and Pearl Harbour; other minor operations in Hong Kong and Shanghai were also included.

Three days later, by another Combined Fleet Operation Order, X day[1] was fixed as from midnight on 7th–8th December.

During these negotiations the United States Government kept in close touch with the Governments of Britain, the Netherlands, and China, and on 10th November the British Prime Minister, in a speech delivered in London, used these words: 'We do not know whether the efforts of the United States to preserve peace in the Pacific will be successful. But if they fail, I take this occasion to say—and it is my duty to say—that should the United States be involved in a war with Japan, a British declaration *will follow within an hour*.'[2]

While these very words were being spoken Japanese air forces were moving into position at Saigon for the assault on Singapore, and the Japanese carrier force which was to take part in the raid on Pearl Harbour was leaving Japanese ports *en route* for its rendezvous at Tankan Wan.

Proposal 'A' having been rejected, the alternative proposal was presented to Cordell Hull on 20th November. Its accept-

[1] The equivalent of D day.
[2] Author's italics.

ance by the United States was unthinkable, for this would have been tantamount to condoning Japanese aggression in China and the abandonment of Mr. Hull's 'four points'.[1]

On 26th November Cordell Hull gave the Japanese Ambassador and the Special Envoy, Ambassador Kurusu, his final conditions which were as follows.

(1) That there should be a non-aggression pact among all nations with interests in the Far East.
(2) That Japan should withdraw her armed forces from China and French Indo-China.
(3) That Japan should withdraw all support from her puppet Government in China.

On that very morning the Japanese fleet which was to make the attack on Pearl Harbour set sail, while the Japanese diplomats were instructed by their Foreign Minister Togo 'to refrain from giving the impression to the United States that the negotiations are broken off'. 'Tell them,' Togo cabled, 'that you are waiting for instructions from your Government.' The Japanese now intended to use these diplomatic exchanges between the two countries in such a way that, under cover of them and before news of their rupture could reach England and America, surprise attacks could be made at the points selected.

On 1st December 1941 an Imperial Conference was called to decide the fatal question, peace or war with the United States of America, the British Commonwealth, and the Netherlands. The decision was made known in these words. 'Our negotiations with the United States regarding the execution of our national policy have finally failed. Japan will open hostilities against the United States, Great Britain and the Netherlands.'

Meanwhile Nomura and Kurusu stayed in Washington doing what they could, in the words of their instructions, 'to prevent the United States from becoming unduly sus-

[1] Page 32.

picious'. At about 10 a.m. (Tokyo time) on 7th December Togo's message to his two envoys breaking off the negotiations began coming in. The message stated that the exact hour for its delivery to the State Department would be telegraphed later.

In a forlorn hope to preserve peace President Roosevelt cabled a personal message to Emperor Hirohito. This message arrived in Tokyo by the afternoon of 7th December, for the Japanese Foreign Office by then was aware of its contents, but it was not delivered to Ambassador Grew until 9 p.m.

When it was decoded the American Ambassador took it to Togo at 12.15 a.m. on 8th December, and asked for a personal interview with the Emperor. Togo told Grew that he himself would hand the President's message to the Emperor.

Half an hour after midnight the American Ambassador returned to his Embassy. In America it was then 10.30 a.m. on 7th December. The Pacific war had already begun.

The International Military Tribunal for the Far East in its judgment dealt with the delay in the delivering of the President's message to Emperor Hirohito in these words. 'No satisfactory explanation of the delay in delivering to Mr. Grew the President's message to the Emperor was given to this Tribunal. Whatever effect that message might have had was precluded by this unexplained delay.'[1]

Before the day ended the Japanese forces had made attacks on Pearl Harbour, on Kota Bharu in Malaya, on the Philippines, on Hong Kong, on Shanghai and on the islands of Guam and Wake. They had made landings at other selected points along the eastern shores of the Malayan Peninsula. They had also crossed the Malaya-Thailand frontier at Pedang Besar, and before nightfall Singapore had experienced its first air-raid. By this monumental diplomatic treachery the Japanese ensured that all the operations scheduled for X day achieved the maximum element of surprise.

[1] Proceedings of the IMT, Far East, page 49,456–9.

Thus began Japan's war with the Western powers, which was to continue with much bloodshed and great bitterness for nearly four years, until the unconditional surrender in 1945.

Throughout its duration, wherever the Japanese forces went, massacre, murder, torture, rape and many other atrocities of a barbarous nature were committed wholesale by officers and men.

The International Military Tribunal at Tokyo said this, in its judgment. 'During a period of several months the Tribunal heard evidence from witnesses who testified in detail to atrocities committed in all theatres of war on a scale so vast, yet following so common a pattern, that only one conclusion is possible. The atrocities were either secretly ordered, or wilfully permitted by the Japanese Government, or individual members thereof, and by the leaders of the armed forces.'

CHAPTER II

THE CHINA INCIDENT

In China, however, war had been going on for more than a decade, but from its very inception after the 'Mukden Incident' until its end in 1945, Japan refused to acknowledge that the Sino-Japanese conflict was a war in the accepted sense of the word.

When the Japanese delegate to the League of Nations in Geneva accepted the resolution which led to the setting up of the Lytton Commission and brought about a virtual truce, he made it clear that his country's acceptance was conditional upon it being understood that the League's action would not prevent the Japanese forces from taking 'punitive' action against 'bandits' in Manchuria.

The hostilities in China constituted, not a war, but an 'incident', and the Chinese troops which resisted Japanese aggression were not soldiers, but 'bandits'.

The adoption of such euphemistic nomenclature afforded a pretext, to the Japanese mind, to maintain that in the conduct of such hostilities the laws and customs of war did not apply and need not be observed.

The Chinese soldiers taken in battle by Japanese troops were, therefore, denied the status of prisoners of war upon the same pretext and many of them were massacred, tortured, or drafted into Japanese labour camps. In one camp alone on the Island of Houshu nearly fifty per cent of a forced labour unit, nine hundred strong, died of starvation or the results of torture.

The campaign, according to the Japanese, was being undertaken in order to 'punish the people of China for their refusal to acknowledge the superiority and leadership of the Japanese race and to co-operate with them'.[1]

[1] Proceedings of the IMT, Far East, page 49,595.

It was the Japanese aim to conduct the war with such barbarity that the Chinese people's will to fight on and defend their homes and their country would be broken. Plans were therefore made to carry out terror air-raids.

In an appreciation of the situation which the Chief of Staff of the Central China Expeditionary Force sent to War Minister Itagaki[1] in 1939, he made the following suggestion:

> The Army and Air Force should carry out attacks upon strategic points in the hinterland in order to terrorize the enemy forces and civilians, and so develop among them an anti-war pacifist tendency. What we expect of offensive operations against the interior is the mental terror they will create among the enemy forces and civilians rather than the material damage inflicted directly upon enemy personnel and equipment. We will wait and see them falling into nervous prostration in an excess of terror and madly starting anti-Chiang[2] pacifist movements.

There could be no clearer evidence that the campaign was, in effect, a punitive war, nor did the Japanese leaders ever cease from declaring that its purpose was to make the Chinese people 'seriously reflect upon the error of their ways', and accept domination by Japan. Nor was that other totalitarian euphemism, extermination, so much favoured by another aggressor nation about the same period, absent from their lips.

Hiranuma in a speech intended to 'stimulate the national morale', which he made in the Japanese Diet in the same year, speaking of the 'China Incident' said, 'I hope the intention of Japan will be understood by the Chinese so that they may co-operate with us. *As for those who fail to understand we have no other alternative but to exterminate them.*'[3]

The proviso upon which the Japanese delegate to the League

---

[1] The same Itagaki who, as Senior Staff Officer at Mukden, took such a prominent part in the Mukden Incident. See page 6.

[2] Generalissimo Chiang Kai-Shek.

[3] Author's italics.

of Nations had made his acceptance of the League's resolution conditional, was used by Japan as a cloak under which the military operations against Chinese troops in Manchuria could continue.

A ruthless campaign for the extermination of these 'bandits' was set on foot. By the end of 1931 the main Chinese Army had withdrawn behind the Great Wall, but considerable resistance was still kept up over a large area by units of Chinese Volunteers, particularly in the country round Mukden, Haicheng and Yingkow.

On one occasion in the late summer of 1932 the Japanese forces, pursuing retreating Chinese volunteer forces, arrived at three towns in the vicinity of Fushun. The inhabitants were suspected of having given aid to the so-called 'bandits' during the operations, and of giving them refuge on their retreat. In all three towns these civilians, among whom were women and children, were dragged from their homes by the Japanese soldiers, lined up along the ditches at the side of the main road and made to kneel down. They were then machine-gunned and the few who survived were bayoneted to death. The total number killed in this way was 2,700 men, women and children, and it was justified by the General Officer Commanding the Kwantung Army as part of the 'programme of exterminating bandits'.

General Koiso,[1] who twelve years later was to become Prime Minister of Japan, in a memorandum which he sent, shortly after this massacre, to the Japanese Vice-Minister for War, wrote: 'Racial struggle between the Japanese and Chinese is to be expected . . . we must never hesitate to wield military power in case of necessity.'

Massacre in the Chinese War was, therefore, justified as military necessity,[2] and it was practised throughout its entirety, reaching its peak in a crime which has long been forgotten in the western hemisphere, the massacre of two

[1] See Chapter XV.
[2] The doctrine of military necessity is discussed in the Appendix, *Some Legal Aspects of War Crime Trials*.

[41]

hundred thousand Chinese civilians and prisoners of war in the first six weeks of the Japanese occupation of Nanking.

One of the accused brought to trial before the International Military Tribunal at Tokyo was General Matsui, who had been Commander-in-Chief in Central China from 1937–8. It was his troops who were responsible for what is generally known as 'The Rape of Nanking', one of the most appalling war crimes of modern times. The account which follows is a very brief summary of the evidence given before the Tokyo Tribunal ten years after the event.

As the Japanese 'Central China Expeditionary Force' approached Nanking early in December 1937 more than half the population fled from the city. At the same time the main Chinese Army retreated, leaving behind some fifty thousand troops to defend Nanking.

On 12th December the Japanese troops stormed the south gate and most of the Chinese troops escaped through the northern and western gates. By the time that the Japanese entered the city on the following morning those Chinese soldiers who had not already evacuated it had doffed their uniforms, abandoned their arms, and taken refuge in the International Safety Zone which had been organized by a few neutrals who had remained behind for that purpose. All resistance had ceased.

The Japanese troops were then let loose like the hordes of Genghis Khan to ravish and murder. As one eye-witness described it, 'the city appeared to have fallen into the hands of the Japanese as captured prey, and the members of the victorious army had set upon the prize to commit unlimited violence'. Small groups of Japanese soldiers roamed all over the city night and day. Many were crazed with drink, but no attempt was made by their commander or their officers to maintain discipline among the occupying forces. They looted, they burned, they raped and they murdered. Soldiers marched through the streets indiscriminately killing Chinese of both sexes, adults and children alike, without receiving any provocation and without rhyme or reason.

They went on killing until the gutters ran with blood and the streets were littered with the bodies of their victims. As one Chinese witness who was there testified, the inhabitants of Nanking were 'hunted like rabbits, everyone seen to move was shot'.

At the lowest computation twelve thousand men, women and children were shot or done to death during the first three days of the Japanese occupation. Rape was the order of the day, and resistance by the victim, or by members of her family who tried to protect her, meant almost certain death. Girls of tender years and old women, neither were spared. Neither youth nor old age was respected, and the evidence given before the Tokyo Tribunal by eye-witnesses of the abnormal and sadistic behaviour displayed by the ravishers defies description and is quite unprintable. Many of the victims, however, were killed after the act and their bodies mutilated, and during the first month of the Japanese occupation approximately twenty thousand cases of rape occurred.

During the next few weeks looting became a pastime and arson a sport. Civilians were stopped in the street, searched, and if they were in possession of nothing of value they were shot.

Thousands of houses and commercial premises were broken into and emptied of their contents. After looting them the Japanese soldiers set them on fire. In the Taiping Road, which was the main shopping centre of Nanking, block after block was destroyed by fire. For no reason at all private houses were set alight, and it was estimated that about one-third of the city was gutted by fire.

The Japanese commanders gave their troops full licence to commit wholesale murder of the male inhabitants of the city on the grounds that the Chinese soldiers, who as related had thrown their arms away, were mingling with the civilian population, as doubtless they were.

They remained, however, for the most part within the so-called International Safety Zone and even had they not done so, their murder could not be justified under international law, for as they had thrown away their arms and were offering no resistance, they were entitled to be treated as prisoners of war.

Nevertheless, under this pretext, thousands of male civilians were rounded up, bound with their hands behind their backs, and marched outside the city walls where they were killed either by machine-gun fire or by bayoneting. In this way more than twenty thousand Chinese men of military age are known to have been murdered.

'This barbarous behaviour of the Japanese Army,' as the Tokyo Tribunal said in its judgment, 'cannot be excused as the acts of a soldiery which had temporarily got out of hand when at last a stubbornly defended position had capitulated. Rape, arson and murder continued to be committed on a large scale for at least six weeks after the city had been taken.'

These events in Nanking appear to have horrified even the Nazis who, within the next six years, were to prove themselves equally adept at wholesale extermination. In a report made to the German Foreign Office by the German Embassy in China reference was made to 'atrocities and criminal acts of an entire army', namely the Japanese troops in Nanking, and the Army itself was characterized as 'bestial machinery'.

But these twenty thousand were not the only soldiers to be killed after capture. As the Japanese forces approached Nanking large bodies of Chinese troops, totalling more than thirty thousand, had laid down their arms and surrendered. Within seventy-two hours they had all been lined up in groups along the banks of the Yangtse River and killed by machine-gun fire.

A very careful estimate has been made of the total number of Chinese soldiers and civilians murdered in Nanking itself during the first six weeks of the Japanese occupation of the city, and by the lowest computation, the number was not less than two hundred thousand. Burial societies, and other organizations which kept reliable records, have accounted for more than one hundred and fifty thousand bodies which they buried. Nearly all these had the hands bound behind the back, and these records obviously did not include the many thousands of bodies which are known to have been destroyed by fire, or thrown into the Yangtse River.

Such is the story of the sacking of Nanking and the mass murder of so many of its inhabitants. All these events were well known to the Japanese High Command at the time they were happening, yet no action was taken to prevent their occurrence or to halt the slaughter. Officials of the Japanese Embassy who entered the city with the Army's advance guard were fully aware of the Army's intentions. Indeed, they even complained to the military authorities about the inadequacy of the military police force in Nanking to deal with the situation and to maintain discipline. The military police unit detailed for this task consisted of no more than seventeen policemen.

As this appeal to the military authorities met with no response, an attempt was made by the Embassy staff, acting through a number of foreign missionaries in Nanking, to let the terrible facts become known in Japan in the hope that the Government would be obliged by the sheer force of public opinion to restrain the Army.

General Matsui himself arrived in Nanking only four days after the entry of his troops, by which date at least one hundred and fifty thousand innocent inhabitants had been massacred. He admitted at his trial that he had heard about the atrocities at his rear headquarters before he moved into the city, and that two days after his arrival there, the whole of the commercial district of Nanking was still burning.

He appears, however, to have been left quite unperturbed, for on the day after his triumphal ceremonial entry into the city he held a religious service in memory of the dead and issued this statement:

I extend much sympathy to millions of innocent people in the Kiangpei and Chekiang districts who have suffered the evils of war. Now the flag of the Rising Sun is floating high over Nanking, and the Imperial Way is shining in the southern parts of the Yangtse-Kiang. The dawn of the renaissance of the East is on the verge of appearing. On this occasion I hope for reconsideration of the situation by the four hundred million people of China.

Two hundred thousand of them were given no opportunity to consider this gracious appeal. Their dead bodies rested in the cemeteries of Nanking, their charred remains lay in the ruins of their burnt out homes, their swollen corpses floated down the Yangtse River towards their last resting place.

General Matsui was on the retired list when he was recalled to active duty in 1937 to take command first of the Shanghai Expeditionary Force and, later, of the Central China Expeditionary Force. Regarding his responsibility for these crimes and his knowledge of them the Tokyo Tribunal said in its judgment:

At the height of these dreadful happenings, on 17th December, Matsui made a triumphal entry into the city and remained there from five to seven days. From his own observations, and from the reports of his staff, he must have been aware of what was happening. He admits he was told to some extent of the misbehaviour of his Army by the Kempei Tai and consular officials. Daily reports of these atrocities were made to Japanese diplomatic representatives in Nanking who, in turn, reported them to Tokyo.

The Tribunal is satisfied that Matsui knew what was happening. He did nothing, or nothing effective, to abate these horrors. He did issue orders before the capture of the city enjoining propriety of conduct upon his troops, and later issued further orders to the same purport. These orders were of no effect as is now known, and as he must have known.

It was pleaded on his behalf that at this time he was ill. His illness was not sufficient to prevent him from conducting the military operations of his command, nor did it prevent his visiting the city for days while these atrocities were occurring. He was in command of the Army responsible for these happenings. He knew of them. He had the power, as he had the duty, to control his troops and to protect the unfortunate citizens of Nanking. He must be held criminally responsible for his failure to discharge this duty.

The efforts made through the foreign missionaries in Nanking to rouse public opinion in Japan met with some success and there were serious repercussions throughout the civilized world. These led to the recall of General Matsui and a number of officers under his command, but no action was taken against any of them and before very long Matsui returned to public life as a member of the Cabinet Advisory Council and was decorated for his 'meritorious services in China'.

Meanwhile the slaughter continued. After the fall of Nanking, Generalissimo Chiang Kai-Shek moved his headquarters to Hankow, and the seat of his Government to Chungking. The Japanese set up a puppet Government at Peiping.

A few days later, in the Hsing Tai district, a party of Japanese gendarmes seized seven civilians in one of the villages who were suspected of being Chinese irregulars. They were starved for three days, then submitted to the usual Japanese torture, and on the fifth day were tied to trees and bayoneted to death.

At another village a party of soldiers who arrived raped all the women, murdered twenty-four of the inhabitants, and burned down two-thirds of the houses before they left. About the same time, in the same province, more than forty inhabitants of the village of Wang-Chia-To were murdered.

In the Shanghai area also, numerous atrocities were committed by the Japanese troops. On the outskirts of Shanghai city itself all the farmhouses were burned down and, after the soldiers had left, the bodies of the farmers and their families, including the women and children, were found. They had been killed in cold blood, for their hands were tied behind them and the bodies had bayonet wounds in the back.

Along the whole line of march, from Shanghai to Nanking, General Matsui's army left a trail of blood and devastation. In village after village which his troops occupied, sometimes for one night only, looting and murder were rife. In Soochow, which was entered early in November 1937, many of the inhabitants who had been unable to flee the city before the arrival of the Japanese troops, whose barbarous reputation was now well known in China, were collected, lined up along the side of the main street, and shot.

During 1938 the campaign was extended further south to Hankow and Canton. On 25th October, General Hata's[1] troops entered and occupied Hankow and proceeded to 'dispose' of the prisoners of war who had fallen into their hands when the city had surrendered.

How these prisoners met their death was told at the Tokyo Trial by an eye-witness, Albert Dorrance, who was manager of the Standard Oil Company. There were, at the time, four American gunboats on the River Yangtse at Hankow when the Japanese entered the city, and it was from the deck of one of these ships that Dorrance witnessed the atrocities.

The Japanese had occupied the city on the afternoon of the previous day, and on the following morning the witness had seen several hundred Chinese soldiers assembled by the Japanese at the customs wharf. At that time, the water being extremely low in the Yangtse River, gangplanks, running about half a mile out into the river bed from its banks, were in use. The Chinese soldiers were taken down these long gangplanks in groups of three or four and then thrown into the water. As their heads appeared above the water they were shot.

Dorrance, with a number of American sailors, was standing on the deck of a gunboat watching this performance. When the Japanese saw that there was an audience they changed their plans. Embarking the victims in small motor launches, they took them a little way down stream until they were out

[1] Later Field-Marshal Hata. See Chapter XV.

of sight of the American ships, and threw them into the water and shot them as before.

But it was not only General Hata's and General Matsui's troops who behaved in this barbaric fashion. In Japan the conduct of the whole Army in China was, by this time, beginning to produce, among the more liberal and less military minded citizens, an unfavourable reaction which had become embarrassing to the Government.

In much the same way as German soldiers, between 1940 and 1945, boasted about their exploits in occupied Europe, sent home gruesome souvenirs of some of their atrocities, and carried in their wallets photographs commemorating many of their worst crimes, so the Japanese troops, in their letters and while relating their experiences to friends and relations when home on leave, told of the many atrocities committed by them and their comrades upon Chinese soldiers and civilians.

According to these stories, one accommodating Japanese company commander gave unofficial instructions to would-be ravishers. 'So that we will not have any problems on our hands, either pay them money or kill them in some obscure place after you have finished.'

A letter which one soldier wrote home contained the following passage, 'the thing I like doing best during battle is plundering. In the front lines the superiors turn a blind eye to plundering and there are some who plundered to their hearts' content.'

Another wrote, 'in my half year at the front about the only two things I have learned are rape and robbery . . . the looting by our armies is beyond imagination . . . the prisoners taken from the Chinese Army are sometimes lined up in a line and shot, just to give us practice in machine-gun traversing fire'.

Yet a third wrote home and told the following story. 'At —— we captured a family of four. We played with the daughter as we would with a harlot. As the parents kept insisting that their daughter should be returned to them, we killed the father and mother. We then played with the daughter again as before, until our unit marched on, when we killed her.'

The fact that letters containing such statements were allowed to be sent home by the Japanese officers without being censored, seems to indicate clearly that these practices were not only allowed and condoned but were not even considered reprehensible. It will be noticed, however, that although the terrible account contained in the third and last letter was not interfered with, the name of the place where the incident occurred was, for *security reasons*, deleted.

These stories, and many others, became so general that War Minister Itagaki found it necessary to take some action to prevent soldiers writing home, or proceeding to Japan on leave, from destroying the Japanese Army's 'good name', as he put it. Special orders were, therefore, drawn up in the military service section of the War Ministry, classified as 'top secret' and issued, on the authority of the Vice-Minister for War in February 1939, addressed to 'All Japanese Army Commanders in China'.

Included in the orders were some of the extracts from the statements and letters of Japanese soldiers given above, and that alone is sufficient proof of their authenticity. The orders stated that this 'objectionable conduct' of returning soldiers was to be stopped. The words 'objectionable conduct', be it noted, did not refer to the war crimes committed by these men, but to the regrettable fact that they had told their friends and relations about them.

The ' Special Order ' ended with these words :

. . . not only does the improper talk of the returned officers and men become the cause of rumours, but it also impairs the trust of the people in the Army and disrupts the unity of the people supporting the Army. . . . I repeat the order again, to make the control of instructions even more strict and consequently to glorify the meritorious deeds, raise the Japanese Army's military reputation and ensure that nothing shall impair the accomplishment of the object of this Holy War.

There is no evidence of whether the 'objectionable conduct' which the Special Order condemned ceased after its publication. The authorities, however, who brought the order into being, did nothing to stop it. Month after month, and year after year, throughout the whole duration of the Sino-Japanese war the Japanese armies continued to fight like barbarians, and brought death and destruction to innocent people and defenceless villages wherever they went.

In 1941, some troops belonging to the Army of General Umezu, which was conducting a campaign to subdue all resistance to the puppet Government of the Emperor Pu Yi, in a single night killed all the members of three hundred families in a village in the province of Jehol, which they then burned to the ground.

Later in the same year, long after Hankow and Canton had been successively occupied, the Japanese forces, converging from both those cities, carried out operations far into the interior.

Entering the city of Wei-Yang in the Kwantung Province, they massacred over six hundred civilians. A witness who was called to give evidence before the Tokyo Tribunal had received a bayonet wound in the stomach on that occasion but had survived to tell the tale. He told the Court that the Japanese soldiers 'bayoncted male and female, young and old, without discrimination'.

Sweeping south from Hankow towards Changsha in the Province of Hunan in September 1941, the troops of one Japanese division forced, under threat of violence, over two hundred Chinese prisoners of war to plunder large quantities of wheat and rice from the granaries there; then, after the return of the prisoners with the loot, the Japanese soldiers, in order to cover up their theft, turned machine-guns on them and mowed them down. Not one survived.

Having entered Changsha they did much as they had done in Nanking, though on a minor scale, and everywhere throughout the Hunan, Kwangsi and Kwantung provinces the Japanese committed wholesale atrocities and other war

[51]

crimes. They raped and they plundered, they burned and they murdered. They illegally recruited women for forced labour and for prostitution. They shot by the thousand prisoners who had given themselves up.

The full extent of these crimes will never be accurately known, but in China they will never be forgotten.

CHAPTER III

THE GENERAL TREATMENT OF PRISONERS OF WAR

THE right of prisoners of war to be properly housed, fed, and humanely treated first became recognized late in the eighteenth century. In early times they were frequently butchered or offered as sacrifices to the gods. If they were not killed they were more often than not enslaved, though they were sometimes exchanged or ransomed.

Their position gradually improved as Christianity spread but it was long before it became accepted that the object of captivity, unlike ordinary imprisonment, was merely to prevent prisoners of war rejoining their own forces and again taking up arms.

By the Treaty of Friendship, made between Prussia and the United States of America in 1785, it was forbidden to keep prisoners of war in convict prisons or to manacle them. They had to be housed in healthy surroundings, allowed exercise and fed in the same way as the troops who had captured them.

Later, during the nineteenth century, the above principles became generally recognized, and at the beginning of the twentieth century, when in 1907 the Fourth Hague Convention was drawn up, 'Regulations Respecting the Laws and Customs of War on Land' were annexed to and made part of it.

During World War I the ill-treatment of British prisoners of war by the Germans[1] drew the world's attention to the shortcomings of the Convention's provisions about captivity,

---

[1] *The Times History & Encyclopedia of the War*, VI (1916), pages 241–8.
McCarthy, *The Prisoners of War in Germany.*
Parliamentary Command Papers 8984 and 9106.

and after a meeting in Geneva of the representatives of forty-seven States the 'International Convention Relative to the Treatment of Prisoners of War' was signed on 27th July 1929.

Japan's representative, who attended the conference, also signed the Convention, but she had not formally ratified it when she went to war in December 1941. Early in 1942, however, Great Britain, the United States of America and other great powers let Japan know that they would, on their part, observe all the provisions of the Convention and requested reciprocity.

The Japanese Foreign Minister, Togo, gave a formal assurance that although she was not bound by the Convention Japan would apply it, *mutatis mutandis*, to all American, Australian, British, Canadian and New Zealand prisoners of war. By this specific undertaking, Japan became morally bound to comply with the provisions of the Convention in all the possible circumstances and, where literal compliance was not possible, she was under an obligation to apply the nearest practicable equivalent.

But in any event the Japanese were formally bound by the Fourth Hague Convention of 1907. In the preamble it was stated that the powers declared, 'realizing that it was not possible at the time to concert regulations covering all circumstances that might arise in practice', that they did not intend that unforeseen cases should be left to the arbitrary judgment of military commanders, and that until a more complete code should be issued, in cases which had not been specifically dealt with in the Regulations, the belligerents remained 'under the protection and principles of the laws of nations as they resulted from the usages of civilized peoples, the laws of humanity, and the dictate of the public conscience'.

It was useless, therefore, for the Japanese leaders to maintain at the Tokyo trial, as they did, that as they had never ratified the Geneva Prisoner of War Convention of 1929 they were under no obligation to treat their captives properly.

The Regulations which were attached to the earlier Convention of 1907 provided that they must be treated humanely and their personal property respected, that all captured troops, including non-combatants, were entitled to prisoner of war status, that work should be neither excessive nor connected with the war, that they must be decently housed, and fed as well as their captors, that a proper record of their particulars should be taken and disclosed to those entitled to ask for them, and that the relief provided for them by organizations such as the Red Cross must be given to them.

Each and every one of these provisions was contravened time and time again. They were murdered, they were bayoneted, they were tortured, they were beaten. They were robbed of their possessions. They were worked night and day in appalling conditions and on prohibited tasks. They were kept in filth and squalor and many of them were starved to death or reduced to living skeletons.

The uncivilized ill-treatment of prisoners of war by the Japanese was the natural outcome of the code of Bushido, which was inculcated into the Japanese soldier as part of his basic training. It was considered cowardly to show one's back to the enemy, and to do so brought dishonour on the family name. The Japanese warriors

> looked upon it as shame to themselves not to die when their Lord was hard pressed . . . their own shame was the shame upon their parents, their family, their house and their whole clan, and with this idea deeply impressed upon their minds, the Samurai, no matter of what rank, held their lives light as feathers when compared with the weight they attached to the maintenance of a spotless name.[1]

The youth of Japan had been brought up, in accordance with this Bushido precept, to consider that the greatest honour was to die for their Emperor and that it was ignominious to surrender to the enemy. It was because it appeared to the Japanese to run counter to this view of military conduct

[1] Jukichi Inouye, *Introduction to Chushingura*. Maruzen Company Ltd. 4th Edition, 1910.

that the Geneva Prisoner of War Convention of 1929 was never ratified by Japan.

The soldiers of all the Western powers who, having fought to the last round of ammunition, find themselves completely surrounded or facing hopeless odds are not disgraced if, in such circumstances, they surrender. By international agreement their names are taken and their relatives informed that they are alive and well.

In similar conditions the only honourable conduct for the Japanese soldier is to fight to the death. He should never surrender, rather he should keep his last round of ammunition for himself or charge the enemy in a final suicidal assault. Even were he taken prisoner after being wounded and unable to move or unconscious, he could never again hold up his head in Japan. He and his family would be disgraced for ever.

This concept of manly duty undoubtedly led to the Japanese soldier having a feeling of utter contempt for those who surrendered to the Japanese forces. They had forfeited all right to any consideration. When the first American prisoners of war surrendered in large numbers in Bataan the Japanese soldier was astounded when they asked that their names should be reported to their Government so that their families should know that they were alive.

Nor did the Japanese soldier make any distinction between those who fought honourably and courageously until an inevitable surrender and those who gave up without a fight. They were all the same to him, they were entitled to no respect for they had lost their honour.

This attitude of mind does much to explain, though it does not excuse, the Japanese Army and Navy's treatment of Allied prisoners of war. As Prime Minister Tojo said when he gave instructions to Commandants of prisoner of war camps, 'in Japan we have our own ideology concerning prisoners of war which should naturally make their treatment more or less different from that in Europe and America'.

From the beginning of the Pacific War the generally

accepted Regulations concerning the custody of prisoners of war and civilian internees were flagrantly disregarded. Prisoners of war were murdered by shooting, decapitation, drowning, and other methods. They died during death marches on which prisoners of war who were sick and quite unfit for any form of exertion were forced to march for long distances in conditions which even fit troops could not have been expected to stand. Many of those who fell out of the column were shot or bayoneted to death by the escort.

There was forced labour in tropical heat, without any protection from the sun, and thousands of prisoners died whilst working on the Burma–Siam railway upon the construction of which they should never have been employed.

In the prison camps the conditions were appalling. The accommodation was inadequate, the sanitation non-existent, and the absence or scarcity of medical supplies resulted in thousands of deaths from disease.

Prisoners were systematically beaten and subjected to a variety of tortures in attempts to extract information from them, or for minor disciplinary offences committed by them in the camps.

Prisoners of war, recaptured after escaping, were shot, and captured aviators beheaded, in the usual Japanese method by sword.

Even cannibalism was not unknown.

The above list is by no means exhaustive, and many other examples of brutality and ill-treatment will be found in the succeeding chapters which describe in some detail these horrible crimes.

The extent of the ill-treatment, however, can be appreciated from this significant comparison. In the European theatres of war 235,473 British and American prisoners of war were captured by the Germans and Italians. Of this number, 9,348, or 4 per cent of the total, died in captivity. In the Pacific theatres of war the percentage was 27.

In addition to actual brutality and ill-treatment, excessive and unlawful punishment was systematically imposed upon

[57]

the prisoners. In an instruction sent to the commandants of prisoner of war and civilian internee camps by Tojo, enjoining them to exercise the most rigid discipline over the prisoners and internees, he wrote:

> Prisoners of war must be placed under strict discipline so far as it does not contravene the law of humanity. It is necessary to take care not to be obsessed with the mistaken idea of humanitarianism or swayed by personal feelings towards those prisoners of war, which may grow in the long time of their imprisonment.

The Geneva Prisoner of War Convention of 1929, which Japan had signed but not ratified and which Foreign Minister Togo had promised to apply, *mutatis mutandis*, to all American, Australian, British, Canadian and New Zealand prisoners of war specifically forbade the following: 'corporal punishment, imprisonment in quarters without daylight and any form of cruelty whatever'. It also prohibited collective punishment for individual acts. Under the Convention escaped prisoners of war, retaken before they had been able to get right away, were only liable to disciplinary punishment.

The Japanese thoroughly understood these provisions, which they were under a moral obligation to observe, for the military authorities in Japan had, in 1934, opposed its ratification upon these grounds, namely that under the Convention 'prisoners of war could not be so severely punished as Japanese soldiers and this would involve a revision of the Japanese Military and Naval Disciplinary Codes to put them on an equal footing, a revision which was undesirable in the interests of discipline'.

Despite Togo's assurances, a regulation was published by the Japanese War Minister in 1943 in the following terms: 'In case a prisoner of war is guilty of an act of insubordination, he shall be subject to imprisonment or arrest, and *any other measures deemed necessary for the purpose of discipline may be added*.'[1]

[1] Author's italics.

This regulation gave *carte blanche* to the Japanese forces, particularly those responsible for the custody of prisoners of war, and under it corporal punishment, as well as torture and mass punishment, was administered. It was the common practice wherever prisoners of war or civilian internees were to be found to inflict corporal punishment upon them for the slightest disciplinary offence or, more often than not, for no offence. In its mildest form it consisted of slapping,[1] beating and kicking. If the victim became unconscious he was revived with cold water and given a second dose. Thousands died of this form of punishment alone for many of them were already wasted by disease and starvation.

Many other forms of cruel and illegal punishment were in common use. Exposing the prisoner to the hot tropical sun for long hours without any protection, suspending him by his arms in such a manner as at times to force the arms from their sockets, tying him up and leaving him where he would be attacked by insects, confining him in a cramped cage for days without food, shutting him up for weeks at a time in an underground cell without light, fresh air and with scarcely any food, forcing him to kneel on sharp objects in a cramped position for long periods of time.

Whenever the Japanese were unable to find the perpetrator of individual acts, mass punishment was employed. That most commonly used was compelling all the members of the group or hut concerned to assume a strained position such as sitting with the legs folded under the body, the hands on the knees with the palms upwards and to remain in that position during daylight for several days.

In the Havelock Road Camp in Malaya the prisoners on more than one occasion, as a collective punishment, were made to run round in a circle without shoes over broken glass whilst beaten with the rifle butts of their Japanese guards.

During the war the Japanese Prisoner of War Regulations were amended so as to permit an escaping prisoner to be

[1] See Proceedings of the IMT, Far East, page 49,702.

punished in the same way as a deserter from the Japanese Army.

> The leader of a group of persons who have acted together in effecting an escape shall be subject to either death, or imprisonment for a minimum of ten years. The other persons involved shall be subject to either the death penalty or a minimum imprisonment of one year.[1]

Under the regulation the death penalty was imposed in nearly every case in which a prisoner had attempted to escape, or had escaped and been recaptured.

Allied prisoners of war were also consistently subjected by the Japanese to insults and public humiliation. The object of this was to impress the other peoples of Asia with the superiority of the Master Race of the East and to lower the prestige of Western civilization.

On 4th March 1942 the following telegram from the Chief-of-Staff of the Korean Army[2] was received by the Japanese War Ministry.

> As it would be very effective in stamping out the respect and admiration of the Korean people for Britain and America, and also in establishing in them a strong faith in [our] victory, and as the Governor-General[3] and the Army are both strongly desirous of it, we wish you would intern 1,000 British and 1,000 American prisoners of war in Korea. Kindly give this matter special consideration.

A reply was sent on the following day to the effect that one thousand 'white prisoners of war' were to be sent to Fusan.

Further details of General Itagaki's plans to exploit Allied prisoners of war for psychological purposes were sent to Tojo later in the month. 'It is our purpose,' Itagaki wrote, 'by interning American and British prisoners of war in Korea to

---

[1] Extract from an Ordinance of 9th March 1943.
[2] Commanded at this time by General Itagaki, one of the Japanese 'major war criminals'.
[3] The Governor-General was General Minami, also one of the Japanese 'major war criminals'.

make Koreans realize positively the true might of our empire as well as to contribute to psychological propaganda work for stamping out any ideas of the worship of Europe and America which the greater part of Korea still retains deep down.'

In May the Commander-in-Chief of the Japanese forces in Singapore was informed that before August the white prisoners of war would be handed over to the Formosan and Korean Armies.

In August the first batch of prisoners who had been captured in the fighting in Malaya arrived in Southern Korea, and were marched through the streets of Seoul and Fusan before a crowd of some 120,000 Koreans and 57,000 Japanese. They had previously been subjected to a very drastic slimming diet by means of malnutrition, ill-treatment and neglect in order that their poor physical condition should invite contempt from the audience whom the parade was intended to impress.

It appears to have been, from the Japanese point of view, an unqualified success. In sending his report to Kimura, the Vice-Minister of War, Itagaki's Chief-of-Staff quoted the remarks of two Koreans who were in the crowd.

'When we look at their frail and unsteady appearance, it is no wonder that they lost to the Japanese forces,' one bystander was overheard to say.

'When I saw young Korean soldiers,' another remarked, 'members of the Imperial Army, guarding the prisoners, I shed tears of joy.'

The Chief of Staff ended his report with this comment: 'On the whole it seems that the idea was very successful in driving all admiration for the British out of the Koreans' minds and in driving into them an understanding of the situation.'

The parade in Fusan was thus described by a British soldier who took part in it:

At about 9 a.m. one thousand British and Australian prisoners of war arrived at Fusan in Southern Korea from

[61]

Singapore after a journey of five weeks in the Japanese transport *Fukai Maru*. As they disembarked the prisoners were sprayed with disinfectant, photographed by Japanese pressmen and then mustered on the wharf for inspection of kit by the Kempei Tai. During this inspection watches, wedding and signet rings and personal photographs were taken by the Kempei Tai and never returned to their owners.

After the search, all the prisoners, including those who were sick, were made to fall in, in column of fours, and were marched round the streets of Fusan between the marshalled Korean inhabitants of the city, with a Japanese officer at the head of the column on horseback and Japanese guards on either side. The march went on all day under a hot sun with only two halts in the playgrounds of two schools where the children were allowed to come close up to the prisoners to jeer and spit at them.

The march ended about 5 p.m. at the railway station where each prisoner was given a small oblong fibre box containing cold boiled rice, a piece of dried fish and a few pieces of pickled cucumber. They were allowed to eat this on the platform as it was the first meal they had eaten since 8 a.m. Before entering the train each man was given another similar box of food to last the next twenty-four hours which was to be spent on the train from Fusan to Seoul.

On arrival at Seoul the prisoners were again marched round part of the town before finally entering the prisoner of war camp which was to be their home for the next two years. As a result of this propaganda march, and the long train journey on starvation rations, several of the prisoners died a few days after arriving at Seoul.

After the success of this first attempt to humiliate Allied prisoners on a large scale the practice became widespread. More than 2,000 miles away, at Moulmein in Burma, in February 1944, twenty-five Allied prisoners of war were paraded through the streets. They were in an emaciated condition and were forced to carry notices in Burmese, falsely stating that they had recently been captured on the Arakan front. They were ridiculed and held up to contempt by a Japanese officer who accompanied the parade.

Frequent protests, formal and informal, against these consistent contraventions of international law were made to Japan by the Allied powers and by the Protecting power, which was Switzerland. Most of them were ignored and, when a reply was given, it was either untruthful or evasive.

There is no doubt that these complaints were known to all the members of the Japanese Government who, even if they pretended at the time to know nothing about the Allied prisoners' plight, must then have been put on inquiry. Copies of the Allied protests were circulated by the Foreign Ministry to all the other Ministries concerned including, of course, the Service Ministries. They were discussed at the bi-weekly meetings of the departmental chiefs of the War Ministry when it was decided whether or not a reply should be given and what form, if any, it should take.

Radio broadcasts were continually being made from Allied broadcasting stations giving details of the Japanese atrocities and warning Japan of the retribution to come. These talks were monitored by the Foreign Ministry and also circulated. It is known that they reached Imperial circles, for an entry was made by Kido, Lord Keeper of the Privy Seal, in his diary for 19th March 1942 to this effect: '. . . the Imperial Household Minister came to the office and told me about Eden's address in Parliament concerning our soldiers' atrocities at Hong Kong, and we exchanged opinions.'

Many detailed protests were sent by the United States Government through the Swiss Embassy and many of them were dealt with by the Foreign Minister Shigemitsu.[1] He accused the State Department of 'distorting and exaggerating the facts' and rejected the protests.

The United States answered this accusation in the following terms: 'The United States Government cannot accept a statement by the Japanese Government impugning its veracity . . . the protests are all based on documentary evidence which cannot be refuted in such an arbitrary fashion.'

[1] See Chapter XV.

British protests met with the same fate. In July 1942 the British Government protested to the Japanese Foreign Minister, Togo, about a photograph which had appeared in a Tokyo newspaper showing British prisoners of war cleaning the streets in Rangoon to the evident amusement of the public. Two months later a further protest was made about the conditions in Rangoon Gaol where British prisoners of war were in custody. The only reply received was to the effect that 'the competent authorities stated after having made a full inquiry that the facts set out in the British protests never happened'.

The following reply from Foreign Minister Shigemitsu to a British protest about the health of the Allied prisoners of war employed on the construction of the Burma–Siam Railway must have seemed incredible to those who knew the facts.

> The Imperial Government, by exercising great vigilance as to the health and hygiene of prisoners of war, takes added measures, such as monthly medical examinations of each prisoner of war camp, to enable sickness to be treated in the first stage.

This was a completely fallacious statement, for these unfortunate prisoners had received no medical attention whatsoever, and had died by the thousand from beri-beri, cholera, malaria and other tropical and deficiency diseases.

The true facts became known after a ship named *Rakuyo Maru* was sunk by torpedo in the South China Sea in September 1944 with 1,300 Allied prisoners of war on board. Only a hundred of the Australian and British prisoners were picked up and when, eventually, they reached home they told the whole story. All the available prisoners in Singapore and Java had been sent to Burma and Thailand to build the new strategic railway. The conditions in which they worked and the terrible treatment they received are described in another chapter.[1]

In reply to the British note setting out all the information

[1] Chapter V.

obtained from these survivors Foreign Minister Togo denied that any atrocities had been committed by the Japanese troops.

The ill-treatment of prisoners of war and civilian internees was at all times condoned by the Japanese Government who failed to impose any or adequate punishment on those whom they knew to be responsible. Furthermore, they did everything to conceal it by preventing the representatives of the Protecting power from visiting the camps, and on the few occasions when such visits were permitted, by refusing to allow the prisoners to be interviewed except in the presence of one of the camp staff.

They also put out propaganda to give the impression that all Allied prisoners of war and civilian internees were well treated. Shortly after the return of the Allied troops to Batavia, after the surrender of Japan, they captured several Japanese propaganda films. One such film had been made for showing in Australia when the Japanese forces conquered the country, as they fully expected to do in those early days.

British, Australian and Dutch prisoners of war and internees were forced to act in this film: many of them subsequently died but quite a few were still alive at the end of the war. It was eventually decided by the Netherlands Indies Government Information Service, known by the initials NIGIS, to send the film to Australia and to try and get together there the same ex-prisoners of war whom the Japanese had compelled, by the threat of starvation, to take parts in the film, and to introduce into it shots from other films which showed the real conditions under which the prisoners and internees had been living when the original film was made.

The film, which was made by the Japanese in 1943, showed the Allied prisoners living a life of comfort and apparent ease. There were scenes shot in a beautiful library, an up-to-date surgery and a well-equipped kitchen, none of which existed in any of the camps in Java, or indeed anywhere else. The scenes taken in the kitchen were, in fact, shot in the de-luxe

F

Hotel des Indes in Batavia which was the Japanese Head-quarters. One day a few Australians were sent out of camp, supposedly to go on a working party. Instead they were marched off to the hotel kitchen where the pictures were taken. Afterwards they returned back to camp to resume their normal diet of what was little better than garbage.

Another scene depicted what was supposed to be a normal day in the lives of the women internees. The script ran something like this:

> *Children singing:* 'Ring around the rosy [sic], pocket full of posy [sic], Ki chu, Ki chu, all fall down.'
> *Women talking:* 'Thank goodness that's finished.'
> 'Excuse me, I am going up to Mrs. Marsh with this dress. I won't be long.'
> 'Fay, come here.'
> 'Lovely weather today.'
> 'Would you like some tea?'
> 'No, thank you, dear, not today, some other time.'
> 'What *are* you worrying about?'
> 'Well, when I came into this camp I did think I would be able to lose weight. Instead of that I have been putting it on daily.'
> 'What *are* you two talking about?'
> 'Oh, it's only Mabel talking about her figure again.'

Explaining, in the revised version of the film subsequently shown in Australia after the war, how the shot in the women's camp came to be taken, a Mrs. Johnson, who was herself there, said: 'For a while conditions in our camp were really not so bad. It was pleasantly situated, the food was good enough and we had reasonable freedom, but we were, in fact, living in a fool's paradise.

'When the Japs had made the scenes which you have just seen—that was the end.

'We were whisked off to the germ-laden, rat-infested, filthy, bug-breeding slums you see in Batavia, a forlorn mass of modern misery, of brutal beatings and indignities, of

degrees of fever, weevils, lice, weevily rice and utter hopeless-
ness. That is what Java meant to us from then on.'

Another scene depicted a man and a woman in a dress shop
where the following dialogue took place:

> 'Good afternoon.'
> 'Gray, do you think this will fit my kid?'
> 'What, the big one?'
> 'No, the new one.'
> 'How many have you got?'
> 'Five?'
> 'Oh, no!'
> 'Yes I have.'

The two customers in the shop who were engaged in this
conversation had been given a sheaf of occupation currency
notes by the Japanese for the purpose, which were taken
away from them immediately the scene had been shot. The
two 'shop girls' were Dutch internees dressed up for the
occasion and given special 'hair-dos'. While it was being
acted the prisoners' guards, with fixed bayonets, were standing by just outside camera range.

But the final indignity was when about five hundred of the
prisoners of war were paraded one morning for what they
thought was a religious ceremony of some kind.

Group Captain Noble of the Royal Air Force, who was
one of those present, has described it thus:

> At dawn one day five hundred of us were assembled in the
> hospital grounds where a large cross had been placed, its base
> inscribed 'Lest we forget'.
> When General Saito and his staff came on parade a religious
> ceremony commenced. It was impressive. We began to think
> that the Nips must have a grain of decency in them after all.
> But when General Saito read his speech, with the cameraman
> shooting, and then re-read it to let them take some close ups
> and we saw the shoddy cardboard cross swaying in the wind,
> and we realized that the barbed wire had been camouflaged
> with broken branches, and the machine-guns were trained on

us hidden behind them, then we tumbled to the farce it was. The reverence with which we Christians observed our faith became no more than a mockery and an insult to our fallen comrades.

At the end of this sacrilegious sequence these words appeared on the screen, 'We treat well our enemy soldiers. We protect them. May their spirits rest in peace in Heaven.'[1]

From the very outset of Japan's entry into the war until her unconditional surrender the murder, torture, ill-treatment and wilful neglect of prisoners of war continued unceasingly. Those who committed these crimes had never expected that retribution would follow for, as one of them said, 'we shall be the victors and will not have to answer questions'.

When, at last, it became apparent that Japan would have to surrender, an organized attempt was made to destroy all documentary and other evidence of the ill-treatment of prisoners of war and civilian internees.[2] The Chief of the Prisoner of War Camps sent a signal on 20th August 1945 to

[1] In some prisoner of war camps, however, the Japanese attitude to the disposal of the dead was beyond reproach. The following statement on the burial of the dead in one of the camps in Java at Tanjong Priok was given by Colonel C. W. Maisey, OBE, who was Senior Medical Officer there during the whole period of his captivity.

At Tanjong Priok we carried out our funeral services in the local cemetery virtually without interference. In the majority of cases the Japanese commandant came to the camp hospital to pay his respects to the deceased. In the hospitals of St. Vicentius and Mater Dolorosa they went to a considerable amount of trouble. A service was held in the hospital grounds, the coffin was placed on trestles, we stood on one side and the Japanese, including a senior staff officer from their headquarters, on the other side.

The Japanese officer would lay a wreath on the coffin, stand back, remove his hat and make a deep ceremonial bow. Our padre would conduct a short service. Then in turn a senior member from each of the Allies would lay a wreath and salute the coffin. . . . As a British soldier remarked, 'They are only decent to you when you are bloody well dead.'

[2] Cf. the plans made by the Germans for the destruction of all real evidence of their crimes in the concentration camps. These provided for the destruction of the camp sites and the liquidation of their surviving inmates which only the rapid Allied advance circumvented.

See *The Scourge of the Swastika*, Chapter VI.

all commands in which prisoner of war camps were situated, and these two extracts are striking testimony of the Japanese guilty knowledge.

(1) Documents which would be unfavourable for us in the hands of the enemy are to be treated in the same way as secret documents and destroyed.

(2) Personnel who ill-treated prisoners of war and internees, or who are held in extremely bad odour by them, are permitted to take care of the situation by immediately transferring or fleeing without trace.

CHAPTER IV

THE MURDER OF CAPTURED AIRCREWS

ONE of the reasons given by the Japanese military authorities for opposing, as they did tooth and nail, the ratification of the Geneva Prisoner of War Convention of 1929 was that this would make it easier for an enemy air force to carry out raids on Japanese cities. If enemy aircrews knew that if they did not return from their mission they would be treated properly as prisoners of war in accordance with international law, the opponents of ratification argued, it would have the practical effect of doubling the range of the enemy's planes.

The effect of air raids on the overcrowded and poorly built cities of Japan was greatly dreaded by the Japanese Government. On 18th April 1942 this fear was realized, for on that day the first Allied air-raids took place when Tokyo and other Japanese cities were bombed by a number of American planes ·under the command of Colonel Doolittle. As their Prime Minister said, it was a great shock to them all.

On the insistent demand of the Japanese Chief of Staff that the death penalty should be instituted for all the airmen who bombed Japan, Tojo introduced retrospective regulations to permit the death penalty being imposed on Colonel Doolittle's aircrews. The provisions of these regulations made them applicable to 'enemy fliers who have raided Japan, Manchukuo or any other Japanese operational area and have come within the jurisdiction of the Japanese Expeditionary Forces in China'. This, of course, included the United States airmen already held as prisoners in China.

Thus a sentence of death or imprisonment for ten or more years became the recognized punishment for the following offences:

Any air attack,
(1) upon ordinary people,
(2) upon private property of a non-military nature,
(3) against other than military objectives, and
(4) 'violations of war-time international law'.

The first three of these offences had been regularly committed by the Japanese themselves in China for a long time. The Chief of Staff of the Central China Expeditionary Force had, as early as 1939, adopted the policy of indiscriminate bombing in order to strike terror into the civilian population. The fourth offence, namely 'violation of war-time international law', was already punishable under the existing international law but only after proper trial, and to the extent legally permitted.

The aircrews of two of Colonel Doolittle's planes, which had had to make forced landings in China, had been taken prisoner and handcuffed like ordinary criminals. The members of one crew had been taken to Shanghai, and the other to Nanking where they were interrogated by the Kempei Tai using their usual methods of torture.

A week after their capture both crews, handcuffed and blindfolded, were moved to Tokyo where they were thrown into cells at the Military Police Headquarters. They remained there in solitary confinement for eighteen days and were again interrogated daily under torture. Eventually, to avoid further suffering, they signed statements which were written in Japanese and which they could not, therefore, understand.

On 17th June they returned to Shanghai, where they remained in gaol for more than two months. During that time they were starved and abominably ill-treated.

On 28th July Tojo's new regulations were circularized to all Commands, including that of General Hata, the Supreme Commander of all the Japanese forces then in China, and the General was ordered to put the American airmen on trial.

The trial, which was held on 20th August, was a farce. Some of the accused were by this time, after all their suffering, unfit to plead or to take any part in the proceedings, neither the charge nor the evidence was translated into English, and they were given no facilities for making their defence. All were sentenced to death. When the proceedings were sent to Tokyo for review, Tojo confirmed three sentences of death, and commuted the other five to life imprisonment. Early in October, the three death sentences which had not been reduced were put into execution.

Thus was the policy of killing Allied airmen, who were captured by the Japanese, initiated, and thereafter large numbers of airmen, who were entitled to the protection of the Geneva Prisoner of War Convention, were similarly put to death. It was the common practice to starve and torture these prisoners for a considerable period before they were tried, more often than not trial was dispensed with, and even if a trial was held it was nothing but a hollow sham.

An American bomber, on a mission from the Philippines to bomb the railway at Saigon, crashed near Cholon in French Indo-China, and the two survivors were taken to the Kempei Tai prison in Saigon and subjected to various forms of torture and repeated beatings. They were taken from the prison, bound, and transported shoeless in a motor car to a secluded spot near the airfield. The Japanese escort consisted of three men commanded by a warrant officer. When they approached the airfield the warrant officer stopped the car, and, in company with a member of the escort, led one of the American airmen into the woods while the remaining two members brought in the second American. The warrant officer made the two men kneel down, one after the other, beside a grave which had already been dug, and then decapitated them. The Japanese party then returned to Saigon, and one of them later committed suicide to avoid arrest by the British. The warrant officer was eventually tried by a British Military Court in Singapore, convicted and sentenced to death by hanging.

The usual defence of superior orders was put forward, although the accused admitted that he was the principal participant in the executions, and that there had been no sort of trial. A plea of superior orders must fail when the act committed is manifestly illegal. Nevertheless the defence put forward may constitute a mitigating factor. Although admitting all the facts the accused, in his petition, did not shrink from making the following appeal:

> Jesus Christ our Master has taught us 'Thou shalt love thine enemy, thou shalt pray for them that curse thee, thou shalt be good unto them that hate thee'—and He Himself practised it. This great spirit of love of humanity as taught to us by the life of Jesus Christ itself left a great impression upon mankind throughout the world. It is your petitioner's humble view that a spirit of love of humanity, as taught to us by Jesus Christ, would give a deeper, more lasting, stronger and better influence upon the history of mankind than threats of rigorous and severe punishment.'

In July 1945 seven American airmen who had been shot down in a B24 were brought to the Seletar Naval Base where they were detained for some time until orders were received from Lieutenant-Commander Okamoto, the local naval commander, for their disposal. After some delay caused, so Okamoto alleged, by having to refer the matter to his superiors for a decision, he ordered his sub-lieutenant to execute them. Arrangements were accordingly made and the eight airmen were beheaded on the Nee Soon rifle range.

At the trial of Okamoto, the sub-lieutenant and a petty officer, at Changi in December 1947 by a British Military Court the following evidence was given by a Japanese named Oka Harumitzu who was one of the cooks at the naval camp.

> About the middle of July 1945 a flight of B24 aircraft came over to bomb Singapore. As they came over the harbour they were strafing two Japanese ships engaged in mine-sweeping and one plane was shot down by the two ships, the destroyer *Kamikaze* and the minesweeper, *Toshimaru*. It crashed into the water and seven survivors were picked up by the two ships . . . they were brought to our camp and so I went out to see them. They were kept in a small prison where previously fourteen or

fifteen other prisoners of war had been imprisoned before they were beheaded.

When I went to see the flyers I noticed that one of them was an officer. He was wearing overalls with a zipper up the front and had a pair of cloth wings sewn onto it above the breast pocket. I was told that he was the pilot. The other members of the crew were wearing fatigues with combat boots but some had only shirts on above the waist.

They were divided into two groups, three were put in one hut and four in another. I looked inside the huts and saw that they were lying on the floor with their hands tied in front of them and were blindfolded. One of the men had an injured leg which was bleeding profusely so that the blood was coming through the bandage. I did not see them get any medical attention. I returned to my duties after I had looked at the airmen and food was sent to them every day for the rest of the fortnight. . . .

Then one morning, about the 4th or 5th August, I saw the following people getting ready to board a truck and carrying their swords [here witness gave the names of five petty officers]. They told me that they were going out to behead the flyers and asked if I wanted to come along. But I didn't like to participate in such things so I didn't go.

About two o'clock that afternoon when the five petty officers had returned I heard them discussing the morning's events. 'It was difficult to cut today,' one of them said. 'In Hikiji's demonstration the neck was cut perfectly,' said another, and a third remarked that one of the airmen ran off so he had to go after him to cut his head off. It appeared that about twenty-five of them had taken part in the execution, and that after the instructor in swordsmanship had given a demonstration the others were allowed to try their hand at it.

I heard nothing more about this incident until after the war was over and I was in the POW camp located at Batobaha. At that time Petty Officer Ton, who was in charge of the execution party on the occasion I have given evidence about, told me that as soon as they heard news of Japan's surrender, he and the other executioners went at once to Niyusun airport, dug up the airmen's bodies, brought them back to camp, cremated them on a big fire on the barrack square and threw the ashes into the sea. The flames did not attract any undue attention as there were fires lit at all the different naval and military establishments at that time to burn all military documents and records before the Allied forces arrived.

The witness Oka said that after the Japanese surrender all naval personnel were warned to keep quiet about these incidents so that the Allies would not get to hear of them. He, however, had volunteered to tell the Allied authorities all about it because he felt that it was not right that honourable prisoners of war who had surrendered should be treated as were these airmen. He considered that those responsible 'should be punished for the good of Japan and humanity as a whole'.

These unfortunate American airmen were put to death merely because the 10th Special Naval Base Unit were short of men and found it a nuisance to have to provide guards for their prisoners. 'What in the world is to be done with these prisoners?' asked the sub-lieutenant of his lieutenant-commander. The lieutenant-commander telephoned to Fleet HQ: 'What are we to do with these prisoners?' Back came the reply: 'Execute them!'

The deaths of these innocent men, who were entitled to be treated as prisoners of war, does not seem to have weighed very heavily on Lieutenant-Commander Okamoto's conscience for he ended a statement which he made under oath, on 11th June 1947, with these words:

The general factors influencing the decision to kill them were:
(1) We could not send them back to Japan.
(2) We could not guard them indefinitely, and
(3) Although the general policy was to send POWs back to Japan or hand them over to the Army authorities, the orders of Fleet HQ had to be carried out.

As far as I know Admiral Imamura never objected to these orders for the execution of any of the prisoners of war, neither did Captain Matsuda, nor Captain Saito, nor myself. I thought at the time that the affair was a bad thing and as a private individual thought these things were pitiful; but I could do nothing against orders from Fleet HQ.

I was not anxious to have the men disposed of. I was interested in the matter only because Lieutenant Kobayahi was unable to guard the men because of his operational duties.

There is no doubt that the order to execute captured Allied airmen was nearly always given or approved by superior military authority in the earlier years of the war, but from the end of 1944 the practice became almost general and automatic.

Before 1945, although the trials were purely perfunctory they were the rule rather than the exception, but in May of that year the Commandant of the Military Police in Japan considered that such proceedings imposed an unnecessary delay in the killing of captured Allied airmen, and sent a letter to each of the Military Police Headquarters complaining of the delay in the 'disposal' of captured flyers, and recommending that in future the Military Police should dispense with courts-martial after obtaining the approval of the District Commander. After receipt of this letter twenty-seven were killed without trial in the Tokai Military District, forty-three in General Hata's command and twenty-four in Fukuoka.

Sometimes the executions were carried out by firing squads, but usually less humane methods were used.

The Army Prison in Tokyo was situated on the edge of the city's principal military parade ground. It was used as a disciplinary barracks for Japanese soldiers under sentence. The prison grounds were small, and surrounded by a brick wall approximately twelve feet high. The buildings were of wood and constructed so close together as to occupy the whole ground space within the walls except for a few alleyways.

One of the cell blocks was shut off from the other buildings by a wooden wall seven feet high. On the night of 25th May 1945 Tokyo was bombed when sixty-two Allied flyers were confined in this cell block. In the other buildings within the prison walls were four hundred and sixty-four Japanese soldiers under sentence. The Tokyo International Tribunal who heard all the evidence about this incident said in its judgment:

> . . . the wooden buildings of the prison, as well as the highly inflammable dwellings surrounding it, were hit and set on fire by incendiary bombs. The prison was completely demolished; and after the fire, it was found that all of the sixty-two Allied flyers had perished. It is significant that none of the four hundred and sixty-four Japanese or any of their gaolers suffered a similar fate. The evidence shows that the fate of the Allied airmen was deliberately planned.

Another method of murdering Allied airmen was employed in China, at Hankow in December 1944, when three Americans, who had been shot down and taken prisoner earlier, were paraded through the streets and subjected to ridicule, beating and torture by the inhabitants. When they had been made to run the gauntlet of public hostility they were saturated with petrol and burned alive. This was personally sanctioned by the Commander of the 34th Japanese Army.

Some Allied Air Force prisoners of war were killed by injection. One American aviator was shot down near Saigon in May 1945, taken prisoner and locked up in the Kempei Tai gaol. He had been badly wounded and burnt about the face yet received no medical treatment for three days during which he was taken to Kempei Tai headquarters daily for interrogation. Then, at last, he was admitted to a military hospital, but even there he was questioned daily by the Kempei Tai in their usual pleasant way.[1]

By the end of June the prisoner was well on the way to recovery, when the head surgeon received a visit from the local Kempei Tai chief. The KT, the doctor was told, had no

[1] See Chapter XIV.

further use for the patient who should now be 'disposed of' in hospital.

When the Kempei Tai chief next visited the hospital about ten days later the prisoner was still there, and alive. The surgeon was then told, politely but firmly, that it was an order from the KT who would take full responsibility. The airman must be 'disposed of' at once.

The following day two surgeons performed an operation on the patient who by now had fully recovered. Under a general anæsthetic an incision was made in the neck to expose the lower end of the right jugular vein. A fatal dose of novocaine was then injected into the jugular vein and the airman died on the operating table in less than two minutes.

All the participants in this crime, the three doctors concerned, and the Kempei Tai captain, were eventually apprehended, tried by a British Military Court and sentenced to death by hanging.[1]

Early in February 1945 an RAF Liberator crashed in Lower Burma and the two officers and four flight sergeants, who formed the crew of six, were captured by the Japanese garrison at Pypon and sent to Myaungnya where they were incarcerated in the civil prison. After the two officers had been interrogated by the Kempei Tai without success the four flight sergeants underwent a similar ordeal. They properly refused to give any military information and were brutally ill-treated.

The interrogation of the flight sergeants was carried out some six miles away from the prison on the fringe of the reserved forest area to which they had been taken for the purpose. Realizing that no information could be obtained from the prisoners, they were marched some two miles further along the road where the main party of Japanese guards was waiting for them. All four airmen were led to the side of a newly dug trench, blindfolded, bound and forced to sit on the edge. They were then beheaded with the Japanese

[1] Majors Mabuchi and Nakamura, Captain Wakamatsu, all of the Army Medical Corps; and Captain Hisakawa of the Kempei Tai.

officer's own sword and the guards were afterwards allowed to carry out bayonet practice on the headless bodies.

These are but a few examples of the butchery of captured Allied Air Force prisoners which, from the end of 1944 until the Japanese surrender, was carried out with increasing regularity and, it would appear from the large volume of evidence available, with considerable enthusiasm.

The following excerpt from the diary of a captured Japanese soldier described his reactions when he was privileged to be a spectator at one of these outrages.

BLOOD CARNIVAL

29 Mar. 43. All four of us (Technicians Kurokawa, Nishiguchi, Yawata and myself) assembled in front of the headquarters at 1500 hours. One of the two members of the crew of the Douglas which was shot down by AA on the 18th, and who had been under interrogation by the 7th Base Force for some days, had been returned to the Salamua Garrison, and it had been decided to kill him. Unit Commander Komai, when he came to the observation station today, told us personally that, in accordance with the compassionate sentiments of Japanese Bushido, he was going to kill the prisoner himself with his favourite sword. So we gathered to see this happen.

After we had waited a little more than ten minutes the escort party came to the guard house and took over the prisoner, who was then given his last drink of water.

The chief medical officer and the unit commander, together with the headquarters platoon commander, came out of the officers' mess wearing their swords. The time has come, so the prisoner, with his arms bound and his long hair cropped very close, totters forward. He probably suspects what is afoot but he is put on the truck and we set out for our destination. My seat is next to the medical officer, and ten guards ride with us. To the pleasant rumble of the engine we run swiftly along the road in the growing twilight. The glowing sun has set behind the western hills, gigantic clouds rise before us, and the dusk is falling all around.

It will not be long now. As I picture the scene we are about to witness, my heart beats faster. I glance at the prisoner: he

[79]

has probably resigned himself to his fate. As though saying farewell to the world, as he sits in the truck, he looks at the hills and at the sea and seems deep in thought. I feel a surge of pity and turn my eyes away.

As we pass by the place where last year our lamented squad leader was cremated, Technician Nishiguchi must have been thinking about him too, for he remarked, 'It's a long time since we were here last.' It certainly is a long time. We could see the place every day from the observation post, but never got a chance to come. It is nearly a year since the squad leader was cremated. I was moved in spite of myself, and as I passed the place I closed my eyes and prayed for the repose of Shimizu's soul.

The truck runs along the seashore. We have left the Navy guard sector behind us, and now come into the Army guard sector. Here and there we see soldiers in the grassy fields, and I thank them in my heart for their toil as we drive on. They must have got it in the bombing the night before last, there are bomb craters by the side of the road, full of water from the rain.

In a little over twenty minutes we arrive at our destination and all get off. Unit Commander Komai stands up and says to the prisoner, 'We are going to kill you.'

When he tells the prisoner that in accordance with Japanese Bushido he will be killed with a Japanese sword, and will have two or three minutes' grace, he listens with bowed head. The flight lieutenant says a few words in a low voice. Apparently he wants to be killed with one stroke of the sword. I hear him say the word 'one'.

The unit commander becomes tense, and his face stiffens as he replies, 'Yes.'

Now the time has come, and the prisoner is made to kneel on the bank of a bomb crater filled with water. He is apparently resigned. The precaution is taken of surrounding him with guards with fixed bayonets, but he remains calm. He even stretches out his neck and is very brave. When I put myself in the prisoner's place and thrill that in one more minute it will be good-bye to this world, although the daily bombings have filled me with hate, ordinary human feelings make me pity him.

The unit commander has drawn his favourite sword. It is the famous Osamure sword which he showed us at the observation post. It glitters in the light, and sends a cold shiver down my spine. He taps the prisoner's neck lightly with the back of the blade, then raises it above his head with both arms, and brings it down with a sweep.

I had been standing with my muscles tensed, but at that moment, I closed my eyes.

SSh . . . it must be the sound of blood spurting from the arteries. With a sound as though something had been cut, the body falls forward. It is amazing . . . he had killed him with one stroke. The onlookers crowd forward. The head, detached from the trunk, rolls in front of it. SSh . . . SSh . . . the dark blood gushes out.

All is over. The head is dead white like a doll's. The savageness which I felt only a little while ago is gone, and now I feel nothing but the true compassion of Japanese Bushido.

A senior corporal laughs loudly, 'Well, he will enter Nirvana now.'

Then a superior seaman of the medical unit takes the chief medical officer's sword and, intent on paying off old scores, turns the headless body over on its back, and cuts the abdomen open with one clean stroke. 'They are thick-skinned these Kato, even the skin of their bellies is thick.' Not a drop of blood comes out of the body. It is pushed down into the crater at once and buried.

Now the wind blows mournfully and I see the scene again in my mind's eye. We get into the truck and start back. It is dark now. We get off in front of the headquarters. I say good-bye to the unit commander, Komai, and climb up the hill with Technician Kurokawa.

This will be something to remember all my life. If ever I get back alive it will make a good story to tell, so I have written it down.

At Salamua Observation Post. 30 Mar. 43.
0110 hours, to the sound of the midnight waves.

N.B. The prisoner killed today was an Air Force flight lieutenant from Moresby. He was a young man, only twenty-three.

G

CHAPTER V

LIFE AND DEATH ON THE
BURMA–SIAM RAILWAY

Early in 1942 Imperial General Headquarters in Tokyo decided that a railway should be built across part of Siam[1] and Burma to link up the two lines already in existence from Rangoon to Ye, in Tenasserim, and from Singapore to Bangkok. The distance between them was about two hundred and fifty miles.

The proposed new railroad was purely strategic, as it was to shorten the line of communication between the Japanese Armies in India and Burma and their rear, and prisoners of war, therefore, should not have been employed on its construction.

Work on the railway was to have been started in June but was not, in fact, begun until November 1942. The Japanese engineers, who were advising Imperial General Headquarters, considered that the work would take five or six years to complete. The military situation could not, of course, admit of such a long delay, and orders were given that the railway must be completed in eighteen months.

Responsibility for carrying out this project was placed upon the Japanese Southern Army, under the command of Field-Marshal Terauchi. A large number of coolies had been recruited as a labour force, but the Field-Marshal's advisers considered that this was insufficient and prevailed on him to suggest to Imperial General Headquarters that Allied prisoners of war should also be used.

Tojo agreed to this proposal, and two groups of prisoners were sent from Singapore, their transfer beginning in August.

---

[1] Siam is used for Thailand in all references to the railway and generally throughout this chapter.

The first, known as 'A' Force, was sent by sea. The second group, which consisted of 'F' and 'H' Forces, went by rail from Singapore to Bangpong whence they were made to march to the various camps along the projected line where they were to be stationed during the period of construction.

Before they left Singapore they had been told by the Japanese General, who was in charge of the prisoner of war administration, that they were being sent to rest camps up in the mountains. This step was being taken, he said, because the food situation there was better and there would, consequently, soon be an improvement in the health of those who, due to the lack of food and the insanitary conditions in Singapore, were suffering from the effects of malnutrition. It was for this reason, therefore, that the sick were to be moved up with the fit prisoners.

They were all crowded into goods trucks, sitting cross-legged with no room even to move, let alone lie down, and there they remained for four days and nights, with no food or water for the last twenty-four hours of the journey and prior to that nothing but a thin vegetable stew.

On arrival at Bangpong they had to march two hundred miles in two and a half weeks, a march that would have taxed the health of fit men, as the route lay over very rough jungle tracks in mountainous country, but many of these men were sick, and all were weak and undernourished. Moreover, it was still the monsoon season, and the march had to be completed in fifteen night stages in constant rain and a sea of mud.

Those who were fit had to carry those who were sick, and there were some two thousand who could not walk. Those who became too sick or weak to march at all were often beaten and driven on by the guards like cattle.

Another group of nearly nine hundred prisoners who arrived on the site of the proposed railway in October had come from the well known 'Bicycle Prisoner of War Camp' in Java. They had been transported in a small ship of about 4,000 tons from Batavia to Singapore, where they boarded a much smaller ship, and after a voyage of over fifteen days eventually arrived at Moulmein.

As usual the conditions on the voyage were very poor. When the party left Batavia it was fifteen hundred strong. They were all crammed into one hold in which there were also four tanks. They were unable to lie down and were only allowed on deck for about five minutes each day. They received daily three small bowls of rice but there was no water available. Many developed dysentery and it was a miracle that only one died before the ship reached Singapore.

From Moulmein the party went first to the base camp at Thanbuyazat, and from there marched thirty-five kilometres into the jungle where it remained until April 1943, when it became a mobile unit, and worked on the whole line up to the Burma–Siam border. The senior officer of the party was Lieutenant-Colonel J. M. Williams of the 2nd Australian Pioneer Battalion, and after it arrived at Thirty-five Kilometre Camp it became known as 'Williams's Force'.

For the first few months Williams's Force was building the embankment of the line, and the work was not too hard although the food was very poor. Later it became extremely scarce, mostly boiled watery rice and scarcely ever any meat. As there were no vegetables provided, the prisoners gathered leaves and cut any green grass that they could find. Starved of all flesh they even had recourse to eating dogs, cats, rats and even the entrails of pigs thrown away by the Japanese whose rations were, at all times, adequate. The prisoners only got the leavings.[1]

[1] Discussing the diet of prisoners of war in the Far East, Russell Braddon wrote in *The Naked Island*, that they

. . . ate anything which was not actually poisonous, even, in Thailand, the fungus of trees.

The only meat it never occurred to the prisoners to touch was human flesh. This may not seem especially remarkable. When, however, one considers that under conditions considerably less atrocious than those of Thailand and Burma the Japanese in New Guinea frequently resorted to cannibalism (and have, many of them, since been proved guilty of the crime and hanged for it) then perhaps the moral strength of the Britisher in situations of extreme and protracted crisis will be better appreciated.

For details of Japanese cannibalism, see Chapter XII.

The huts in which these prisoners lived had usually been previously occupied by the native coolies and were already in an insanitary condition. They were made of bamboo and atap and were generally sited on low-lying ground. During the rainy season it was normal for there to be at least six inches of mud throughout the entire camp, both outside and inside the huts.

'In one camp,' Lieutenant-Colonel Williams stated in his evidence before the Tokyo Tribunal, 'we spent five months in a very crowded area . . . where for the first three weeks there was no roof on our building. I complained to the Japanese commander about the accommodation and he said that they were equally crowded. In fact, twenty-three officers and twenty-three other ranks of my Force occupied the same space as three Japanese soldiers.'

Owing to the deterioration of the Japanese military situation early in 1943, the need for a supply line to their forces in Burma became more urgent, and an order came from Tokyo insisting that the railway must be completed by August of that year. This decision was referred to in a *Report on Employment of War Prisoners on Siam–Burma Railway Construction* prepared by the Japanese Government itself:

When counter-attacks by the British Indian Army and the bombing of our communications rapidly became fiercer, and the situation in this area considerably worsened after the rainy season of 1942 our sea transportation from Malaya to Burma gradually became more difficult. . . . It became evident that if things were left as they were till the end of the next rainy season communication with Burma would be almost entirely interrupted . . . as, however, the rainy season of 1943 set in earlier than usual the conditions in the jungle worsened from April onwards and the victims of the work gradually increased. Confronted with these bad conditions, Imperial General Headquarters at last postponed the target date for completion of the railway for two months.

During this last period, May to October 1943, which was

[85]

known by the code name of 'Speedo', the conditions were at their worst for all the prisoners of war employed on the project. It rained almost incessantly and Williams's Force moved from camp to camp at frequent intervals. The men had very little clothing and were hardly ever dry. They were worked like slaves, leaving camp about five or six in the morning, and often not returning before midnight. All the time they were getting weaker and weaker.

Between April and October over two hundred of them died. Each morning some men would be found dead in their huts. To spur the prisoners on, so that the railway would be finished on time, the Japanese guards 'belted the men hourly with bamboos and rifle butts, or they kicked them. I have seen them use a five pound hammer and anything they could lay their hands on. One man had his jaw broken with a blow from a rifle butt because he bent a spike while driving it into the rail'.[1]

There was only one issue of some two hundred and fifty blankets for the whole force of eight hundred and eighty-four. The majority of men were without blankets. At one time a few rice sacks were issued to the prisoners to keep them warm but, shortly afterwards, they were withdrawn as they were wanted for rice.

In May 1943 Williams's Force moved to Sixty Kilometre Camp. As it arrived a number of dead bodies were being carried away. It was later discovered that they had recently died from cholera. The camp had previously been a coolie camp and was covered with filth. So dirty and insanitary was it that Lieutenant-Colonel Williams ordered his men to burn the bamboo sleeping slats, to tear down the sides of the huts and burn them and to scrape about an inch of soil from the whole surface of the camp. Shortly afterwards several prisoners were taken ill with cholera and died, for there were no proper medical supplies.

At Eighty Kilometre Camp there was a makeshift hospital for 'No. 5 Group, Prisoner of War Thailand Administration'.

[1] Lieutenant-Colonel Williams.

Here lay men who were so ill that they were physically incapable of doing any work. They were deposited there to die, for the Japanese told them, 'No work, no food.' When Williams's Force arrived at the camp the death rate was about five a day. His men took them what food they could, and on one occasion killed two cows belonging to the Japanese camp staff and distributed the meat to the starving invalids under cover of darkness.

Senior Japanese officers frequently visited these camps, but they never appeared to inspect the huts and never questioned any of the prisoners.

Lieutenant-Colonel Williams protested regularly about the conditions, but he was always told that the orders were that the railway must be completed in the shortest possible time and that nothing could be done to improve the prisoners' lot.

One of the witnesses who gave evidence before the Tokyo Tribunal about the conditions on the Burma–Siam railway was Colonel Wild, who worked on the project until November 1943. As he could speak Japanese he acted as liaison officer between the prisoners of war employed on the construction of the railway and the Japanese officers. He visited many of the camps and was able to speak at first hand of the conditions in them. The following is an extract from his evidence.

Q. Substantially was there any difference between the living conditions and treatment of prisoners of war in these various camps?

A. None.

Q. Will you describe one of them as an example?

A. When I entered Songkrei Camp on 3rd August 1943 I went first to a very large hut accommodating about seven hundred men. The hut was of the usual pattern. On each side of an earthen gangway there was a twelve feet wide sleeping platform made of split bamboo.

The roof was inadequately made with an insufficient quantity of palm leaves which let the rain through everywhere. There were no walls, and a stream of water was running down the earthen gangway. The framework of the hut was bamboo tied with creeper. In this hut were seven hundred sick men. They were lying two deep along each side of the hut on the split bamboo platform. Their bodies were touching one another down the whole length of the hut. They were all very thin and practically naked. In the middle of the hut were about a hundred and fifty men suffering from tropical ulcers. These commonly stripped the whole of the flesh from a man's leg from the knee to the ankle. There was an almost overwhelming smell of putrefaction. The only dressings available were banana leaves tied around with puttees, and the only medicine was hot water.

There was another hut further up the hill of similar design in which so-called fit men were kept and one well-roofed and better constructed hut occupied by the Japanese guards.

Q. Was there any bedding supplied?

A. None whatever.

Q. What did they have to cover them from the rain?

A. When we first entered these working camps not one of them was roofed at all for the first few weeks. The monsoon had already broken and during those weeks the men had nothing whatever to cover themselves from the rain except banana leaves.

If he had the strength each man cut a couple of banana leaves and put them over his body.

Q. Was any roofing material ever received?

A. In my own camp, of which I was in command, Lower Niki, we got a lorry load of atap palm which was enough to roof half the hut in which the worst of the sick were lying. In Niki Camp no atap palm was ever received but we got some rotten leaky canvas.

In the other four camps, after a few weeks, enough atap palm was supplied to roof all the huts with about half the amount that was necessary.

Again, this does not apply to the Japanese and Korean guards, who always had a proper roof over them.

Q. By the middle of July 1943, that is ten weeks after you had left Singapore, what was the state of 'F' Force as a whole?

A. We had seventeen hundred deaths by that time, and seven

hundred men out of seven thousand were going out to work. Of these seven hundred, we British officers considered that three hundred and fifty should have been lying down sick.

Even when the prisoners returned to camp at night after a gruelling working day of eighteen hours, weary to death, they were allowed no rest or quiet. Every Japanese soldier had to be saluted at all times whenever one was seen. This meant standing up and bowing sometimes a dozen or two dozen times a night.[1] Failure to do this resulted in certain punishment. Sometimes, because one prisoner had failed to salute correctly, a whole hut of men would be dragged outside to stand to attention for a couple of hours.

One Japanese officer, because he disliked the smell of one of the hospital huts close to his guardroom, emptied the hut of all the sick and crowded them into another hut already full to overflowing. One party of fifty sick men, who should have been in bed, were forced to work for three weeks clearing the jungle in front of the commandant's house so that he could obtain a better view of the valley.

Many prisoners of war were executed at the Burma end of the railway in 1942 and 1943. Two groups of Netherlands East Indies officers, who had attempted to escape, were shot in the cemetery of their camp, and a number of Australians were shot for the same reason a few months later.

In April 1943 the commandant of one camp called all the prisoners together one morning and told them that their lives were of no consequence, and that the railway had to be built irrespective of any suffering or deaths.[2] The following extract,

[1] Proceedings of the IMT, Far East, page 13,031.
[2] Reichsführer Himmler had similar ideas about the Russians when he wrote:
    What happens to the Russians does not interest me in the slightest. Whether other nations live in prosperity or starve to death interests me only in so far as we need them as slaves for our culture. Whether 10,000 Russian females fall down from exhaustion while digging an anti-tank trench interests me not at all so long as the trench is finished for Germany.
See *The Scourge of the Swastika*, Chapter V.

therefore, from the Japanese Report already referred to makes strange reading.

> We should like to declare that the Japanese troops participated in the joys and sorrows of the POWs and native labourers in the construction work, and they by no means completed, or intended to complete the work only at the sacrifice of POWs.

When they were well enough to work the prisoners were kept at it till they dropped, when they went sick they were starved, but the whole time, sick or well, they were subjected to great brutality. The hours of work varied from twelve to twenty a day with no days off. 8 a.m. till 10 p.m. was a normal day's work. Protests were of no avail.

About the middle of July 1943, when the Japanese were becoming desperate in their efforts to complete the line before the end of the year, the senior officer in one of the camps was summoned by a Japanese officer who told him that as the railway was required for operational purposes it had to be finished by the target date at all costs, irrespective of the number of British and American prisoners who might lose their lives. It was no use, the Japanese officer said, the Allies quoting the Articles of the Geneva Convention for they had themselves contravened them 'by sinking hospital ships and by running down civilian internees with steam rollers'.

The line was to be completed by August, and when this did not happen the Japanese became infuriated and during the last few weeks of its construction, the prisoners on some of the sections had to work from 5.30 a.m. until 2 a.m. on the following day. An account of the programme of work for part of 'F' Force from 13th to 16th September 1943 was given by one of the witnesses at the trial of major war criminals at Tokyo, Lieutenant-Colonel C. H. Kappe, who was allowed to refresh his memory from a diary which he kept during his incarceration.

> On 13th September I was informed by Lieutenant Fakuda

that the men must be prepared to work all through the night, as the railway was only a few kilometres to the north and it was necessary that the line should reach Sonkurai, three kilometres to the south, by the 16th. Owing to the heavy rain, however, the work ceased at 10.30 p.m., the men having been out since 5.30 a.m. On the 14th reveille was at 5.30 a.m., and, despite heavy rain all day and throughout the evening, the prisoners were forced to remain out until 2.30 a.m. on the 15th. Again they were roused at 5.30 a.m., after only three hours' rest, and were worked until midnight, and on the next day, which was the 16th, they continued working from 5.30 a.m. until 10 p.m.

Of the original 3663 prisoners who left Singapore for Siam as members of 'F' Force in April 1943, 1060 failed to return, representing approximately 29 per cent of the Australian contingent. The British lost 59 per cent of their strength and the entire Force lost 44 per cent.

When the survivors returned from the railway after its completion in December their condition was, according to the evidence of one witness who saw their arrival, pitiable. 'They were in a shocking condition, suffering from serious attacks of beri-beri, malaria, tropical ulcers and extreme debility. The loss of weight was simply appalling, averaging about seventy pounds per individual; 80 per cent of them had to be admitted at once to hospital.'

Some reference should be made to the coolie labour employed on the railway construction for they received, if such a thing were possible, even worse treatment. A native labour force was recruited by means of false promises or pressed into service. It consisted of Burmese, Tamils, Javanese, Malayans and Chinese who numbered about 150,000. At least 60,000 of them died. These coolies were kept in camps along the railway line, and from 1st August 1943 until 31st March 1945[1] a Japanese unit known as the 19th Ambulance Corps was responsible for their medical care and attention. It was com-

[1] Although the construction of the railroad was, to all intents and purposes, completed by December 1943 a number of prisoners of war and thousands of coolies were kept on the spot for maintenance work.

manded by a Major Kudo and, according to Japanese Army custom, took from him the name of 'Kudo Batai'. The conduct of the Japanese towards these coolies was characterized by complete indifference to their sufferings and a callous disregard for their lives.

Several hospitals were set up at different places on the railroad, the principal one being at Kanburi where, also, the unit headquarters were located. In all these so-called hospitals there was inadequate accommodation, and a shortage of food and drinking water. The sick were neglected, if not entirely ignored by the medical staff, and abandoned to die. Each hospital had a 'Death House', a hut where the sick, both male and female, were left unattended and without any medical comforts. The 'Death House' was nothing but an ante-room to the mortuary. It was the Japanese method of getting rid of useless mouths to feed. If the patients were not taken off by disease, malnutrition finally did away with them.[1]

A member of the Japanese staff at Kanburi told one of his orderlies that he would gain much favour by clearing the 'Death House' quickly. The orderly took the officer at his word, for both living and dead were speedily removed and buried together.[2] Out of 1200 coolies placed in the 'Death House' at Kanburi Hospital, only ten survived.

Medical supplies which were available and should have been given to the patients were deliberately withheld, and some were even bartered by Nishimura, the camp dispenser, for the services of Siamese prostitutes. The coolies were at all times beaten, and were also subjected to other forms of physical violence, by way of punishment for minor disciplinary offences, upon the express orders of Major Kudo.

They were bound, stripped naked and left out in the sun, sometimes for three successive days. This punishment was

[1] It was a German, Field-Marshal von Rundstedt, who said, 'Malnutrition is better than machine guns.'

[2] From the affidavit of a Major P. F. Murphy, which was used at the trial of Major Kudo and eleven other members of the 19th Ambulance Corps by Military Court in Singapore in October 1946.

occasionally varied by making the victim hold a heavy log or stone above his head. Women and children were also tied up and exposed to the sun for several hours at a time. Many of the coolies of both sexes and of all ages were also subjected to obscene brutalities, which cannot be described here, in order to gratify the perverted sadism of their captors.

The evidence given against the unit commander, Major Kudo, at his trial included many accusations of rape and indecent assault. At his evening drinking parties many young Tamil women were forced to dance naked to please his guests who then raped them. One young woman who was outraged in this manner died a few weeks later, and her husband went out of his mind.

Another member of the camp staff at Mezali, named Onodera, dragged a nineteen year old Indian girl from her tent, raped her, and after forcing a number of coolies to rape her also, committed unspeakable outrages upon her with strips of lighted bamboo. According to an eyewitness, who gave evidence at Onodera's trial, the wretched girl became unconscious and died that night.

The coolies were supposed to receive wages for their work. Kudo refused to pay them, and in the place of money issued them with vouchers which could only be exchanged for goods in the canteen which he himself ran as a private business. The prices were excessive, and the resulting profit, which went into Kudo's pocket, high.

The death rate in these hospitals was very high, and the lowest reliable estimate is 42,000, but not all the coolies working on the railway died of disease or malnutrition.

In February 1944 about twenty-five escaped from Niki Camp and, upon being recaptured, were imprisoned in a hut in the vicinity of Kanburi Hospital. They were then given an injection of some reddish fluid. They all died in agony and showed symptoms consistent with mercurial poisoning. Evidence of this was given at Kudo's trial by the affidavit of Lieutenant-Colonel Benson, who commanded 'L' Force, which was composed of thirty prisoner of war medical officers and two hundred orderlies, sent to Siam to assist Kudo Batai. Six months later a number of Indian prisoners of war, also at Kanburi, suffered a similar fate.

At his trial Tojo told the Tribunal that he instructed the Chief of the Prisoner of War Information Bureau to investigate complaints which had reached him about the conditions in the labour camps along the whole length of the railway.

The investigation was, in fact, made by someone else, Wakamatsu, who was head of the General Affairs Section of the Japanese General Staff. In August Wakamatsu inspected the Burma–Siam railway area and, in due course, made a verbal report to the Chief-of-Staff, General Sugiyma, and the Vice-Chief-of-Staff, Lieutenant-General Hata.

The following is an extract from Wakamatsu's evidence.

I visited Rangoon, Bangkok and a portion of the railroad from the Siam end. It was during the rainy season and the work was not progressing satisfactorily. I made this inspection because I had been receiving reports from time to time which showed that the progress of the work was not satisfactory. The reports also contained information that the physical condition of the prisoners of war working on the railway was poor, and that the death rate was very high. I had heard that cholera was epidemic and that caused me considerable worry. I saw the labourers at work on the railroad and noticed many cases of beri-beri and dysentery amongst them. I also inspected the feeding of the prisoners and it was unsatisfactory, the quantity and quality being below the required standard. I orally reported the results of my inspection to the Chief and Vice-Chief-of-Staff and recommended a two months' extension of the deadline for the completion of the railroad. . . . Many deaths of prisoners of war resulted from the building of this railway. The causes were epidemic diseases and unfavourable weather.

The construction outfit did not have a proper supply service. There were not enough trucks, and the truck road which was made in April parallel to the permanent way suffered bridge wash-outs, and could not be used for some time. It was intended to be used during the rainy season, but this proved to be difficult and prisoners and other workers had a difficult time as a result. Because there were not enough trucks, it was thought necessary to use more men, and because more men were employed the food situation became more difficult. I recommended to the Commander of the Southern Army that more trucks should be used and fewer men.

The results of Wakamatsu's inspection eventually came to the ears of Tojo. The only action he took was to court-martial one Japanese company commander who was reported to have dealt unfairly with the prisoners of war.

As the Tokyo Tribunal said in its judgment,

. . . the court-martial of one company commander was so insignificant and inadequate as a corrective measure, in view of the general disregard of the laws of war by those in charge of prisoners of war on this project, and the inhumane treatment to which they were subjecting the prisoners, as to amount to condonation of their conduct.

The chief concern of the Japanese Government and the Imperial General Staff was that the railway should be completed in time to use it in resisting the Allied advance in Burma. The cost in lives and suffering mattered nothing. The prisoners of war could be driven like slaves, beaten, tortured and murdered by their Japanese and Korean guards so long as the target date was kept. They could die like flies of disease or malnutrition so long as the work went on.

Out of 46,000 Allied prisoners of war who were employed on this work, 16,000 died, and many thousands more will suffer from the effects of their ill-treatment for the rest of their lives.

So the Imperial General Staff got its railway, but at what a cost of human life and human suffering. Each mile of this 'Railroad of Death' was paid for with the lives of sixty-four Allied prisoners of war, and two hundred and forty coolie slaves.

CHAPTER VI

THE MASSACRE AND MURDER OF PRISONERS OF WAR

THE killing of Allied prisoners of war by the Japanese was not an uncommon practice. Many were massacred immediately after capture. Other mass killings occurred in prisoner of war camps for a variety of reasons. On Hainan Island, for example, in May 1943 a number of prisoners were murdered in an effort to prevent smuggling. At Saigon, in French Indo-China, in December of the same year, a similar crime was committed in order to discourage the unauthorized use of secret radios, and on Amboina Island a number of prisoners were slaughtered for accepting food from the local inhabitants.

There were murders committed on the high seas, such as the beheading of some American prisoners of war aboard the *Nitta Maru*,[1] and a number of massacres in anticipation of a Japanese withdrawal or an Allied attack, the object apparently being, in either event, to prevent the prisoners from being liberated by the Allied forces.

When the Japanese captured Singapore their troops went through the first floor of the Alexandra Hospital and bayoneted every person there, then entering the operating room, where a soldier was undergoing an operation, they bayoneted the patient, the anæsthetist and the surgeon. From there the Japanese soldiers went to the second floor, and to other parts of the building, removed the patients and nurses and massacred them all.

When the Japanese invaded Hong Kong on 8th December 1941 St Stephen's College at Stanley was one of the hospitals to which wounded soldiers were taken. Before the war it had been a school for boys. About 6 a.m. on Christmas Day 1941

[1] See Chapter VII.

the Japanese troops entered the hospital. James Barrett, who came from Quebec, was a Canadian Army Chaplain at the time and was in the hospital when the soldiers came in. He saw five Japanese soldiers bayonet about fifteen wounded men while they were still in bed.

On that day there were about a hundred and sixty patients in the hospital and seven nurses. The Japanese proceeded to herd together all who could walk, both patients and staff, and put them into a store room. All of them were entitled to be treated as prisoners of war or protected persons.

At the Tokyo trial Mr. Barrett gave the following evidence:

> After we had been there for about an hour the Japanese moved us up to a smaller room. Until then the nurses had been with me, but as we were being moved from the store room to the smaller room they were taken away. I saw one of them beaten over the head with a steel helmet, kicked, and then slapped in the face by a Japanese soldier. In the small room ninety men were placed with me, some of the hospital staff and some of the wounded men. The room was so small that we could not have all sat down together, and it was necessary for the very sick or wounded men to lie down as best they could and when they could.
>
> After we had been in the room a little while a Japanese soldier came to the door, made us put up our hands and took my watch, my ring and some money which I had in my pocket. Later, another Japanese soldier entered with a sack of ammunition, and threw cartridges in our faces. Yet a third came in, a few minutes later, and removed two riflemen. Immediately afterwards we heard screams coming from the corridor outside.
>
> We remained in this room until 4 p.m. when a Japanese soldier entered and gave us to understand by sign language that Hong Kong had surrendered.[1]

[1] As indeed it had. The following is the last paragraph of the GOC British Troops in China's Despatch on the operations in Hong Kong from 8th–25th December 1941.

At 15.15 hours I advised H.E. The Governor and C-in-C that no further military resistance was possible and I then ordered all Commanding Officers to break off fighting and to capitulate to the nearest Japanese Commander as and when the enemy advanced and opportunity offered.

The next day I made a tour of the hospital. It was in a dreadful state. I found the two men who had been taken out of our room. Their bodies were badly mutilated, their ears, tongues, noses and eyes had been cut away from their faces. About seventy or more wounded men had been killed by bayonets while in their beds. Many more were seriously wounded. None of the victims had been armed, nor was the hospital anywhere near the battle area. There were no armed troops or battle positions in the vicinity. I found the dead bodies of the commanding officer of the hospital, and his adjutant, on the ground floor. They had been badly mutilated.

I was anxious about the nurses as I had not seen them again after their separation from the rest of us. During the morning I saw four of them coming towards me. They were in a terrible state, and had experienced dreadful things during the night. They had been assaulted by Japanese soldiers and one of them told me she had been forced to lie on top of two dead bodies and had there been raped several times.

None of us had yet seen the three other nurses. Later in the morning one of the nurses came to me and said that a Japanese soldier wanted her to go with him out of the hospital into the grounds. She asked me to accompany her. I did and took a RAMC sergeant along with us. In the bushes, covered with branches, we found the bodies of the three dead nurses, one of whom had her head practically severed from her body. . . . I started to organize burial parties but the Japanese soldiers made us light a fire and cremate all the bodies in and around the hospital. I cremated about one hundred and seventy bodies. Some came from the hospital itself, and others from the fields surrounding it.

During the fighting which took place in Hong Kong between the first assault and the capitulation, about two hundred British, Canadian, Indian, and Chinese troops, who had been taken prisoner, were imprisoned in a small hut with insufficient space to lie down.

In the early morning of 20th December the hut was hit by a British trench mortar bomb, and several prisoners of war were killed or wounded. Those who tried to leave the building were bayoneted to death by the sentries. Those who were able to walk were subsequently marched off to North Point. While on the march one prisoner fell out, and was at once killed by the bayonet of one of the escort. A party of St. John Ambulance wearing Red Cross brassards came out of their shelters and surrendered. They were all killed in the same way.

When the Japanese troops entered Soebang, in Java, in March 1942, they removed a nurse and her patients from the military hospital and massacred them with women and children of the civilian population.

Some prisoners were killed merely to provide an afternoon's sport for the battalion commander. One such instance occurred in New Guinea in October 1944. The Japanese officer concerned applied to his Divisional Headquarters for an American prisoner of war to be provided as the victim.

In a statement which this officer made, during an investigation conducted after the war, he said, 'I asked if I could get an American prisoner of war and kill him.' The Commander of the 36th Japanese Division was most co-operative and sent him two prisoners. When they arrived at the unit they were blindfolded, stabbed in the back with bayonets, and then decapitated with shovels.

During the battle of north-western Johore, in January 1942, an ambulance convoy containing a number of sick and wounded Allied soldiers was captured by the Japanese. The patients, and the RAMC personnel and drivers were all removed from their ambulances and killed by shooting, bayoneting, and burning alive after being saturated with petrol. In the same month, at Katonga, also in Malaya, another ambulance convoy was fired upon by Japanese machine-gunners. The medical personnel and the wounded were all taken prisoner, roped together, and shot in the back.

There was a great similarity to be found in most of these massacres. The victims were first bound and then shot, bayoneted or decapitated with swords. In most instances the victims were shot, and then bayoneted by Japanese who went among the wounded giving the *coup de grâce* to those who still

[99]

remained alive. On frequent occasions they were killed on beaches with their backs to the sea, or on the edge of a cliff where they were shot and thrown over.

When the Japanese captured Amboina Island on the 3rd February 1942 there were about eight hundred Australian troops on the Ambon side of the island, and three hundred on the Lala side. The former were imprisoned in Tan Toey Barracks, near Ambon, and their experiences as prisoners of war are described in Chapter VIII. Those who were taken prisoner on the other side of the island, two hundred and ten of them, met a terrible fate.

The Japanese force landed on the beaches at 2 a.m. on 31st January, and on 3rd February captured the aerodrome. Their casualties were no more than one hundred. Ten Australians were captured on the morning of 1st February and taken to a place called Sowacoad. Before the Japanese left Sowacoad these prisoners were bayoneted to death. This was done, according to a statement made by the local Japanese commander, by order of Rear-Admiral Hataki-yama, who was in command of the invasion force, 'because,' he said, 'prisoners were likely to become a drag upon the movement of the Admiral's forces,' who planned to advance until they made touch with the Japanese troops who had landed near Ambon.

On 4th February fifty-one more prisoners, who had been captured on the previous day, were giving the Japanese some anxiety as they felt they had not enough spare men to guard them. One or two had even managed to escape. The Admiral, on hearing of these escapes, became annoyed and sent an order to the local commander of the naval landing force, to kill all the prisoners in their hands. The lieutenant who carried out these orders has given the following description of the massacre. His name was Nakagawa.

In compliance with this order I took about thirty petty officers and men to Sowacoad. In a coconut tree plantation, about two hundred metres from the airfield, we dug holes and killed the prisoners of war with swords or bayonets. It took about two hours. The way in which the murder was carried out was as follows: I divided my men into three groups, the first for leading the prisoners of war out of a house where we had temporarily confined them, the second for preventing disorder on their way from the house to the plantation, the third for beheading or stabbing the victims.

They were taken one by one to the spot where they were to die, and made to kneel down with a bandage over their eyes. The members of the third troop stepped out of the ranks, one by one as his turn came, to behead a prisoner of war with a sword or stab him through the breast with a bayonet.

The prisoners were all Australian and their number included four or five officers, one of whom I am sure was a major. All the corpses were buried in the holes which we had dug. I was the only Japanese officer present. . . . When it was all over I reported its completion to my adjutant.

There were, however, still some two hundred Australian and about sixty Dutch prisoners of war. Thirty of them, who objected to the work which they were being made to do, protested, and were killed in the same way as the others had been. This happened on 5th February.

On 17th February, while the Japanese officers were at lunch, the commanding officer of Nakagawa's unit, whose name was Hayashi, said that he intended to kill off all the remaining prisoners of war, and two days later Nakagawa was given the order to carry out this massacre. On 20th February, therefore, Nakagawa paraded about ninety men and marched them to another coconut plantation about one hundred and fifty metres away from the scene of the first massacre, and two hundred metres from the headquarters of the Japanese detachment at Laha.

The rest of the story is told in Nakagawa's own words:

I divided my men into nine parties, two for bloody killings, three for guarding the prisoners on their way to the place of execution, two for escorting the prisoners out of the barracks, one to be on guard at the spot where the prisoners were to be killed, and one in reserve for emergency.

The prisoners of war were brought by truck from the barracks to the detachment headquarters, and marched from there to the plantation. The same way of killing was adopted as before, i.e. they were made to kneel down with their eyes bandaged and they were killed with sword or bayonet. The poor victims numbered about two hundred and twenty in all, including some Australian officers.

The whole affair took from 6 p.m. to 9.30 p.m. Most of the corpses were buried in one hole, but because the hole turned out not to be big enough to accommodate all the bodies an adjacent dug-out was also used as a grave.

The Japanese Admiral responsible for these atrocities was never brought to trial, for he was killed later in the war.

On 12th February 1942, three days before the surrender of the British forces in Malaya, sixty-five Australian Army nursing sisters with about two hundred women and children and a few elderly men were evacuated from Singapore on a small ship, the *Vynor Brook*. The sisters were mostly members of the nursing staff of the 13th Australian General Hospital at Singapore.

On the morning of 15th February, a party, consisting of the ship's officer and several women civilians and nurses, went ashore on the island of Banka to a small native village to get some help for the wounded who were on board. They were refused aid, and learned that the island was already occupied by the Japanese.

That night the passengers on the *Vynor Brook* saw a ship being shelled in the Banka Straits, just off the island, and two hours afterwards a lifeboat arrived with about twenty-five English soldiers on board.

Next morning the whole party decided to give themselves up, and a ship's officer went to find some Japanese to whom they could surrender. Later, the ship's officer returned with a party of fifteen Japanese soldiers under the command of an officer.

The party from the *Vynor Brook* were formed up on the beach near Muntok, on the island of Sumatra, in two groups. The men together in one, and the Army sisters and a civilian in another. Half the group, consisting of men only, was then marched away by the Japanese soldiers out of sight behind a headland. The Japanese shortly returned and marched the rest of the group away in the same direction. A few minutes later a lot of rifle shots were heard and when the Japanese soldiers returned they were cleaning their rifles and their bayonets.

Evidence of all this was given before the Tokyo Tribunal by an eye-witness, Vivien Bullwinkel, a captain in the Australian Army Nursing Service. Describing what happened subsequently she said, in answer to the question, 'At that time, who was left on the beach?'

A. There were twenty-two Army sisters, one civilian, and about ten or twelve stretcher cases that had been wounded in the bombing of our ship and the shelling of the other one.

When they had finished cleaning their rifles and bayonets the Japanese officer ordered twenty-three of us [the nursing sisters and the civilian] to march into the sea. We had gone a few yards into the water when they commenced to machine-gun from behind. I saw the girls fall one after the other until I was hit. The bullet that hit me entered my back at about waist level and passed straight through. It knocked me over and the waves gradually washed me up on to the beach. I continued to lie there for ten or fifteen minutes, and then I sat up and looked around. The Japanese party had disappeared. I then dragged myself into the jungle and became unconscious . . .

Q. What happened then?

A. When I regained consciousness, I decided to come down to the beach in order to get a drink. On my way to a fresh water spring that was there, somebody spoke to me. On looking round I saw that it was one of the English soldiers who had joined us on the Sunday night. He was one of the stretcher cases and he had been bayoneted by the same party of Japanese that had shot the girls on

Monday morning. All the other stretcher cases had like-wise been bayoneted and left for dead.

Sister Bullwinkel then learned from the English soldier, whose name was Private Kingsley and who was a very sick man, that it was Wednesday and she had, therefore, been unconscious for two days.

Of the party of men who had been taken round behind the headland to be murdered, only two survived. They had dashed into the sea and managed to get away. Of the Army Nursing Sisters, Sister Bullwinkel was the sole survivor.

On 4th February 1942 the Japanese captured a party of twenty-four Australian soldiers at Tol, after landing at Rabaul in New Britain. They all belonged to the Army Medical Corps, and were wearing Red Cross armbands when taken prisoner which the Japanese soldiers immediately removed.

On reaching Tol their captors ransacked the prisoners' packs, and took all their personal belongings from them including rings and watches. Their pay books were also taken from them, and they were tied together in groups of three with their hands bound behind their backs with rope. One of them has thus described what then took place.

They marched us to a plantation about half a mile beyond Tol in the direction of Rabaul. We were ordered, by signs, to sit down on a slight rise on the track which led from the road to the plantation. . . . They then began to take the men down the track in twos and threes. I was in the last party which numbered three.

The officer, still using signs, asked whether we would rather be bayoneted or shot. We chose the latter. When we reached the end of the track, three Japanese with fixed bayonets took us over and walked on behind us. All three in my group were then knocked to the ground, and as our hands were bound behind our backs and we were also tied together we were unable to move.

[104]

The escort stood over us and bayoneted us several times. I received five bayonet wounds, but I held my breath and feigned death though still alive. As the Japanese were moving off the man next to me groaned. One of the Japanese soldiers came running back and stabbed him once more. By this time I could hold my breath no longer. When I drew a deep breath the soldier heard me and inflicted six more bayonet wounds. The last thrust went through my ear into my mouth severing an artery on the way. The member of the escort seeing the blood gushing out of my mouth assumed that I was at last dead, covered the three of us with coconut fronds and vine leaves and left.

I lay there for approximately one hour when I decided to try and get away. I managed to undo the cord which bound me to the other two and started to walk towards the sea, which was only fifty yards away. After taking a few steps I collapsed. It seemed only a short time before I regained consciousness. I then tried to saw through the bonds round my hands with the iron heel of my boot, but without success. Eventually I managed to get my leg between my two hands and, raising it, chewed at the cord until it came apart.

The exact number of prisoners of war killed in New Britain after capture is not known but a military court of inquiry which investigated the atrocities estimated the dead at not less than one hundred and fifty. The killings were flagrant contraventions of the Hague Convention of 1907, to which Japan was a party, and which forbade the killing or wounding of an enemy who, having laid down his arms, or no longer having means of defence, has surrendered at discretion.

All these Australians had surrendered, some under the white flag, and all were entitled to be treated as prisoners of war.

Even worse atrocities were committed near a Japanese headquarters at Waga Waga. Despite their horror the details are given here to illustrate the devilish sadism to which the Japanese troops sometimes gave way.

Waga Waga is near Milne Bay, Papua, where the Japanese troops landed on the 25th August 1942, and the following is an extract from an affidavit made by Captain Kendall of the 18th Australian Infantry Brigade:

About 1st or 2nd September 1942 at Waga Waga in Milne Bay we captured the headquarters of a Japanese Marine Regiment. In clearing the jungle around these headquarters for our defensive position, I saw the bodies of two Australian soldiers who had been members of the 61st Militia Battalion.

One of these bodies was lying on the ground with his hands tied together in front of him, and his trousers pulled down around his knees, and tied down to his boots by his belt. He had the tops of his ears cut off and about twenty knife or bayonet wounds in the body. His hands were tied in front of his chest and his forearms were cut as though he had been trying to protect himself. His buttocks and genitals had been frightfully mutilated.

About six feet away, the other body was tied to a tree, with his hands behind his back. He had six small wounds on the upper arm.

The ground around the base of the tree was very disturbed and it was apparent that he had lain there for some days before he eventually died of his wounds. Both these bodies were found by Captain Kendall not more than fifty yards from the Japanese headquarters.

In the same area of jungle two other soldiers had been tied to a sago palm facing inwards with their arms lashed around its trunk. Both had several bayonet wounds all over the buttocks and in the rectum. Another soldier, who had also been tied to a tree, appeared from his wounds to have been used as a bayonet training dummy.

Captain Kendall's affidavit continues:

On the track leading from Waga Waga to Lillihi I saw the body of another Australian soldier with his hands tied behind his back, lying face downwards. He was tied with string. He had a wound on his leg with a field dressing on it, and had the top of his head cut right off. The top portion of the skull was lying forward as if it had been cut through with a heavy knife or sword and had been chopped from the rear. He also had lacerations criss-crossing his back and shoulders. They appeared to be knife or sword wounds, and had cut right through the shirt into his flesh.

Two days later a Japanese soldier was captured at Ahioma. He spoke English and I showed him the bodies of the two Australian soldiers whom I have previously mentioned. He told me that he was attached to the landing party, and that the ill-treatment and torturing of Australian troops was done by the order of their officers so that the Japanese soldiers would fight and not surrender, because the same things would be done to them now that these atrocities had been committed on the Australians.

There is certainly no reason to doubt that the massacre of prisoners of war in New Britain and New Guinea was the result of superior orders. Before the landings pamphlets had been dropped warning the Allied troops that all who resisted the Japanese invasion would be killed.

There were other massacres of prisoners of war during the Japanese occupation which were committed because, through starvation, they were no longer able to work and had become an incubus to their captors. Such massacres are known to have taken place at no less than fourteen different places between April 1942 and August 1945. One of these was committed on Wake Island in October 1943.

Part of this story has been described by a lieutenant-commander in the Imperial Japanese Navy, named Tachibana, who was then serving with a unit on Wake Island which had custody of nearly one hundred Allied prisoners of war.

On the 7th [October], just after sundown, I don't remember the time, the commanding officer [Rear-Admiral Sakibara] and I were at the command post. Then, all of a sudden, he gave this order. 'The headquarters company leader is to use his men and shoot to death the prisoners of war on the northern shore.' It was so sudden that I was startled but I knew that the CO was a careful man and that he wouldn't come to a conclusion unless he had given it plenty of consideration. When I was a cadet at the Naval Academy he had been my instructor. I didn't, therefore, have any doubt and thought it was justifiable to execute all the prisoners of war according to the situation that night.

At 5.30 p.m. that very afternoon a new officer, named Lieutenant Ito, had just arrived from Kwajalein by plane to take over command of the headquarters company and shortly after his arrival the CO's order was passed on to him by Lieutenant-Commander Tachibana.

When Lieutenant Ito arrived at the beach where the massacre was to take place he saw the prisoners—there were ninety-six of them, sitting side by side in one rank with their backs to the sea. They had been blindfolded and their hands were bound behind their backs. Behind them stood the firing squad. A platoon commander reported that everything was ready and was told by the company commander to 'go ahead as ordered'. When the prisoners had been shot Lieutenant Ito returned to the command post to report.

Nearly two years later, on the night of 15th August 1945, news of the Japanese surrender reached Wake Island. It had been announced on the radio, but as no signal had been received from the Naval General Staff in Tokyo the Japanese commander refused to believe it. An Imperial Rescript confirming the news arrived the next day.

On 18th August Rear-Admiral Sakibara ordered all officers from platoon commanders upwards to muster at his quarters. When all were present he addressed them in these words: 'I have just heard over the radio from Melbourne that all criminals of war whether they were ordered or were the officers who gave the orders will be punished.' After making this announcement he stood staring at the floor for some time but said no more. A few minutes later he dismissed all present.

Two days later Sakibara again mustered all company commanders and said: 'The case concerning the prisoners of war will be like this. I have thought up a good story. Half of them were killed in the bombardment on the 6th October 1943. The remainder escaped the following night and resisted recapture with rifle fire. A fight ensued and they were all killed.'

Two days later the prisoners' remains, which had been buried where they died on the northern shore, were exhumed and reburied on the eastern shore of the island.

At Sakibara's trial he pleaded that he was merely obeying orders. The announcement that the excuse of 'superior orders' would not be accepted as a valid defence where the act committed was, on the face of it, unlawful and in violation of the unchallenged rules of warfare, must have come as a shock to Japanese officers.

Their views on the criminal responsibility of officers in the Services, who commit crimes under the orders of a superior, were clearly stated by Vice-Admiral Abe when interrogated, after the capitulation, about the Wake Island massacre which had taken place within the limits of his command:

Because the Japanese Military Forces are under a strict discipline, by a rigorous chain of command which originates in the supreme prerogative of command of His Majesty the Emperor, and penetrates from him at the top down to a private at the bottom, the primary and supreme duty of a military man is absolute submission to an order . . . among hundreds and thousands of Japanese military men, has there ever been one person who thought that he could be charged with his own acts which he has committed pursuant to an order? It is beyond the understanding of the Japanese that such things could be penalized.[1]

Other methods of slaughter were occasionally used; for

[1] The defence of 'superior orders' is discussed in the Appendix.

example, mass drowning, when at Port Blair in the Andaman Islands in August 1945 civilian internees were put on board a ship, taken out to sea, and forced into the water.

A combination of drowning and shooting, similar to that carried out at Hankow[1] was used at Kota Radja in Indonesia where, in March 1942, Dutch prisoners of war were put on barges, towed out to sea, shot and thrown into the water.

At Tarakan, in Borneo, two months earlier, another batch of Dutch naval prisoners of war had been massacred in much the same way as their comrades at Kota Radja. They were put on board a Japanese light cruiser and taken to the spot where their own ship had fired on a Japanese destroyer. There they were decapitated and thrown into the sea.

'A particularly cruel and premeditated massacre of American prisoners,' as the International Military Tribunal for the Far East called it, occurred on 14th December 1944 at the prisoner of war camp above the bay of Puerto Princesa on the Philippine Island of Palawan.

There were about one hundred and fifty prisoners in this camp. Two-thirds of them were in the United States Army and the remainder belonged to the Navy Marines, and on that day in December, one hundred and forty-five of them lost their lives. In the early morning the prisoners had gone out to work but they were brought back at noon which caused them some uneasiness as it seemed a little strange.

They had been threatened before that if Japan lost the war they would all be killed, and when the first American air-raids had begun at Puerto Princesa in October 1944, they were told that if the Americans invaded Palawan all the prisoners of war would be killed.

While the prisoners were having lunch, after their return to camp, two air-raid warnings were sounded and extra guards were placed round the compound. During the early afternoon another air-raid warning was sounded and the

[1] See Chapter II, page 48.

prisoners were driven into their air-raid shelters and told to remain there as there were 'hundreds of American planes approaching'.

The shelters were very cramped, only four feet six inches high, and with very narrow entrances. They were also very small and to get all the prisoners in, every one had to sit bunched up, his knees under his chin.

What happened then can best be described in the words of one of the five survivors, Gunnery Sergeant Douglas William Bogue of the United States Marine Corps.

No sooner had we got under cover than I heard a dull explosion and incessant screaming, laughing and the shooting of machine-gun and rifles. As I was near the entrance of my shelter I stuck my head out to see what was taking place. The first thing I saw was a black pillar of smoke coming from the entrance of A Company shelter. It appeared to me that about fifty to sixty Jap soldiers, armed with rifles, hand grenades, light machine-guns, and carrying torches and buckets containing gasoline, were attacking the A Company shelter which was next to mine. The buckets of gasoline were thrown into the entrance of the shelter and a lighted torch was then thrown in to ignite the gasoline: and, as the men were forced to come out on fire, they were bayoneted, shot, clubbed, or stabbed. I saw several men staggering about, still in flames, and saw them fall down shot. Some of the Japanese attacking force then branched off and attacked the north-east entrance of C Company's shelter and the north entrance of B Company's shelter.

Due to the confined space the whole attack was visible at a glance. I saw several Japanese shooting and stabbing with their bayonets directly above where Stidham was lying helpless on a stretcher.[1] I saw one man whom I presumed to be Dr Mango with his clothes smouldering, staggering towards the Japs with his arms outstretched, when he was mowed down by

[1] Stidham was one of the prisoners of war in Puerto Princesa Camp who was paralysed through a wound received in a previous air-raid. He had to be carried about on a stretcher and, due to the size of the shelters' entrances, he could not be got inside and was left outside the entrance during air-raids.

a Japanese soldier with a light machine-gun. Other American prisoners of war, who were coming out of these narrow entrances, were shot as they emerged, or mown down as they made for the fence above the cliff.

The Japanese soldiers participating were yelling, and in such a manner that it seemed to me as if they were enjoying their task. Lieutenant Sato was running about with his sword drawn, giving orders, urging his men on. Before I withdrew my head the Japanese guards outside the fence had commenced a covering fire over the entrances that the Japanese attacking force had not yet attacked, in an endeavour to keep the men down [the shelters] until the attacking force could get to them and mop them up. I told Sceiva and Kozuch, who were in the same shelter as I, what was taking place and that our only escape was to get out of the entrance one at a time, and try and get through the fence above the bluff and get down to the beach.

I then quickly emerged from the entrance of my shelter, and somehow scrambled through the double barbed wire fence. Hanging on to the bluff I yelled back to Sceiva and Kozuch that they could make it now. In the few seconds that I was exposed I was hit by a bullet in the right leg. Kozuch was next to try, and Sceiva was directly behind him. Both of these men were shot down hanging partly through the fence and lying across the shelter. I could see the bullet holes in Kozuch's back as he was hanging on the wire.

A number of other men were now scrambling down this cliff from C Company's shelter where they had a previously arranged escape hatch. This escape hatch was made due to indications that we had received through conversations with the Japanese that just such a thing as this might take place.

At the southern entrance of B Company's shelter I saw one man crawl under the barbed wire fence and tumble down the bluff. I then let go of the bluff and scrambled down the cliff to the water's edge. Upon arriving there I noticed the bodies of two American prisoners of war lying face downwards, half in the water. They had been shot in the back. The Japanese taking part in the attack were standing along the barbed wire fence above the bluff, and shooting at the men who had managed to get over it, either through the fence or the escape hatch.

It was then that I was joined by two other prisoners named

Ayres and Hale. I told them I was going to follow up close to the rocks on the beach around to the south-west by the dock area, and try to get into the underbush, circling from there into the jungle. Neither Ayres nor Hale agreed with my plan and attempted to swim the bay, but both lost their lives. Hale, after swimming approximately thirty yards from the shore, was brought under fire by the Japanese on the bluff and, after a few shots had struck the water alongside of him, he was hit. Rolling over on his back he said, 'They've got me,' and drowned.

After seeing Ayres and Hale killed I proceeded around the rocks towards the dock area I previously had in mind, and after going about thirty yards the rocks ended and I stumbled on three Japanese sailors . . . attempting to set up a Lewis gun to cover the path which I had just come over. I had no alternative but to jump on these three sailors in an attempt to get the machine-gun away from them. We finally fought out into the water where, due to their weight, I fell under the water and remained holding them under with me, forcing them finally to release their hold on the gun and on me. They then tried to get back on to the beach.

Coming out of the water myself, I pulled the actuator[1] back on the Lewis gun and managed to kill all three sailors. But seeing another machine-gun being set up a little further down the beach I was forced to return the way I had come, in an effort to find a hiding place amongst the rocks.

In order to crawl into a small crevice to hide, I was forced to get rid of the machine-gun which I threw into the water. While in this crevice I could easily discern the difference between the Japanese hollering and laughing, and the Americans' screams being killed. I could also distinguish the smell of burning flesh and the odour of dynamite.

Very soon afterwards a Japanese landing barge patrolled within a few feet of the rocks where I was hiding. They were looking for prisoners who had managed to get away. Any who were found were shot from the barge. Patrols continued to comb the rocks and beaches for the rest of the day and about 9 p.m., along with the other four survivors, I swam the bay and managed, after a few days in the jungle, to join up with the Filipino guerrillas.

[1] Cocking handle.

About forty other prisoners succeeded in escaping from the compound by throwing themselves over a fifty feet high cliff on to the beach below. Four of them survived and joined up with Bogue. Men on the landing barges were patrolling the bay; these were the barges which Bogue saw, and the sentries on shore fired on these prisoners. Many of them, badly burned and wounded, were lying on the beaches moaning in agony and were buried alive by the Japanese patrolmen.

One such prisoner, who had managed to reach the water and had struck out to swim across the bay, was recaptured and brought back to land where Japanese soldiers, prodding him with their bayonets, forced him to walk along the beach. One Japanese guard poured petrol on this prisoner's foot and set fire to it. Ignoring his entreaties that he be shot, the Japanese soldiers deliberately set fire to his other foot and to his arms and hands. They mocked and derided him in his suffering and then bayoneted him until he collapsed. Thereupon they poured petrol over his body, and watched the flames devour it.

After the American forces landed at Puerto Princesa on the 28th February 1944, a search of the prisoner of war enclosure was made and some identity discs, certain personal belongings and fragmentary records of the slaughtered American prisoners of war were found. A fortnight later seventy-nine skeletons were discovered and buried by 601 Q.M. Company of the United States Army. Twenty-six of them were found in one excavation piled up to a height of four or five feet. Bullets had pierced the skulls which had also been crushed with blunt instruments. The smallest number of bodies was found in the largest shelters which were nearest the cliff and furthest away from the prison building. Many prisoners from these shelters had, presumably, found it easier to get away over the cliff only to be shot later on the rocks or on the beaches. Most of the bodies were found huddled together at spots furthest away from the entrances. In two dug-outs ciosest to the cliff some bodies were found in prone positions with the arms extended in front of them and the result of a pathological examination showed that these men had been trying to dig their way to freedom.

A report on this atrocity was embodied in a protest sent by the United States Government through the Swiss Legation to the Japanese Foreign Minister, Togo, on the 19th May 1945. The protest ended with these words:

> Such barbaric behaviour on the part of the Japanese armed forces is an offence to all civilized people.
>
> The Japanese Government cannot escape punishment for this crime. The United States Government demands that appropriate punishment be inflicted on all those who directed or took part in it. It expects to receive from the Japanese Government notification that such punishment has been inflicted. The United States Government further demands that the Japanese Government take such action as may be necessary to forestall the repetition of offences of so heinous a nature and assure the United States Government that such outrages will not again be inflicted upon American prisoners of war in Japanese custody.

The protest was handed personally to the Japanese Foreign Minister by the Swiss Minister on the 3rd June 1945. A month later the Japanese Foreign Ministry let the Swiss Legation know that a reply would be made to the protest after an *immediate investigation*, but up to the day on which Japan surrendered no such reply had been received.

There is ample evidence that most of these massacres were ordered by commissioned officers, some of whom were high-ranking Admirals and Generals, and carried out under the supervision of their subordinates. This evidence has come from many sources, from captured Japanese orders, from battle reports, from the diaries of Japanese soldiers and from the statements, affidavits and testimony of a large number of Allied ex-prisoners of war.

[115]

Battle reports of military units and police reports of the military police contained accounts of massacres which had been carried out, together with details of the number of victims killed and the *number of rounds of ammunition expended*. In more than one prisoner of war camp documentary evidence was found of orders from high authority to kill prisoners of war.

The war diary of one such camp in Formosa contained an entry giving the reply which had been sent in answer to an inquiry from the adjutant of the 11th Military Police Unit stationed on the island. The unit had written for details of the 'extreme measures' to be taken against prisoners of war. The method to be employed in carrying out such extreme measures was dealt with, in the reply, as follows:

> Whether they [the prisoners] are destroyed individually or in groups, or however it is done, with mass bombing, gas, poison, drowning, decapitation, et cetera, dispose of them as the situation dictates.
>
> In any case, the object is not to allow the escape of a single one, to annihilate them all and to leave no trace.

During the last six months of the conflict unmistakably clear orders were issued from the War Ministry itself by the Vice-Minister of War, Shitayama, to prevent our prisoners of war from falling into Allied hands.

The order stated, among other things, that the policy for the 'handling of prisoners of war in these times, when the situation is becoming more pressing, and the evils of war extend to the Imperial Domain, Manchuria and other places, will be found in the enclosed summary. We hope that you will follow it, making no mistakes'.

The 'Policy' was described in the enclosure as being to make every effort, and to spare no pains, 'to prevent the prisoners of war from falling into the enemy's hands'.

CHAPTER VII

THE PRISON HULKS

PRISONERS of war, when transported from place to place by sea, fared no better than they did in the prison camps, for the ships used were veritable prison hulks. The prisoners were packed into the holds and coal bunkers with no air and inadequate sanitation. Many of them were already weak from starvation and disease, and on the voyage they received no medical attention or supplies. The rations were meagre, drinking water was in short supply, and the prisoners were generally kept below decks for the whole voyage. The ships were unmarked and were thus subjected to Allied attacks from sea and air in which many of the prisoners on board perished.

In its judgment, the International Military Tribunal for the Far East thus described the method employed to conserve space in these ships.

Wooden stages or temporary decks were built in empty coal bunkers and holds, with a vertical space of only three feet between. The space allotted to prisoners on these decks was an area six feet by six feet per fifteen prisoners. They were compelled to sit cross-legged during the entire voyage. Space was conserved also by the elimination of proper sanitary facilities. Those provided consisted of buckets or boxes which were lowered into the hold or bunker with ropes, and were removed in the same manner for emptying over the side. Drippings from these containers added to the general insanitary conditions. Many prisoners were suffering from dysentery when taken on board, and their excreta fell freely through the cracks of the wooden stages upon their comrades below. To save space for the preparation of food, the prisoners were served uncooked food, or food that had been prepared before sailing. For the same reason, an inadequate supply of water was carried. To

[117]

add to the horrible conditions which prevailed, prisoners were not allowed on deck.[1]

One of the first of these voyages was made in January 1942 when a Japanese ship, the *Nitta Maru*, put in at Wake Island to take on board 1235 American prisoners of war and civilian internees and transport them to Yokohama and Shanghai.

As each prisoner went on board he was forced to run the gauntlet, during which time he was beaten and kicked by the ship's crew. This was a recognized pastime on many prisoner of war sea transports. The prisoners were then placed in three separate holds which contained several temporary decks, each with about three feet of headroom. The men were already very exhausted when they reached the ship, and having to run the gauntlet did not improve their condition. The holds were very crowded and there was no room to lie down except in shifts.

The voyage lasted seventeen days, and for the whole of that time the prisoners remained below, but on reaching Yokohama, the *Nitta Maru's* first port of call, ten of them were allowed on deck, and their photograph was taken for propaganda purposes.

Before embarking, each prisoner was issued with a copy of the 'Regulations for Prisoners' which were in force aboard all prison ships. Regulation I provided the death penalty for a dozen offences. Those disobeying orders and instructions, showing any sign of opposition, talking without permission or raising the voice, walking about or climbing ladders without orders would 'be punished with *immediate death*'. The Regulations went on to make it clear that the Navy of the Great Japanese Empire would try not to punish all with death, and that those who obeyed all the rules of the Japanese Navy, and co-operated with Japan in constructing the 'New Order of Great Asia' would be well treated.

---

[1] This statement is not completely accurate as there were one or two voyages during which prisoners were allowed on deck for about five minutes per day.

The Japanese guards were allowed to search the prisoners at any time, and when they did this, to the accompaniment of much beating and slapping, they removed all the prisoners' belongings such as watches, rings, money, pens, pencils, articles of toilet, clothing, and even their personal papers, letters, and family photographs which they held most dear.

There were no latrines for the prisoners and the usual bucket routine, already described, was the only means by which they could relieve themselves. The insanitary and filthy condition of the holds was aggravated by the fact that so many of the occupants were suffering from diarrhœa or dysentery, and no means of cleaning the decks or themselves were provided.

Until the ship reached Japan the heat was tropical and the atmosphere below stifling. During the whole trip the prisoners had to live in those dark, steamy holds, half starved, thirsty, filthy, and were beaten and humiliated daily. Many healthy young Marines, who had only been taken prisoner less than three weeks earlier, contracted tuberculosis and other ailments as a result of their ill-treatment and privations.

There was a Japanese medical officer on board but he flatly refused to treat the prisoners who were wounded or sick.

When the ship reached Yokohama on 18th January the weather was very cold and the prisoners had no warm clothing. Many of them fell sick with exposure. There was worse to come.

On the second day out from Yokohama, Captain Saito, the Japanese OC Troops, called Chief Petty Officer Kohara to his cabin. Kohara had been posted to the *Nitta Maru* for the duration of this voyage for prisoner of war guard duty. When Kohara got to the cabin Saito showed him a piece of paper which purported to be an execution warrant for five of the American prisoners of war on board. After Kohara had read the document Saito ordered him to carry out the execution, but the chief petty officer, according to his own story, 'flatly refused'. The order was repeated and again refused. Saito then warned his subordinate that this was a serious matter,

[119]

that he was giving Kohara a direct order and that he must carry it out with his 'Japanese sword'.

Kohara thought the matter over and quickly decided that an order from his Captain was an order from his Emperor and must be obeyed. The reflection that if he did not do so the next execution might well be his own, Kohara admitted, also influenced his decision. But he did not like having to make it, and returned to his cabin 'feeling ill'.

Shortly afterwards he was informed, while still in his cabin, that all was ready for the execution to take place. When he reached the quarter-deck he saw five American prisoners of war lined up on the port side. The Japanese guards were posted all round them.

Captain Saito came on deck, mounted a small dais in front of which the five victims were paraded, and read out their names from a piece of paper, the same document he had previously shown to Kohara. He then addressed the prisoners in these words. 'Since you have committed a crime, it will do no good to the world to let you live. I hope you will find happiness in the next world. When you are born again I hope you will become peace-loving citizens.'

Saito stepped down from the dais and ordered Warrant Officer Yoshimura to execute the first prisoner, who was blindfolded and bound with his hands behind his back. He was then made to kneel down on a small straw mat. Yoshimura stepped forward, raised his sword and struck the prisoner hard across the side of the neck but failed to sever the head. He aimed a second blow which also did not decapitate the American who took some little time to die.

Petty Officer Takamura was chosen to behead the second prisoner and succeeded in beheading the victim with one stroke of the sword.

Then came Kohara's turn. This account of what happened is in his own words:

Next Captain Saito called out, 'Senor "Gocho".' I answered, 'Yes.' I was scared and shaking. I stepped forward to where the third American prisoner of war was kneeling on the deck. I raised my sword to strike him. Being unable to bring myself to deliver the stroke, I lowered my sword. I opened my eyes, and I saw the red hair above his eye bandage. As Captain Saito was standing right beside me and had ordered me to do this duty I raised my sword again and attempted to strike. A second time I could not, so I lowered my sword once more.

Then realizing that I was acting on orders from the Emperor of Japan, I closed my eyes, raised my sword and brought it down 'whang'. When I opened my eyes the body of the American prisoner was lying at my feet. His head was severed from his body. I had carried out Captain Saito's orders.

After the last man had been beheaded the bodies were mutilated by soldiers of the 'Prisoner of War Guard Detachment' and thrown overboard.

On the following day the ship reached Shanghai and the other prisoners of war having been put ashore, she sailed for Kure. During the voyage from Shanghai to Kure, Saito called all the prisoner of war guards to his cabin and presented each of them with rings and watches which had been taken from the prisoners. Kohara was given, and accepted, a wrist watch and a gold ring.

There is no doubt that there was never any charge, nor any trial, nor any execution warrant. When Kohara went ashore at Kure he found the purported warrant in the pocket of his coat, and as he said in his statement:

I am sure that Captain Saito did not report the execution of the five American prisoners of war to his superiors at the Kure Naval Training Station, otherwise he would have needed the warrant to substantiate the charge and sentence.

On 25th September 1942 a draft of 1816 British prisoners of war was embarked in the *Lisbon Maru* at Hong Kong for transport to Japan. They were packed into three holds. The Royal Navy prisoners were in No. 1 hold, which was in the forecastle, the 2nd Battalion Royal Scots contingent and the prisoners belonging to the 1st Battalion The Middlesex Regiment and a number of small units were all in No. 2 hold which was just forward of the bridge. In No. 3 hold, which was aft, the prisoners were mostly Royal Artillery. There were also two thousand Japanese troops on board who were returning home.

There was, as usual, not enough room for all the men to lie down at the same time, and each unit worked out a scheme whereby their men could lie down in shifts.

At the start of the voyage the food, by Japanese prisoner of war standards, has been described by some of the prisoners as 'average'. There was an adequate supply of drinking water, but no facilities for washing. The prisoners were allowed to go on deck at intervals to join the queues waiting to use the latrines.

At about 7 a.m. on 1st October, just before morning roll call, there was a loud explosion. The ship's engines stopped and all the lights went out. The prisoners could only guess what had happened, and a few men, who were up on deck for the usual purpose, were immediately sent below and extra sentries were posted on the hatches to prevent any prisoners leaving. No prisoners of war were injured by the explosion, and they learned later that it had been caused by a torpedo which had hit the *Lisbon Maru* in one of her coal bunkers.

On board was Nimori, who had been chief interpreter to the prisoner of war camp staff in the Hong Kong Area from early 1942. He wielded far more power than his appointment would indicate, for he exercised executive authority over the British and Canadian prisoners and was at all times brutal and callous.

After the explosion, Nimori gave orders for the hatches to be battened down. Tarpaulins were placed over them and fastened with ropes. On many occasions during the following day and night the senior British officer, Lieutenant-Colonel Stewart, appealed to Nimori to have at least some part of the hatches open, as the prisoners were dying of suffocation and the water supply had run out.

At 4 a.m. next day, in response to repeated requests for water, Nimori, who had a sadistic sense of humour, appeared at one of the hatchways and let down a bucket full of urine.

Many of the prisoners were suffering from dysentery or diarrhoea, but requests that they be allowed to visit the latrines on deck were consistently refused. Nor were any receptacles provided for use below as an alternative measure.

The conditions below can well be imagined. They were worst in No. 3 hold, which was making water, and the prisoners had to man the pump. They were so exhausted from the heat and complete lack of fresh air that a man could only manage about six strokes at the pump before he fainted. Several men had died before the first night was over; two of them were suffering from diphtheria.

During the night, as the *Lisbon Maru* was filling up rapidly, the Japanese troops were taken off by another ship which then took the transport in tow.

Early in the morning of 2nd October, about twenty-four hours after the torpedo had struck the *Lisbon Maru*, she gave a sudden lurch and it became evident that she was beginning to settle. Lieutenant-Colonel Stewart had organized a small party to try and break out of the hold, and they were all standing by to begin the operation when suddenly the ship stopped.

The party succeeded in making a small opening and two officers, Lieutenants Howell and Potter, together with the prisoners' own interpreter and one or two others, climbed through it on to the deck. As they were walking towards the bridge to request an interview with the ship's captain they were fired upon by the Japanese guards. Howell was hit and subsequently died of his wounds. The rest of the party reported back to Lieutenant-Colonel Stewart and told him that the ship was very low down in the water and was about to sink.

Immediately after the return of the deck party, Japanese

guards came to the opening and fired a few shots into the hold, wounding two more officers. Suddenly the ship gave another lurch, settled down by the stern, and water began pouring into No. 2 hold through the opening in the hatch.

Lieutenant G. C. Hamilton of the Royal Scots who was in No. 3 hold has told the story of what then happened:

As soon as the ship settled the men stationed at the hatch cut the ropes and the canvas tarpaulin, and forced away the baulks of timber, and the prisoners from my hold formed into queues and climbed out in perfect order.

The men from the other two holds broke out at the same time, but many in the aftermost hold were trapped by the inrushing sea and drowned before they could get out.

When we emerged on to the deck the Japanese opened fire at us, and continued firing after the men had jumped over the rails into the sea.

When I came on to the deck there were no Japanese left on the ship at all, although when the first lot of prisoners reached it some half dozen guards were still there. All the prisoners in the three holds, who had not been suffocated or drowned, managed either to climb up on deck themselves or were hauled up by the others.

About three miles away I could see some islands and a swift current was running in their direction. Four Japanese ships were standing by, but they appeared to be as inhospitable as the rocky islands for they showed no signs of wanting to pick up any of us. Ropes were dangling from these ships into the water but any prisoners who tried to climb up them were kicked back into the sea.

I struck out for the islands, but after swimming for about half an hour I saw that the Japanese had changed their tune and were beginning to pick up the prisoners. Being still a long way from land I turned and swam for one of the Japanese ships. When I reached it someone threw me a rope and some of our own men helped me on board. A few prisoners managed to reach the islands, but many were lost on rocky coast.

There were a number of Chinese junks and sampans about. These had come from the islands. The Chinese in them picked up several of our men and treated them with great kindness, gave them food and clothing from their meagre supplies, and looked after them until the Japanese landing parties came to recover them.

The ship that picked me up was a small patrol vessel which carried on with its patrol for about three days and then put into Shanghai when the picked up survivors were landed. There all the survivors were eventually assembled on the quayside. Many were completely naked and most of us only had shorts or a shirt. During the time I was on the patrol vessel we were kept on deck under a tarpaulin which leaked badly, and food consisted of four hard-tack biscuits and two small cups of watered milk per day, with a bowl of soup on the third day. Two men died during this time and the cold and exposure had a serious effect on our future health.

By 5th October all the surviving officers and men had been assembled at the docks in Shanghai and when the roll was called nine hundred and seventy answered their names. Of the eight hundred and forty-six who failed to answer all but about half a dozen lost their lives. The other six, it was afterwards learnt, had managed to escape with the help of the Chinese.

While they remained on the dockside awaiting re-embarkation on the *Shinsei Maru*, in which they were later transported to Japan, the prisoners were neglected and abominably ill-treated. Nimori addressed them, and left them in no doubt that their survival was a great disappointment to him. 'You should', he told them, 'have gone with the others.'

Many of them were so ill and weak that they could hardly stand, but when they tried to sit down Nimori beat them unmercifully with his sword, and ordered the guards to do likewise. They were kept there without food and without clothing, except what they had received from the Chinese, from noon on 4th October until 8 a.m. on the 5th. Before they re-embarked, Nimori ordered them to hand over all that was left of their clothing. One regimental sergeant-major who refused was promptly kicked in the testicles.

There can be no doubt that the Japanese had originally

intended to let all 1,816 prisoners drown and then to say that the torpedoed ship had sunk instantaneously and had given them no time to effect a rescue.[1] The Japanese troops and crew had all been transferred to another vessel during the night, and the crew and all the guards, save six, had been withdrawn. The prisoners were, meanwhile, battened down.

Had they been transferred to one of the four ships which were standing by all night there is no reason why they should not have all survived. It was only after they realized that many of the prisoners were being picked up by Chinese junks and sampans that the Japanese changed their minds and began to do the same.

Very few, however, would have escaped had not the ship's stern settled down on a sandbank. This allowed more time for the men to get out of their holds and jump into the sea.

The interpreter, Nimori, was primarily responsible for all that happened on the *Lisbon Maru*, and the officer in command of the guards, Lieutenant Wado, had no real authority. From the very first day of the voyage Nimori indicated his attitude to the prisoners of war, which was one of utter disregard for their fate. When the senior British officer complained about the battening down of all the hatches, as a result of which many died from suffocation, Nimori said, 'You have nothing to worry about, you are bred like rats, and so can stay like rats.'

Nimori's activities were not solely confined to the voyage of the *Lisbon Maru*. He made another voyage a few months later, again as interpreter, on a transport named *Toyama Maru*, which was taking a draft of Canadian prisoners of war from Hong Kong to Japan.

During the voyage some of the prisoners, who had been given sweaters by the Red Cross, sold them to their guards in exchange for food. This came to the ears of Nimori who held a kit inspection. One prisoner, a Canadian soldier named Rifleman Doucet, of the Royal Rifles of Canada, was unable

[1] In the *Nippon Times*, an English language newspaper published in Japan, this very version of the sinking of the *Lisbon Maru* was reported.

to produce his sweater on the inspection. Nimori and a Japanese corporal then set about Doucet in a most brutal manner. He was beaten with a belt, hit all over the body, knocked down, and while on the ground was kicked in the stomach. After this assault Rifleman Doucet had to be carried below, and was very ill for the remainder of the voyage. He never recovered and about a month later he died at Marumi Camp in Japan.

Nimori was eventually tried in Hong Kong, in October 1946, by a British Military Court upon eight war crime charges and was found guilty. As all the charges involved similar incidents of great brutality, some of which led to the ultimate death of the victims, the sentence of fifteen years' imprisonment could hardly be considered severe.

Towards the end of October 1942, eleven hundred prisoners of war, who had been captured in Java, were shipped to Singapore *en route* for Japan. A few days after their arrival at Singapore they were embarked on the *Singapore Maru*, a very old cargo boat of about 5,800 tons, and without any proper ventilation. During the voyage sixty of the prisoners died, and many more died after the ships arrived in Japan on 20th November.

After the war the captain of the ship, Ship Master Nishimi Yoshimari, together with the Japanese OC Troops and two draft conducting officers, was tried by a British War Crimes Court at Singapore for 'being concerned in the ill-treatment of a draft of British prisoners of war resulting in the death of sixty and the physical suffering of many others'.

At the trial, Lieutenant-Colonel E. R. Scott gave evidence. He stated that he was senior British officer on board, that the ship was overcrowded, the food inadequate, medical supplies scarce and the sanitation deplorable.

Prisoners of war began to die soon after the ship left port. On arrival at Cap St Jacques (Saigon) he asked that all the sick prisoners should be disembarked, but this request was

THE KNIGHTS OF BUSHIDO

refused. On arrival at Takao, on the island of Formosa, he again asked that one hundred sick prisoners of war should be taken off. The request was partially granted, and twenty were put ashore. Although the ship was already overcrowded to the limit, another six hundred Japanese troops were embarked, bringing the number of Japanese up to twelve hundred. The wretched prisoners had, therefore, to be packed into the lower holds and the so-called sick-bay removed to the bottom of the after hold. On arrival at Moji, in Japan, two hundred and eighty prisoners were too weak to walk off the ship. They were later taken ashore and within six weeks one hundred and twenty-seven died of malnutrition, dysentery or pellegra.[1]

So many prisoners of war died in this way, and still more arrived at their destination too weak to work, that even their captors began to recognize that valuable assets were going to waste. As early as December 1942 an order was issued from the War Ministry calling attention to this wastage.

> Army Asia Secret Order No. 1504 [dated 10th December 1942]. Recently, during the transportation of prisoners of war to Japan, many of them have been taken ill or have died, and quite a few of them have been incapacitated for further work due to their treatment on the journey, which at times was inadequate.

Instructions then followed that those responsible for the transport of prisoners should ensure that they arrived at their destination 'in a condition to perform work'.

The order, however, had no real effect and the condition of prisoners of war, who were transported by sea, upon arrival at their destination had improved so little by the beginning of 1944 that another order was issued on 3rd March to 'all units concerned' by the Vice-Minister of War, Tominaga.

This order contained the following observations:

> In announcements by the Prisoner of War Administration, the use of prisoners for labour has already been stressed. Al-

---

[1] A disease marked by cracking of the skin and often ending in insanity.

though this has directly helped to increase our fighting strength, the average prisoners of war's health condition is hardly satisfactory. Their high death rate must again be brought to your attention. In the light of the recent intensified enemy propaganda warfare, if the present conditions continue to exist, it will be impossible for us to expect world opinion to be what we would wish it.

But in any event, it is absolutely necessary to improve the health condition of the prisoners of war *from the point of view of using them satisfactorily to increase our fighting strength.*[1] It should be added that although efforts must be made to utilize the space in ships for transporting war prisoners, it is necessary that the purport of 'Army Asia Secret Order No. 1504' of 1942 be thoroughly understood in handling war prisoners at this juncture.

If this order ever reached Lieutenant-Colonel Anami, who commanded a number of prisoner of war camps on the Ambon group of islands, it was certainly not passed on by him to his subordinates.

One of these camps was at Weijami on Amboina Island. Towards the beginning of September 1944 Allied aircraft raided the town of Ambon and inflicted great damage. The Japanese decided, as a result of these raids, to move the prisoners of war, and a party of some five hundred British and Dutch embarked on the *Maros Maru* at Amboina on 17th September. This small ship of about 600 tons had formerly been owned by the Dutch, and was scuttled at Batavia prior to the capitulation in March 1942. The Japanese had salvaged her in 1943.

The senior officer of the party, Flight-Lieutenant W. M. Blackwood, RAF, gave a graphic account of the embarkation in an affidavit which he made, and which was produced as an exhibit at the trial of the Japanese major war criminals in Tokyo.

On the morning of embarkation it rained for the first time for many days. My party marched barefoot, some had wooden

[1] Author's italics.

sandals, in a glutinous sea of liquid mud which covered the sharp coral surface of the road. With guards harassing us to hurry, the beri-beri crippled being pushed and bullied, and the stretcher bearers being goaded into a shambling trot, we made the jetty in about half an hour. There the stretchers were laid in the mud, fully exposed to the pitiless rain, although there were some empty huts available close by. After everybody was soaked, a few straw mats were produced and draped over those who were most ill, and whose delirious groans fell without response upon the ears of our guards.

After a wait of nearly three hours, barges were brought alongside and we were ferried across the creek to where our transport lay at anchor.

When we drew alongside I could scarcely believe that all five hundred of us were expected to get aboard. When I realized that the holds were full and battened down, and we were to travel as deck passengers, I was staggered.

First of all the baggage was dumped on the hatch covers and an attempt was made to distribute the fit men, walking patients, and stretcher cases in the gangways and narrow deck spaces. The effect was like a London tube train in the rush hour. No level space could be found for the stretchers, and the sick men were subjected to acute discomfort, and an ordeal which it was at once obvious they could not sustain for a long sea passage. After protest, the baggage was removed from the hatch covers, but settling into this terribly cramped space with sodden kit bags was almost impossible.

Worse was to come. Firewood for the cookhouse fires on the voyage was brought alongside. Picture a small ferry boat, with a maximum beam of not more than thirty feet, and a space of about forty-five feet from the after bulkhead of the forecastle to just abaft amidships, available for our whole party. The remainder of the deck, all the deck works and housings were out of bounds, so the measure of the overcrowding can be gauged. When the firewood had been brought on board and stacked the deck space was full to the gunwale ... two wooden boxes slung over the ship's sides were all the latrine accommodation provided. Into these boxes our palsied men had to drag themselves after climbing over piles of wood, a journey fraught with difficulty for a fit man, let alone one who was ill.

The first night at sea must have been a nightmare. It was rough, and the *Maros Maru* kept shipping seas which swept across the deck with every roll of the vessel, tossing helpless stretcher cases about the deck like flotsam. One man died before morning came.

When the prisoners embarked they were already worn out by fifteen months of working like slaves, and were weak and ill from malnutrition and constant ill-treatment. Beri-beri soon became prevalent. Day after day, men who were grievously ill lay on the hatch cover fully exposed to the pitiless sun, and although the senior British officer made frequent requests for some shade to be provided, it was not until thirty prisoners had died from thirst and exposure that an awning was erected.

The allowance of drinking water was less than half a pint a day, and to add insult to injury the prisoners, who were suffering the pangs of thirst, had on several occasions to lie helpless on deck while their Korean guards bathed in the drums of drinking water.

One day a prisoner, weakened by hunger, was climbing over the ship's rail to visit one of the latrine boxes when he fell overboard. The ship put about and the man was picked up, whereupon all the officers were paraded and lashed with a rope's end by one of the guards as a punishment for not keeping their men under proper control.

By this time the prisoners were dying like flies and their bodies were thrown overboard after sandbags had been tied to their legs by the Japanese to ensure their sinking. On 21st September the *Maros Maru* arrived at Raha Moena on the island of Celebes. A Japanese junk then came alongside and about another one hundred and fifty prisoners, British and Dutch, under the command of Captain van der Loot, came aboard. These men were the sole survivors from another Japanese transport which had been attacked by a Liberator, set on fire and sunk. Almost all the members of this party were stark naked, and paralysed from beri-beri.

The *Maros Maru* was already full and overflowing, and the

arrival of these extra prisoners caused utter chaos. There was previously no room for all to lie down, now there was scarcely room for a man to sit down properly, but somehow they were squeezed on board.

Flight-Lieutenant Blackwood thus described the gruesome scene :

> All the men lay spread out on the uneven bundles of firewood blistering horribly in the tropical sun. Tongues began to blacken, raw shirtless shoulders to bleed, and all vestige of sanity deserted many. The night air was filled with the yells and screams of the dying, the curses of the worn-out trying to get some sleep, and the chronic hiccoughing that afflicts a man about to die of beri-beri.
>
> Scenes of indescribable horror became commonplace. Picking their way through the tangled mass of humanity lying about on the narrow ship, orderlies carried the naked wasted bodies of the dead to the ship's side where, unheard except by those on the spot, the burial service for those who die at sea was read before casting the body with its sandbag overboard. One youngster, delirious with sunstroke, shouted the thoughts of his disordered mind for thirty hours before he became too weak to utter another word. Just before he died he grabbed a full tin, that was being used as a bed-pan, and drank the contents greedily, thinking it was water, before he could be prevented.

When the ship reached the northern end of the Gulf of Boni the engines, which were very old and almost unserviceable, broke down. As neither the Japanese nor the Javanese crew had much mechanical knowledge or experience, the Japanese lieutenant in charge of the prisoners, Lieutenant Kurishima, appealed to the prisoners of war to carry out repairs. At this time the death rate had reached a total of eight a day, and it became obvious that the longer the voyage lasted the higher the death rate would become. Petty Officer Platt, of the Royal Navy, and two other prisoners volunteered, therefore, to repair the engines and to maintain them and supervise their running for the remainder of the voyage.

When the *Maros Maru* reached Macassar any prisoners who were still fit enough were used to unload her cargo and some of the ammunition. This made it possible for some of the men to go below, and although there was still no room to move they were able to get out of the sun.

The ship remained at anchor in Macassar harbour for forty days, and although some coconuts, cucumbers, mangoes and local sugar were brought on board the prisoners continued to die in large numbers. During the time the *Maros Maru* remained at Macassar one hundred and fifty nine prisoners died.

A sigh of relief went up from the prisoners when at last, after replenishing stores, the ship again set sail, for the end of this nightmare voyage seemed a little nearer. But there was disappointment in store. For another forty days the *Maros Maru* stood off a small island near Macassar, and by the time she set sail on the last leg of the voyage the total number of deaths had reached two hundred and fifty.

The Japanese commander, Lieutenant Kurishima, his senior NCO Sergeant Mori, and the interpreter did nothing to ameliorate the conditions on board. On the contrary, they treated the prisoners with consistent brutality.

One incident has been described by Flight-Lieutenant Blackwood:

> One night, as a sick Dutchman lay dying he began hiccoughing loudly at regular intervals. Sergeant Mori appeared on the bridge and threatened to beat all the sick unless the dying man was given an injection to keep him quiet. This was done but within half an hour he was awake again and hiccoughing as before. Sergeant Mori repeated his threat and another injection was given. Yet a third time the hiccoughing started. The Japanese Sergeant came back on to the bridge and, yelling at the top of his voice, threatened to come down and lay about him with a stick among the stretcher cases. A third injection was given but the Dutchman was never heard again for he died.

Eventually, sixty-seven days after she had sailed from

Amboina, the *Maros Maru* reached Sourabaya in Java. Out of six hundred and thirty prisoners who had been on board, only three hundred and twenty-five were still alive, or nearly alive, for most of them were mere ghosts of their former selves, half starved, half demented wrecks of humanity, diseased, dirty and crawling with vermin.

In the same month as the *Maros Maru* sailed from the island of Amboina 1750 European prisoners of war, six hundred Ambonese prisoners of war and 5500 Indonesian coolies recruited for slave labour were shipped from Java to Sumatra by steamer. The ship was a cargo boat of about 5000 tons.

The conditions on board were similar to those on all the other transports and to describe them would be useless repetition. On one occasion a British prisoner of war went mad and jumped overboard. The Japanese thought this extremely funny until he began to strike out for the shore which was not far off. He was brought back, and orders were given that all prisoners must now be battened down in the holds. The only way they could be got below was by beating them and this was done. Eventually they were crammed into one hold standing upright without room to move. A few hours later, after the ship had sailed and was out of sight of land, the hatches were removed and the prisoners allowed on deck.

When she was about twenty-five miles off the west coast of Sumatra the ship was hit by two torpedoes. One torpedo exploded in one of the holds occupied by some of the coolies, and within twenty minutes she sank. Those of the prisoners who were on deck or who were not trapped below jumped into the sea.

The Japanese commander and the guards got away in one of the lifeboats, but when some of the prisoners tried to save themselves from drowning by clinging on to the lifeboat's gunwale, one Japanese guard, who was armed with a large axe, chopped their hands off or split their skulls open.[1] The escort of two vessels, a destroyer and a corvette, initially picked up about four hundred survivors, but those who were very weak and later became unconscious were thrown back into the sea.

The survivors, who numbered two hundred and seventy-six Europeans, three hundred and twelve Ambonese and only three hundred coolies out of the original 5500, were taken to Padang prison after arrival in Sumatra. Nearly all were entirely naked, and the only clothing issued to them by the Japanese prison authorities was one pair of shorts per man. They were very badly treated and had to sleep on the bare concrete floors of the prison building. The lack of sanitation in this prison was such that within ten days forty-two of the survivors had died.

It made no difference even if the prisoners were women. An Australian nursing sister, named Nesta Gwyneth James, was one of a party of women prisoners of war and civilian internees who embarked on a very small ship for a voyage from Muntok to Palembang in April 1945.

There was a large number of stretcher cases among them and the sisters had to carry the stretchers, together with their own luggage, down the long pier at Muntok to where the ship was lying.

There they had to load everything on to a tender and, later, from the tender on to the ship. One patient died on the dockside and another on the tender, and both nursing sisters and patients remained on deck during the whole of the voyage without any shade or other protection from the weather.

The weather was cold at night and they had no warm clothes and no blankets. In the day time the sun blazed down on them and, as Sister James stated in her evidence, 'it got so

[1] Affidavit of one of the survivors, Isaac Samuel Dixon, see page 13,297 of the proceedings of the IMT, Far East.

hot that the nursing sisters could hardly touch the patients—
they were burning'.

As usual there was no sanitation, and seventy-five per cent
of those on board were suffering from dysentery or diarrhœa.
Several more died on the voyage, and when the ship arrived
at Palembang, although the nursing sisters were themselves
physical wrecks, they had to carry all the stretcher cases on
shore, and put them on the train which was to take them to
their new prison camp.

Throughout the entire period of the Pacific War this
method of transportation by sea of Allied prisoners of war
continued unabated. Members of the Government and
government officials in all the Ministries concerned were well
aware of the practice and its results. Such measures as were
taken to improve the conditions in these ships, totally inadequate as they were, were designed solely to preserve the
ability of the prisoners to perform useful work in the prosecution of the war. That was all that mattered. For their responsibilities in accordance with the recognized laws and customs
of war, the Japanese showed no concern.

CHAPTER VIII

THE DEATH MARCHES

THE Japanese Army habitually contravened the laws and usages of war when moving prisoners of war from place to place. The conditions in which they were transported by sea, packed into holds and coal bunkers with no air and inadequate sanitation, have been described in the preceding chapter, 'The Prison Hulks'.

Prisoners were also forced to march long distances without food and water and without rest. Sick and wounded were forced to march in the same way as the fit. Prisoners who fell behind on these marches were beaten, tortured and murdered.

Much evidence is available regarding this practice, and the fact that its existence was known to the Japanese Government and the military authorities.

One of the outstanding examples, though not the first, was the Bataan march, which took place in April 1942. At 2 a.m. on 9th April 1942 Major-General King, who was in command of the American-Filipino forces in Bataan, sent two of his staff officers forward under a flag of truce to make an appointment for him to meet the commander of the Japanese force with a view to surrendering. Shortly after dawn the American officers returned, having made contact with the enemy, and Major-General King went forward with his two aides in one car followed by the two staff officers in another. During their journey, although both cars carried large white flags, the American parlementaires were repeatedly attacked with light bombs and machine-gun fire from low-flying Japanese aircraft, and had to take cover.

By 10 a.m. they reached Lamao, the headquarters of a Japanese infantry division. Their commander interviewed

Major-General King and explained that he had no authority to treat with the American commander, but that he had informed General Homma who would send an officer with full authority to negotiate the surrender terms.

An hour or so later General Homma's chief-of-staff arrived to discuss the surrender on behalf of his commander-in-chief. The rest of the story is told in Major-General King's own words:

> I was concerned only with the treatment that my men would receive, and whether they would be treated as prisoners of war. The Japanese officer demanded my unconditional surrender. I attempted to secure from him an assurance that my men would be treated as prisoners of war. He accused me of declining to surrender unconditionally and of trying to make a condition. We talked back and forth in this vein for some time, I should guess about half an hour. Finally he said to me, through the interpreter, 'The Imperial Japanese Army are not barbarians'. With that assurance I had to content myself and surrender.
>
> In destroying arms and equipment in preparation for surrender I had reserved enough motor transportation and gasoline to transport all my troops out of Bataan. I endeavoured, prior to surrender, to secure an assurance that this might be done. I pleaded, after my surrender, that this should be done, offering to furnish personnel as might be required by the Japanese for this purpose or to assist in any way they might require. The Japanese told me that they would handle the movement of the prisoners as they desired, that I would have nothing to do with it, and that my wishes in that connection could not be considered.

The prisoners were marched in intense heat along the road to San Fernando, Pampanga, a distance of about seventy-five miles. They had all been on short rations for a considerable period before their capture, and there was a high percentage of sick and wounded prisoners among them; nevertheless, the sick and wounded were also forced to march with the others.

Those who fell by the roadside and were unable to continue, and they were many in number, were shot or bayoneted. Others were taken from the ranks, beaten, tortured and killed. The march lasted nine days, the Japanese guard being relieved at five-kilometre intervals by fresh guards who had been transported in the American trucks.

For the first five days the prisoners received no food, and never any water except what they were able to drink out of caribou wallows and ditches along the highway. Some food was thrown them by Filipinos, and occasionally they broke ranks and grouped themselves round a well, a wallow or a ditch to slake their thirst. Whenever this occurred the Japanese guards opened fire on them.

Throughout the march their escort maltreated them. They were beaten, bayoneted and kicked with hobnailed boots. Dead bodies littered the side of the road.

Staff-Sergeant Samuel Moody of the United States Regular Army has described what happened to one of his friends, a Sergeant Jones:

> My friend Sergeant Jones had a severe case of dysentery caused from drinking the muddy caribou wallow water. When he fell to the rear due to his condition he was beaten and stuck with a bayonet. Later he died from his wounds.

A graphic description of this march was given in evidence at the Tokyo trial by a soldier of the United States Army, D. F. Ingle, who at the time of the American surrender was a patient in a field hospital. He had been admitted to hospital suffering from pneumonia, but shortly after admission he was slightly wounded during an attack made on the hospital by a Japanese aircraft, although it was clearly marked by a Red Cross.

When the Japanese arrived, Ingle was lying on a stretcher with a temperature of 105 degrees. A Japanese soldier prodded him in the back with a bayonet and ordered him to sit up, which Ingle did as quickly as possible. The Japanese then proceeded to relieve him of his watch, his ring, his wallet and all his personal belongings, with the exception of two photographs which Ingle managed to convince the soldier were of Ingle's mother.

Despite the fact that the American was obviously very ill he was forced to join the death march. During the whole nine days he received neither food nor water except what he obtained, like the other prisoners, from the caribou wallows, and other water holes. Ingle's testimony continued:

The water in the ponds and in the ditches was so polluted that it was highly dangerous to drink, and that which came from the artesian wells was of such a small amount that when great numbers of men tried to get it, the Japanese troops would simply raise their rifles and fire into the group, and when the smoke and dust had cleared away it showed that pure water could cause your death as well as that which was polluted.

The Filipino civilians tried on many occasions to give us food, but they did so at the risk of their lives and, indeed, many lost their lives so doing. Apart from that, only an occasional sugar cane patch offered the chance of food, but to try and get some was courting death.

I remember particularly an Episcopalian chaplain named Day. He had contracted dysentery by drinking foul water from a stream or pond beside the highway, and it had become necessary for him to answer the call of nature every few minutes. His usual procedure was to step smartly out of the ranks, relieve himself, and slip quickly back into the column. He had perfected the drill and it had become only a matter of seconds. On one occasion, however, he was spotted by one of the guards and bayoneted. From then onwards he had to be helped, and I was one of those who did so. Taking it in turns, for the remainder of the march, two men at a time had to assist the chaplain to keep up with the others. He was given no medical attention, and had it not been for the help given him by his comrades he would have been left at the roadside to die, or shot and his body thrown on the side of the road.

Ingle was unable to say how many he saw shot or bayoneted because it had become such a commonplace occurrence, and after the first few hundred he stopped counting.

On the sixth day of the march the prisoners were informed, through an interpreter, that if they would hand over their watches, rings and other valuables they would be given food. By then, however, few of them had anything left, for most of them had been 'frisked' by the guards before the march began. Those lucky enough to have any valuables left willingly parted with them, with the result that on the evening of the sixth day the prisoners each received one teacupful of rice.

On the ninth day the prisoners received the welcome news that they would have to march no further. They were going to ride the rest of the way to Camp O'Donnell. Their relief on hearing the glad tidings was short lived, however, for they were then crowded into very small Filipino railway coaches, a hundred men to each coach. So overcrowded were they, that there were many who, during the whole trip, never touched the floor. Hundreds fainted from lack of air, and many died of suffocation.

It is not known exactly how many died on the move from Bataan to Camp O'Donnell, but the evidence indicates that not less than eight thousand American and Filipino prisoners lost their lives during the journey.

Murata, who had been sent to the Philippines in February 1942 by War Minister Tojo as adviser on civil affairs, drove along the Bataan–San Fernando road, and saw the dead bodies on the side of the highway in such great numbers that he even spoke to General Homma about it. After that Homma, at least, could not plead ignorance.

Tojo admitted that he, also, heard about the march in 1942 from many different sources. He was told, he said, that the prisoners had been forced to march long distances in the heat, and that many deaths had occurred. He also admitted that the United States Government's protest against this unlawful treatment of prisoners of war had been discussed at the bi-weekly meetings of the Bureaux Chiefs in the War Ministry soon after the march took place, but no decision was arrived at, and he left the matter to the discretion of the heads of departments concerned.

The Japanese forces in the Philippines were never called upon to make a report on the incident, and Tojo did not even discuss the march with General Homma when the General paid a visit to Japan early in 1943.

The first time Tojo ever made any inquiries was on his visit to the Philippines in May 1943, when he discussed it with Homma's chief-of-staff, who gave him all the details. Tojo took no action, however, and at his trial explained his failure to do so in these words, 'it is the Japanese custom for the commander of an expeditionary army in the field to be given a mission, in the performance of which he is not subject to specific orders from Tokyo, but has considerable autonomy'.

This can only mean that according to the Japanese method of waging war such atrocities were expected to occur, or were at least permitted, and that the Japanese Government was not concerned to prevent them.

That these atrocitities were repeated in other theatres during the Pacific War can rightly be ascribed to the condonation of General Homma's conduct at Bataan.

Although the Bataan death march was the worst of them all, it was not the first. In February 1942 Dutch prisoners of war in Timor, who were suffering from wounds, hunger, malaria and dysentery were marched for five days with their hands tied behind their backs, and were driven and beaten along by their Japanese and Korean guards like a herd of cattle.

Similar marches were forced upon Indian prisoners in British New Guinea during 1943 and 1944.

The Sandakan–Ranau marches early in 1945 were undertaken for different reasons. The Japanese were expecting an Allied landing at Kuching, and the object of moving the prisoners a hundred miles inland to a camp on the eastern slope of Mount Kimabula was to prevent their liberation.

This move took place in a series of marches between January and May 1945, the first beginning in February, and the last at the very end of May.

In February a batch of British and Australian prisoners, totalling four hundred and seventy, made a similar march. These prisoners left the camp in parties of about fifty, one party a day. Each party was accompanied by a Japanese escort of one officer, three NCOs and fifteen private soldiers.

The prisoners, who were very weak, having been existing for the last few days before their departure on a ration of five ounces of weevily rice and a little tapioca, dropped out all along the line of march. In addition to carrying their own food and equipment they were made to act as porters for the escort. As they fell out they were immediately shot.

An Australian private soldier, named Botterill, has given a short account of what happened to his party.

At one time the only food that forty of us had was six cucumbers. When we were about a week away from Ranau we crossed a large mountain, and while we were making the crossing two Australians, Private Humphries and a corporal whose name I cannot remember, fell out. They were suffering from beri-beri, malaria and dysentery and just could not continue any further. A Japanese private shot the corporal, and a Japanese sergeant shot Humphries. Altogether we lost five men on that hill. As we were going along men would fall out as they became too weak to carry on. We would march on and then, shortly afterwards, hear shots ring out and the sound of men screaming. When this occurred there was always a Japanese guard who had stayed behind to 'take care' of the stragglers.

Those who took part in the earlier march were perhaps a little more fortunate than their comrades who did not leave until May, for they were not in quite such bad shape as the second batch, and out of the fifty men who left Sandakan with Botterill thirty-seven reached Ranau. But their good fortune was not to last for long, for by the end of June, only six of the four hundred and seventy who had left Sandakan in February were still alive.

All their Japanese guards, however, had survived and most of them, except for a few who had contracted malaria, were in quite good health.

The last party to leave Sandakan for Ranau began their march after the closing down of the Sandakan prisoner of war camp at the end of May 1945, which will be described in the following chapter.

When the party left Sandakan it numbered five hundred and thirty-six; when it arrived at Ranau there were only one hundred and eighty-three of them alive.

The length of each day's march was trivial, not more than an average of six and a half miles, but very few of the prisoners were fit to walk more than a mile a day, and many of them could hardly stand. For such as these the terrain was difficult. The first three miles was through low lying marshland, there were many creeks to ford and the going was muddy slush. The next forty miles was over higher ground, but it was studded with short steep hills, covered with brush and there were many rivers to be crossed. The last forty-six miles was mountain country.

Before the march began each party of fifty was issued with a hundred-pound bag of rice, and the leader was given a sheet of paper and told to make a nominal roll of the prisoners in his charge.

On the first day there was a halt after two hours' marching and by then, in one party alone, twelve had already fallen out and were never seen again. What happened to those who could not keep up will be seen later. Warrant Officer Sticpewich,[1] who gave evidence at the Tokyo trial, was in command of one of the parties of fifty. According to his evidence the march lasted for twenty-six days by which time he had only thirteen men left. The only food was a small quantity of rice daily, and on the third day the Japanese withdrew thirty-two pounds of rice from each party.

As Sticpewich's party marched on they saw what happened to the stragglers from the party ahead of them. They were

[1] See page 193.

These Sikh prisoners were used as live targets for rifle practice by their Japanese captors in Singapore. A marker hangs over the heart of each and the stakes in front bear the butt numbers. A bayonet thrust (*below*) ensured that no victim survived the shooting

In the six weeks after the Japanese capture of Nanking, it has been estimated that 200,000 Chinese were massacred in the most brutal manner. Here, bound prisoners were used as targets for bayonet practice. As their comrades look on, the Japanese soldier in the centre of the picture gives a final death-thrust, while the one in the foreground goads his victim into position for the *coup de grâce*. Other Chinese prisoners (*below*) were buried alive by their captors

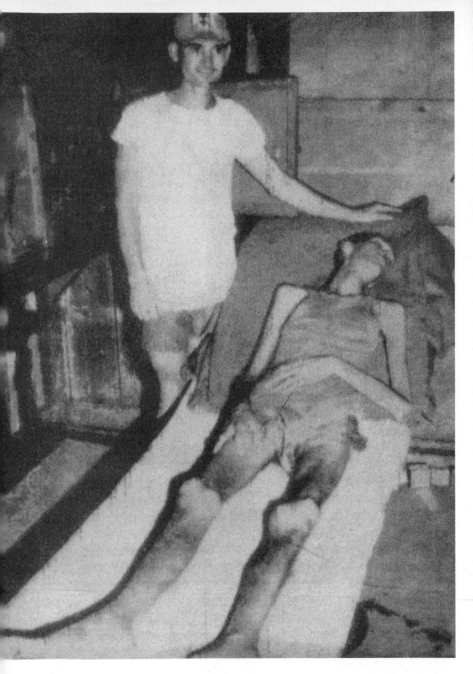

The effects of deliberate malnutrition and mistreatment are shown in this photograph of a prisoner of war from the Aomori Camp near Yokohama, taken four days after his liberation on 27th August 1945

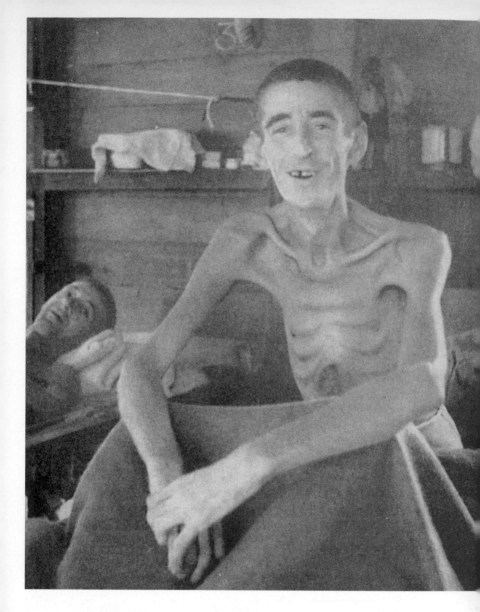

John Sharp of Leicester—one of the worst treated of all the prisoners of war to survive. Attempting to escape while working on the Burma–Siam railway, he was captured and for three years two weeks was held in the torture gaol in Singapore, of which twelve months was spent in solitary confinement

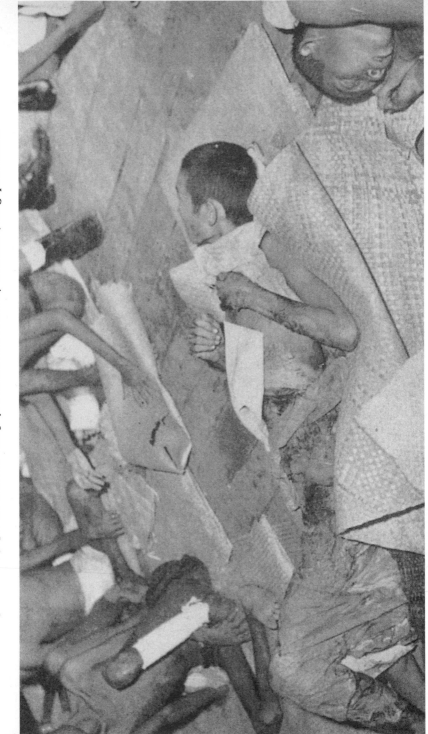

An occupant of the Japanese Labour Camp (for native slave labour) at Seletar, Singapore Island

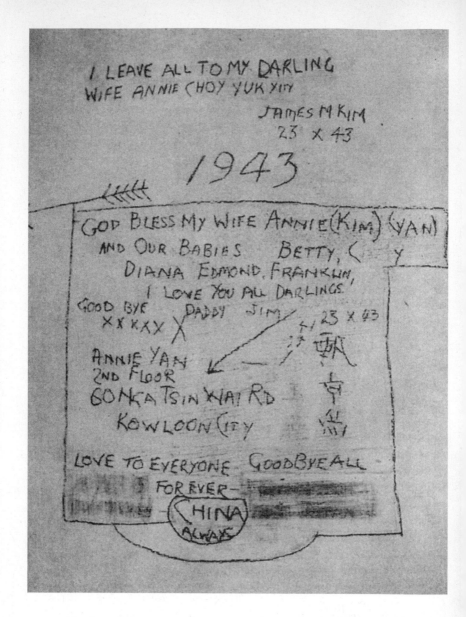

The last Will and message of James M. Kim, an Anglo-Chinese member of the Hong Kong Defence Force. The reason for and manner of his execution are unknown, but the Japanese had, apparently, made every effort to erase this 'writing on the wall' in a cell of Stanley Gaol, Hong Kong

Co-Prosperity. The remains of a hundred men, women and children of Manila who, on 2nd February 1945, were shot and bayoneted to death by the Japanese on the suspicion that members of their families belonged to Philippine guerrilla bands. Those murdered included pregnant women and babies a few months old

Escaped civilians told of the Filipino below who was tortured by Japanese soldiers to make him tell where rice might be hidden, and then killed, near Infanta, Luzon Island

The 'Nippon Golden Arrow', used to carry prisoners of war to working camps on the Burma–Siam railway

THE FOLLOWING ILLUSTRATIONS ARE
REPRODUCTIONS OF ORIGINAL PAINTINGS
AND DRAWINGS BY
LEO RAWLINGS

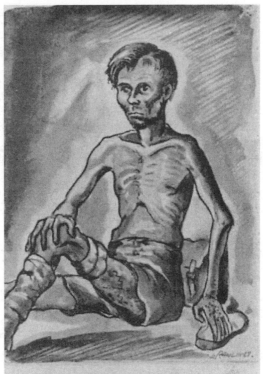

The average condition of thousands
of men returning from working
in the jungles of Thailand & Burma

Leo Rawlings was captured at the fall of Singapore,
spending three and a half years as a prisoner of the
Japanese, during which time he was put to work on the
notorious railway. While a prisoner, he made over a
hundred eye-witness paintings of the conditions under
which the prisoners lived, producing them under the
most difficult conditions, with Chinese Indian ink,
paints, crushed sandstone, clays and vegetable juices

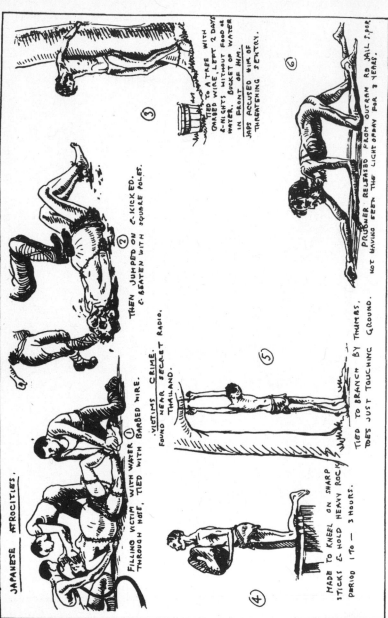

Some Japanese pastimes in punishment for minor crimes. The artist experienced similar treatment to the one shown in Fig 4.

Men had to parade for work often in pitch darkness & pouring rain. Most of them underfed and ill & scantily clad. (Thailand & Burma.)

As men contracted cholera they were isolated in a tent away from the rest of the camp. Doctors did everything possible for them, but few recovered from this terrible scourge.

Small sores quickly developed into horrible ulcers which had to be scraped in order to clean them. No anesthetic was available for this agonising proce

When the railway was finished men returned in thousands, many almost naked, too ill to crawl about & rotten with fever, dysentery & ulcers.

Men on the march through Thailand. Miles of this devilish country are under water during the Monsoon period. Many of us had no boots or foot covering at all, this made no difference to the Japs.

Part of the journey was done by train. Rations were very bad, about 1 pint of rice & a small piece of dried fish was a days food. When the train stopped we would beg, buy, or steal food from the local natives.

Hospital Ward in Thailand. All types
diseases were treated in this hut from
dysentery to Ulcers and Malaria.
Cpl. RAWLINGS the ARTIST, has tooth removed by Capt Winchester A.I.F

Bridge building was one of the wo
jobs, conditions included working
to the waist in fast flowing rivers

At many camps no accommodation
was available so we slept out under
trees & hedges. It was usually raining

Below is the operating theatre at
Khanburi camp Maj. Fagan A.I.F.
did 30 operations per day for 3 month

The meaning of Japanese occupation. This Chinese civilian was first bound and his eyes were then gouged out

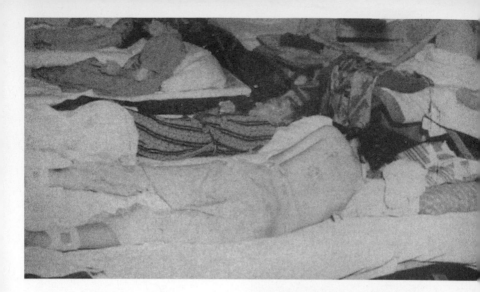

Mrs. Elena Maldonado of Ermita, Manila, who was bayoneted in the back and machine-gunned by Japanese soldiers when she attempted to help other women who were also bayoneted

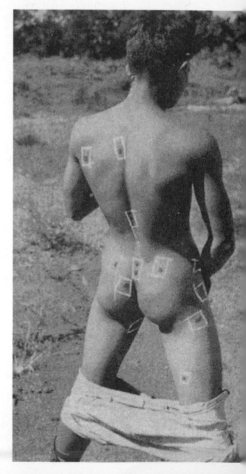

Musebio Linatok, of Lipa, Luzon, who bears the scars of bayonet wounds inflicted upon him by the Japanese

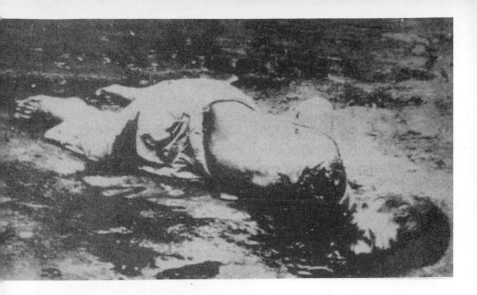

Street scenes in Japanese-
occupied Singapore

The bodies of dead Japanese—killed by Japanese forces to prevent capture in August 1945—lie in an evacuated Japanese hospital area in the Bayombang area, Luzon

These Javanese labourers bayoneted to death and then left by the retreating Japanese as American troops captured Noemfoer Island, Dutch New Guinea, in July 1944

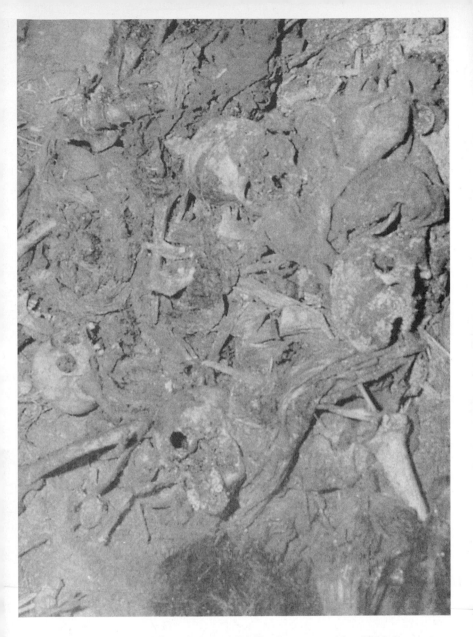

Cave No. 3 in Tuba, Benguet, Philippines, was identified by
Fernandez Aldonand Felipa Malasmas as the scene of the murder
by the Japanese on 10th April 1945 of over fifty Filipino men,
women and children. This picture is evidence of the atrocity

Mr. A. Raven, a Yorkshire architect, at seventy the oldest prisoner in Stanley Gaol, Hong Kong, demonstrates the all-purpose lathe he made with material 'scrounged' from the Japanese guards

General Hideki Tojo

The seven accused at the
'Chinese Massacre Trial'

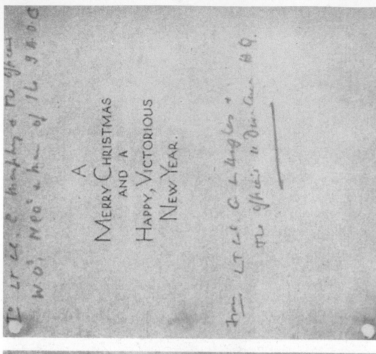

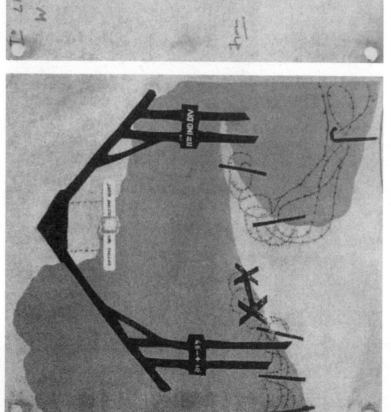

The Christmas card circulated in a Singapore prisoner of war camp in 1944. The drawing is of the ornamental gate erected by the inmates for the visit of the Japanese C.-in-C., Far East. (*See page* 204)

pushed on with the barrel of a rifle, or thumped in the back with the butt. If they could still move they struggled on, but those who were too ill to go on were just left behind.

Three Chinese witnessed one incident which happened on the line of march near the fifteen milepost on the Sandakan–Ranau road, where they lived.

About the end of May or it may have been early June 1945, a large number of Australians and other Allied servicemen were being marched along the Labuk road from the prisoner of war camp at Sandakan.

They arrived at the fifteen milepost at approximately 11 a.m. They stopped there and had a meal. At about 2 p.m. four Allied planes came over and the party scattered. . . . About 5 p.m. the Japanese guards ordered the prisoners to get up and fall in. All obeyed except seven who were too ill to walk and had arrived hobbling on sticks. Two Japanese guards and one Malay soldier remained behind when the others marched off. The guards then started to urge the seven men along, kicking them and hitting them with their own sticks. Although they were very weak the Japanese guards succeeded in beating them along for about thirty yards. The two Japanese guards then took the rifle from the Malay soldier, and driving the prisoners off the road started shooting them in the back.

They were just behind Chin Kin's house. Four of the prisoners were instantaneously killed, and two others were wounded. One managed to get away and hid a little further up the road. The two Japanese guards, together with their Malayan comrade, carried on in the direction of Ranau without waiting to examine the prisoners whom, presumably, they believed to be dead. The prisoner who had run further up the road and gone into hiding was found by one of the Kempei Tai on the following afternoon.

This soldier first went into his house next door, brought his rifle, and shot the other two men, who were still alive, through the head.

The shooting of these two men took place as the three of us were digging a grave for the four men who had been shot the previous evening. The Kempei Tai soldier then left the spot where we were going to bury the six prisoners, and started looking around. We then heard a shot fired, but were too afraid to go and look in the direction whence it came, and continued to dig in the garden as though we had heard nothing. When we had finished burying the six dead prisoners we went to look for the seventh, the one who had escaped and tried to hide. We went in the direction from which we had heard the shot fired and there we found him lying dead. He had been shot in the stomach.

There is no doubt of the truth of the story told by the three Chinese for it was fully corroborated, with a few minor variations, by the criminal himself in a statement which he made, after the war, to a Japanese interpreter attached to the United States Army.

Sergeant Hosotani, for that was his name, stated that he was living temporarily in a hut near the fifteen milepost as he was suffering from malaria. One morning in June 1945 a Corporal Katayama, who was known to him, and who had passed through the village with a number of prisoners on the previous night, came back and told him that if he found any British or Australian stragglers he was to shoot them. When the first lot of prisoners had been shot behind Chin Kin's house by Katayama's guards Hosotani had been asleep, but he was told about it by the Chinese next day.

It was on the way back to his hut after telling the Chinese to bury the dead prisoners that he came across two more. These, he said, were sitting down because they had beri-beri. He went into the house and borrowed a rifle from a Malay police boy who was living with him and shot the two prisoners in the head.

I only shot the prisoners because Corporal Katayama told me to. I was too sick to bury the bodies so I asked Chen Kay to do so. I did not know about another prisoner being shot until Nako, the civilian employee interpreter of the Kempei Tai unit, told me afterwards that he had shot a prisoner at the seventeen milepost. This took place the same day as I shot the two prisoners.

The guards who shot the seven prisoners on their way through the village belonged to the Okamura Unit and, in the words of Hosotani himself, 'they shot them because they could not walk to Ranau and therefore they eliminated them'.

The adjutant at Sandakan, Lieutenant Watanabe, who went on this march as second-in-command to Captain Tanakua, has also given a full account of the march itself, and the killing of the survivors after the arrival of the remnants of the party at Ranau.

The move from Sandakan to Ranau was made on orders from Army headquarters. Air-raids in the Sandakan area had recently become very heavy, and an Australian landing was thought to be imminent.

Watanabe confirmed that only one hundred and eighty-three out of five hundred and thirty-six reached their destination, and that apart from fifty-nine who escaped, ninety prisoners 'were ill and were put out of their misery by being shot. They asked for death rather than be left behind'.

Watanabe appeared to be unaware that to have left them behind to die on the mountains in North Borneo would have been no less a crime, yet that was apparently the alternative proposal. Nor did he reveal what befell the remaining two hundred and five.

There can, however, be no doubt about their fate, for Tanakua's orders to his troops were 'to dispose of sick POWs and to see that none were left behind'. Watanabe described himself as 'i/c the disposal', though he was not present at any of the killings. But he knew perfectly well what the procedure was.

I moved with the rear group with the exception of Fukushima's party. Each morning all those POWs who were unable to travel were placed in groups for Fukushima and Tsuji.[1] The disposal was done behind me, and I never knew who killed them.

[1] Fukushima was an officer and Tsuji a sergeant-major.

The dead bodies of those who were shot in this way were dragged into the jungle before Fukushima's murder squad moved on.

The above are but five examples of what was a common practice, accepted and followed by the Japanese Army and the Prisoner of War Administration, when moving prisoners of war from one place to another.

CHAPTER IX

THE PRISON CAMPS

T H E general attitude of the Japanese to Allied prisoners of war has already been described in Chapter III, and other chapters have dealt with the murder of captured aircrews, the transport of prisoners by sea in appalling conditions, the so-called 'Death Marches', work on the Burma–Siam Railway and the massacre of Allied prisoners on or shortly after capture.

This final chapter on the treatment of Allied prisoners of war describes conditions in some of the many prison camps in which thousands lost their lives, and where death was often a merciful release from unendurable suffering.

Early in 1942 the Japanese Government undertook to take into consideration the national customs and racial habits of their prisoners and internees when supplying such things as food and clothing, but this promise was never kept. When large numbers of prisoners began to die or become ill from malnutrition it must have been obvious to the Japanese authorities that one of the causes was that owing to their different national dietary customs and habits, the American, Australian, British, Dutch, and French prisoners could not remain healthy on the rations issued.

In October 1942 orders were issued to all commandants of prisoner of war camps that 'in view of the consumption of rice and barley by the workers in heavy industries in Japan', the rations for prisoners of war and civilian internees, who were officers or civilian officials, should be reduced to a maximum of four hundred and twenty grams a day. Eighteen months later the ration was further reduced, and although by this time deficiency diseases were widespread, the well-known 'no work, no food' instructions were issued by Tojo to all camp commandants.

The Japanese Army and Navy's own prisoner of war regulations required them to keep a reserve supply of medicines and medical equipment sufficient for one year's use. These regulations were frequently observed only by confiscating Red Cross supplies, and even then most of these were used for the benefit of the Japanese. The failure to provide the prisoners with adequate medical supplies was common to all prisoner of war camps without exception and was a contributory cause of the deaths of many thousands of prisoners and internees.

The Japanese prisoner of war regulations also provided that barracks, temples and other buildings should be used as camps, and that those who employed the prisoners on war production should provide them with shelter from the elements. In many camps both the shelter and the sanitation were inadequate. Atap huts with mud floors furnished the only accommodation in most of the camps situated on islands in the Pacific.

Furthermore, it was the common practice to make the prisoners build their own camps in such places, and until the huts or shelters were completed the prisoners had to live in the open and were exposed to the weather at all times.

Sometimes, indeed, the prisoners were spared the labour of building their own camp by taking over a site previously used for another purpose, but this could, also, have its disadvantages. A former Japanese labour camp at Lahat in the Molucca Islands was converted into a prisoner of war camp in August 1944, but when the British and Dutch prisoners arrived to occupy it they found it full of dead Javanese, its former occupants.

Anything was good enough for an Allied prisoner of war. When Itagaki was planning to house two thousand British and American prisoners in three theological schools in Korea, the Vice-Minister of War, Kimura, inquired whether the intended accommodation was not too good for them.

The terrible conditions in some of these camps, and the miserable existence which their occupants led, are described below.

AMBOINA

On 3rd February 1942, when the island of Amboina, which is south of Ceram in the Molucca Archipelago, fell to the Japanese, eight hundred and nine Australians and three hundred Dutch prisoners of war were captured, and taken to Tan Toey Barracks, two miles outside the town of Ambon. The two nationalities were separated inside the barrack compound by a barbed wire fence. Eight months later five hundred of these prisoners were removed to Hainan Island. The others, except for those who were killed or died, remained on the island until they were liberated on 10th September 1945.

For the first few months the food was adequate and reasonably good. After that, until July 1943, it was enough to keep the prisoners in moderate health, but insufficient to keep them fit enough for the hard work which they had to do. After July 1943 the ration scale fell rapidly, and latterly each prisoner received no more than four ounces of rice and four ounces of sweet potatoes per day. During this period of scarcity of the prisoners' food the Japanese fed well, never less than fifteen ounces of rice per day, a liberal ration of fish, and plenty of vegetables.

Malnutrition became serious in 1945 and forty-two prisoners died in May, seventy-two in June, and ninety-four in July.

Accommodation also was very good in the early stages, for the prisoners were confined in the same barracks which they had occupied before the Japanese invasion. But that enviable state of things, unusual enough in a Japanese prison camp, was not to endure for long. In July 1942 eight of the huts were taken over by the Japanese and used for storing ammunition, and four months later a bomb dump of two hundred thousand pounds of high explosive and armour piercing bombs was established inside the camp area. The dump was situated within a few yards of the camp hospital, within a few feet of the Australian officers' sleeping quarters, and only twenty-five yards away from another compound in which were interned two hundred and fifty Dutch women and children.

Protests made to the authorities through the camp interpreter about the location of the dump were met with the reply, 'Remember your status as prisoners of war. You have no rights. International Law and the Geneva Convention are dead.' A request for the camp hospital to be marked with the Red Cross was also refused.

On 15th February 1943 at 11.30 a.m. the dump was bombed by Allied aircraft. The first string of bombs fell on one of the huts used as a bomb store and set it on fire, but the dump did not explode immediately. There was clearly little time to lose, and every effort was made to evacuate the hospital and remove a number of Dutch women and children injured. There were about fifty patients in the hospital several of whom could only be removed as stretcher cases.

Before much could be done the dump blew up. Six Australian officers, four other ranks and twenty-seven Dutch women and children were killed, and twenty more Australian prisoners of war were badly wounded.

The camp itself was almost completely devastated and the surviving Dutch civilians were moved to the town and quartered in the Bethany Church. Here they were very overcrowded, there were no adequate sanitary arrangements and the church was in a part of the town which became a continual target for Allied aircraft. In August 1944 the Ambon area suffered another heavy aerial bombardment when it was attacked by twenty-four Liberators, and there were many more casualties among the prisoners of war.

From the end of 1943 onwards the physical condition of the prisoners of war inevitably deteriorated, as food became scarcer and disease more prevalent. All were thin and emaciated, many could only walk with the aid of sticks and crutches, and the average loss of weight was about eighty pounds. Nevertheless the prisoners, despite their weakness, were still worked as hard as ever and many died from sheer exhaustion.

What the prisoners called 'long carry' was one of the main causes of the rise in the death roll. 'Long carry' was described by a witness who gave evidence in the Tokyo trial in these words:

> The 'long carry' was a name which the prisoners gave to the task of carrying cement and bombs between two villages, approximately eight miles apart, and the route was over a very tortuous track. The prisoners were required to carry, firstly, ninety-pound bags of cement over this track, and when the first task was completed, and it took them about three weeks, they had to carry a large number of one hundred and fifty pound bombs over the same route, one bomb between two men. They were kept at it from 6.30 a.m. until 5.30 p.m., seven days a week. The prisoners on this work were driven on like slaves by the Japanese guards, and the ground over which they had to move was so rough that sometimes they could only manage it on all fours.
>
> After a week of this back breaking work none of the men was fit to continue, but there was no respite, and they were made to carry on until they dropped. Many prisoners collapsed unconscious.
>
> Each day the Japanese requisitioned at least fifteen men more than it was possible to supply. The Japanese then called out all the sick, and selected the other fifteen from those they considered capable of doing the job. Many of them could only walk with the aid of sticks, yet they were forced to take these heavy weights over the 'long carry' course.

The guards who accompanied these working parties were armed with pistols, and each carried a pick handle or its equivalent and the prisoners were driven along with blows when necessary.

A prisoner named Wilkinson who should really have been

in hospital was one of those whom the Japanese officer in charge of working parties forced to work on 'long carry', though palpably unfit. One morning, when the working party was found to be below the requisitioned strength, the Japanese guards went the rounds of the sleeping quarters and any prisoner who was found lying on his bed was beaten until he got up and joined the parade. A guard saw Private Wilkinson lying on his bed covered with a blanket. He pulled the blanket off and had struck several blows before he realized that Wilkinson was dead. He had died of malnutrition, the effects of beri-beri and utter exhaustion. At least sixty per cent of the men engaged on 'long carry' were dead within three months of its completion.

The most trivial disciplinary offences were dealt with by corporal punishment, or minor forms of torture. A defaulter would be forced to stand in front of the guard with a heavy boulder held high above his head for any period from an hour to two or three hours, forced to stand to attention for long periods but with the knees slightly bent, or forced to assume the 'press up' position and hold it for a long time until, at last, he collapsed. The Kempei Tai cigarette end torture was also very popular with the guards. Such punishments were a daily occurrence.

A Private Tait, while on a working party, attempted to steal a pair of binoculars belonging to one of the Japanese guards. He was caught in the act and beaten by the guards who were on the spot. On the return of the working party to camp the offence was reported to the commandant who ordered that Tait be again punished, and that the punishment should be administered publicly outside the guardroom. An eye-witness has given the following account of this incident.

> I was forced to be present throughout the whole of the punishment which consisted of one hundred strokes with a pick handle. When Tait was no longer able to stand he was beaten whilst on the ground. When he lost consciousness he was doused with cold water in an attempt to bring him to. Efforts

to get the punishment reduced met with no success, and I was twice beaten for trying to intervene.

Twice he became unconscious and twice he came to again. On the second occasion I got permission for him to be admitted to the camp hospital.

Next morning the camp manager, Ikenchi, visited the hospital and saw Tait in bed. He beat him up with a walking stick, and then gave an order that he should lie on the concrete floor with one blanket. This outrageous ill-treatment aggravated the beri-beri from which Tait was suffering at the time of the assault. Six months later he was dead.

When the Allied forces reached Amboina on 10th September 1945, after Japan had capitulated, of the five hundred and twenty-eight Australians who stayed there after the two large drafts went to Hainan Island on 26th October 1942, only one hundred and twenty-three were still alive.

HAROEKOE

In April 1943 there were indications in Sourabaya that there was shortly to be a big movement of Allied prisoners of war. A mammoth medical parade had been held whose object was clearly to select all prisoners who could conceivably be considered fit for work. A board of Japanese medical officers had sat behind a table, past which all the prisoners had to file, stripped to the waist. Only the halt, the maim, and the very sick were not selected.

After a voyage of about seventeen days aboard the *Amagi Maru*, in the usual appalling conditions prevalent on all the Japanese transports for prisoners of war, the draft arrived at the island of Haroekoe and in pouring rain its human cargo, some two thousand British and Dutch prisoners, was ferried ashore to the new camp.

Forwarding a report on the 'Treatment of Allied POWs on the Island of Haroekoe' to the Air Officer Commanding, Royal Air Force, Java, in November 1945, the former Allied commanding officer of the camp, Squadron-Leader Pitts of the RAF, wrote, 'the treatment meted out to prisoners of all ranks was so barbarous and inhuman that it is to be hoped that action will be taken against the individuals who were responsible and whose names are listed in Appendix "E" '.[1]

This was no exaggeration. From the moment the prisoners left Sourabaya their treatment by the Japanese guards had been fiendish. As one of them, Dr Springer,[2] wrote in a report made from extracts from his diary, 'officers, doctors and soldiers were beaten and kicked throughout the voyage, mostly without understanding the reason for the punishment'. Nevertheless, they fondly hoped that conditions ashore would be better.

We still believed in humanity even from the Nips, but that proved to be silly. Even now, while writing this report [November 1945] and reading my notes I get the impression that the Nips were out for wilful murder. When we told them our fear for the future regarding the danger of spreading an epidemic of dysentery, and that we expected many death cases, we often got the answer, 'nice when dead'.

The transfer of all these prisoners of war from Sourabaya to Haroekoe, a small island south of Ceram in the Molucca Archipelago, was with the intention of employing them on the construction of a new military airfield.

The new camp was built on the slopes of an undrained swampy slope. It consisted of a few bamboo structures, they could hardly be called huts, for many of them had no sides

---

[1] All the Japanese included in this list, except a few who could not be traced, were later tried by British Military Courts.

[2] Dr R. Springer belonged to the Dutch Army Medical Service and this was said of him in Squadron-Leader Pitts' report:
This officer was entirely responsible for all the surgical work carried on in the POW camp, Haroekoe. Although at times suffering from ill health himself, he always made himself available for any emergency which arose, performing his duty under the most difficult conditions and in a manner which instilled the highest degree of confidence in his patients. His devotion to duty was a shining example of medical tradition and was responsible for the saving of a great many lives.

and all had uneven floors and inadequate roofing. A latrine trench had been dug parallel with each hut, but when the prisoners from Java arrived it had been raining heavily for some days, the trenches were full to the brim, and excreta was floating on the top. Every effort was made by the prisoners themselves to improve the accommodation but it was a heartbreaking task. Drains were dug around each hut in an attempt to divert the streams of rain water which otherwise flowed over the prisoners as they slept, but the Japanese would not issue enough tools, and so the drainage system was only a partial success.

Six days after their arrival, Squadron-Leader Pitts was ordered to have two shifts, each of six hundred men, ready for work on the airfield. It was not easy to supply so many workers, for there was already a serious outbreak of dysentery in the camp and many hundreds were quite unfit to do any work. As the outbreak grew into an epidemic the difficulty in producing enough men was fast becoming insuperable, and for this failure to meet the Japanese demands the officers were paraded and beaten.

On 14th June 1943 all the sick who were able to walk were paraded, and Sergeant Mori with the camp interpreter, Kasiyama, walked round the ranks hitting over the head all those who he thought were malingering and fit enough to work.

From then on it was work or starve; no work, no food. This rule had the blessing of no less a person than General Uemura who was Director of the Prisoner of War Administration Section of the Military Affairs Bureau of the War Ministry. In June of the previous year he had issued this direction:

Although the working of prisoner of war officers and warrant officers is forbidden by the regulations of 1903, the policy of the control authorities is that in the present situation in our country, where no person eats without working, these POWs must be set to work.

But the direction originated from a very much higher source than General Uemura. In May 1942 Prime Minister Tojo himself had issued instructions to the commander of a division, who had a prisoner of war camp under his command, in which he said, 'the present situation of affairs in this country does not permit anyone to lie idle, doing nothing but eating freely. With that in view, in dealing with prisoners of war, I hope you will see that they are usefully employed'.

A few weeks later he sent the following similar instructions to newly appointed commandants of prisoner of war camps:

> In Japan we have our own ideology concerning prisoners of war which should naturally make their treatment more or less different from that in Europe and America. In dealing with them you should, of course, observe the various regulations concerned, and [here Tojo rapidly added a cautionary and characteristic reservation] aim at an adequate application of them. . . . At the same time, you must not allow them to lie idle, doing nothing but enjoy free meals, for even a single day. Their labour and technical skill should be fully utilized for the replenishment of production, and a contribution thereby made toward the prosecution of the Greater East Asiatic War for which no effort ought to be spared.

'The application of these instructions', the Tokyo Tribunal stated in its judgment, 'accounts, at least in part, for the constant driving and beating of the sick and wounded prisoners, and those suffering from malnutrition, to force them to labour upon military works until they died from disease, malnutrition and sheer exhaustion.'

In pursuance of these instructions the prisoners of Haroekoe, who were still working on the aerodrome, were given extra rations, but they were not issued from the store. They were deducted from the rations given to those men who were only well enough to undertake duties in camp.

On 21st June, the camp was inspected by a major in the Japanese Army Medical Service after which he paraded all the officer prisoners and coolly informed them that the rising incidence of dysentery was all their fault: 'All you have to do,' he said, 'is to kill all the flies and cut your finger nails and the epidemic will die down.'

All their fault? This is an extract from Dr Springer's diary written about a month before that inspection:

> Still diarrhoea cases in increasing numbers. . . . The sick are too weak to go to the lavatories, we have not enough tins and buckets inside the barracks for the purpose, so they go outside, outside in the mud which is drenched with faeces and alive with maggots.

The death rate by July 1943 was mounting rapidly and vitamin deficiency was producing sores and ulcers.

> The dead were buried in a plot of ground quite close to the camp. At first a few planks were available to make coffins, but when this supply ceased crude boxes were made from green bamboo. In the unceasing rain men too sick to march to the aerodrome scratched shallow grooves in the coral ground for graves. At the height of the dysentery epidemic fourteen men were buried in one grave and tens and twelves were quite common.
>
> The officer in charge of the burial party was given one small guttering candle to guide the way for his stumbling bearers across the uneven ground. At all funerals one of the Japanese camp staff attended, more, it is felt, to ensure that no one escaped them than to pay homage to the dead.[1] Mori, the camp sergeant, turned up on one such occasion very drunk indeed and was quietly sick into the open grave before the body was covered.[2]

Sgt. Mori was one of three who helped to make life in Haroekoe camp a perpetual hell. The other two were Lieutenant Kurishima, the camp commandant, and Kasiyama, the camp interpreter.[3] It was Mori, however, who really ran

[1] But see footnote on page 68.
[2] An extract from Squadron-Leader Pitts' report.
[3] See Chapter VII.

the camp, for Kurishima was a lazy nonentity. This sergeant was responsible for the discipline of the prisoners, and it should not have been a difficult task, for most of them were far too ill and weak to resist authority. All they wanted was to be left alone in peace and quiet.

But this did not suit Mori, who was a sadistic brute, and in their treatment of the prisoners the camp guards took their cue from him. He belaboured all and sundry with anything which was handy, a three-inch leather belt, bamboo poles, or failing them he used his feet and his fists. These beatings were generally administered at a parade of the whole camp, for Mori liked an audience. He beat the prisoners for the most trivial offences, or for none. He beat them because they were too ill to fend for themselves. On one occasion he beat all the officers who were dismantling a hut built of rotten bamboo, merely because, when the main supports were removed, the rest collapsed, and on another occasion the Senior British Officer in charge of the prisoners was slapped across the face sixteen times, and a Japanese slap was something to remember, because some of his men had refused to accept boots which had been issued to them and were too small to wear.

There can be few Allied prisoners of war who were not at some time slapped by members of the prison camp staffs or by the Kempei Tai. It was, from all accounts, extremely unpleasant, not just a playful slap but a good stout smack which often left a bruise. It remains doubtful, therefore, whether, had the prisoners known of it, the apologia for this practice which was given by Prime Minister Tojo when interrogated by the Allies in March 1946, would have lessened the pain or the humiliation of the victims.

I want to say something now about the feeling with regard to slapping on the side of the face. In Japanese families, where the educational standard is low, slapping is usual as a means of training. In the Japanese Army and Navy, although it is forbidden, it continues, in fact, because of the influence of the customs of the people. This, of course, is a custom that ought to be corrected, it ought to be stopped, but I don't think it is a crime. It is something that comes from custom.

Kurishima, when he was commandant of the camp at Sourabaya, had a good reputation amongst the prisoners. He helped them to obtain extra food and cigarettes, and he himself never used violence. At Haroekoe he abdicated his power to Sergeant Mori to whom he virtually played second fiddle.

Nevertheless, had he attended properly to his duties and realized his responsibility, as camp commandant, for the lives and well being of the prisoners in his charge, the camp might have been a better place. He did not, however, and maintained a callous indifference to the suffering of the sick whose pitiable condition appeared to cause him unconcealed amusement. According to the official report on this camp, already referred to, 'not even the dead escaped his jocularity. On several occasions he suggested that the bodies [of prisoners who had died] be taken to the kitchen and made into beefsteak. Although these remarks were made in jest[1] they are an indication of his reaction to the tragedies which were taking place and for which he was responsible'.

It may seem strange that of the two men, Kurishima and Mori, the former was more disliked and despised than the latter, but so it was. Squadron-Leader Pitts had this to say of Mori and the published extracts from Dr Springer's diary substantially support the view.

Psychologically he had a split personality,[2] being in part an untamed and brutal savage and, in a much lesser degree, a placid harmless human being, possessing a strong personality and intelligence and, in his more docile moments, generous to a large degree. In all his activities he leant towards the theatrical, having an intense desire for publicity and popularity, the latter being made evident by his distributions of gifts

[1] This suggestion was not always made jocularly. In New Guinea it was put into practice. See Chapter XII.
[2] See the Epilogue to *The Scourge of the Swastika*.

of food or cigarettes after a 'beat-up' of the prisoners. It must be said that first and last he is a soldier with some fine but indefinable quality, perhaps the absence of meanness, which, suppressed though it was, won for him a certain admiration which was not accorded to any other Japanese . . . it is difficult to appreciate how one man can indulge in such bestial and brutal savagery upon another, and still be regarded with a certain amount of esteem, yet such a state did indeed exist.

As time passed, the sick list and the death roll went on mounting. At the peak period there were more than 1,300 prisoners in hospital, and of the remaining seven hundred and forty a large percentage were treated daily for ulcers, sore feet and many other ailments.

About the middle of July 1944 the camp was broken up. Five hundred prisoners were sent to Amboina for further work and the remainder were returned to Java on the *Maros Maru* under the command of Flight-Lieutenant Blackwood.[1]

As far as can be ascertained, of the original number of 2,070 British and Dutch prisoners who left Sourabaya for Haroekoe in April 1943 less than 50 per cent were still alive at the end of the war.

JAVA—CYCLE CAMP

In April 1942, one month after they had surrendered to the Japanese, 2,600 British, Australian and American prisoners of war were sent to a Dutch barracks, which had been built to accommodate a thousand Dutch native troops. This became known as Cycle Camp, and although the barracks later housed as many as five thousand prisoners the buildings and sanitary arrangements remained the same.

The first batch of prisoners was soon reinforced by the arrival of five hundred naval officers and ratings, survivors from two naval vessels, the *Perth* and *Houston*. They arrived in a shocking state of neglect and ill-health, with scarcely any

---

[1] The terrible story of their voyage has been told in Chapter VII.

clothing, and the majority unable to walk without assistance. Since their capture they had received no medical attention and 80 per cent had malaria, or dysentery, or both. A request made to the Japanese commandant to provide dressings, medicaments, towels, soap and blankets for them was refused, and nothing at all was done for these wretched prisoners.

In July an attempt was made by the Japanese to get all the prisoners in Cycle Camp to sign a form promising to obey all orders of the Japanese Army, but everyone refused to sign unless the words 'subject to the oath of allegiance I have already taken' were added. On 3rd July the two senior Australian and American officers, Brigadier Blackburn and Colonel Searle, undertook to obtain the signatures of all the prisoners, provided those words were added; but the commandant insisted that the forms must be signed unaltered.

That afternoon large numbers of the prisoners were beaten to induce them all to come to their senses, and while this was going on Brigadier Blackburn was summoned to Japanese HQ in Java and warned by a staff officer that unless the prisoners all signed as directed the supplies of food and medical stores would be 'progressively reduced'.

On the following morning, 4th July, machine guns were sited all round the perimeter and extra guards were brought into camp. A notice was posted up on the notice board to the effect that the lives of the prisoners could no longer be guaranteed. Blackburn and Searle were then placed in close arrest and locked up in the guardroom, while all the other officers were marched out of camp under an armed guard.

As he was being marched to the guardroom, Brigadier Blackburn had managed to shout orders to some of his men that they were to sign the form without any conditions, and this was passed on to the others. They were then herded into their huts and, to the accompaniment of much beating with rifle butts and sticks, they all signed. In the evening the two senior officer prisoners of war were released from the guardroom, and after they had been shown the signatures of all their men they, too, signed the forms. The prisoners' compliance was rewarded with an orgy of savage beatings of officers and men which continued indiscriminately for a month.

In December of the same year Brigadier Blackburn and about sixty other prisoners left Java for Formosa. With them, in a very old and filthy ship which took them as far as Singapore, was the Governor-General of the Netherlands East Indies. At Singapore they changed ships but the usual conditions which have already been described in Chapter VII, prevailed in both ships. On 30th January, after what must have seemed an interminable journey, the *Ake Maru*, as the second ship was called, reached Formosa.

KWARENKO CAMP, FORMOSA

On arrival at the new camp the form signing business began all over again. The draft of prisoners was paraded and addressed by the camp commandant. He told them that they were regarded as criminals for having fought against Japan, and that it was only by the kindness of the Japanese Government that they were permitted to remain alive. Whether they continued to live would depend on their behaviour.

He then produced a document which he read to them. It was a form which, he said, every prisoner must sign. It was an honourable undertaking to obey every Japanese order and not to attempt to escape. Brigadier Blackburn was called up to the table and ordered by the commandant to sign. The Brigadier said that he could not do so, for it was his duty to escape if possible.

What happened to the Brigadier after that was told by him to the International Military Tribunal for the Far East when giving evidence on 2nd December 1946 in Tokyo.

> I asked him what penalty he proposed to apply to me if I refused to sign. He shouted out at me to sign at once. I said that I would sign when he chose to answer my question. He then aimed a blow at me with his fist, which I succeeded in

dodging, and called up a squad of sentries and I was led off to the guardroom. I was there ordered to empty my pockets and take off all my clothes. I started to do so, the Japanese sentries assisted me by ripping them off, and just when I had nearly completed undressing a Japanese officer came into the guardroom. He gave an order and two sentries immediately placed themselves, one on each side of me. He then stepped up to me and struck me very violently and repeatedly on the jaw. He finally drove me into a corner of the guardroom where I tripped over some boxes and fell down. While I was on the floor he kicked me and then turned away and the guards thereupon pulled me to my feet again.

They then ripped off the rest of my clothes, took me along to a small cell about twelve feet by six and put me into it. The cell was absolutely bare except for a concrete slab in the centre to act as a latrine. I was suffering from a very bad cold at the time and in February the cold at Kwarenko is very intense. I was coughing almost incessantly and in about an hour's time was shivering violently. An armed sentry had been posted outside the entrance to my cell, and threw my trousers to me. I found that every button had been cut off. For about six hours I was alternately made to stand or sit to attention for. half an hour periods. When I first entered the cell I had asked for a drink of water; but this was refused. After about six hours I fell asleep and when I woke up at half-past six in the morning I asked, once again, for a drink of water and some food, but both requests were refused.

About an hour later a Japanese officer with the official interpreter came into my cell and asked me if I would sign the form. I said that I would do so only under protest, and I again asked him for a drink of water and some food. About 11 a.m. the next day he came back again and again to ask me whether I would sign. On my again telling him that I would only sign under protest he informed me that I must stay there without food or sleep or water; but actually, about an hour later, a sentry handed me a small mug of cold water and, shortly afterwards, a handful of cooked rice. I remained in the cell all day, and at hourly intervals was made to stand or sit at attention. With my bad cough I began by evening to feel very feverish. At 9 p.m. I was at last allowed to lie down.

[165]

Next morning, soon after waking up, my clothes were thrown into the cell. All the buttons had been cut off. I put on my clothes and some time later was taken by a Japanese officer to the guardroom, where the form was again put in front of me to sign. I stated that I would only sign under duress, but my signature was, nevertheless, accepted.

The policy of forcing the prisoners to sign forms undertaking not to escape was quite common and orders had been issued on the subject by the War Ministry early in 1943:

As soon as prisoners of war have been imprisoned, they will be administered an oath forbidding them to make an escape. Prisoners of war who refuse to take the oath mentioned in this paragraph shall be deemed to have intentions of escaping, and shall be placed under strict surveillance.

Strict surveillance was a euphemism for being confined on reduced rations and subject to torture until the oath was taken. At Singapore, for example, in August 1942, sixteen thousand prisoners, who had refused to give the parole demanded, were herded into a barrack square at Selarang and kept there without food or latrine facilities for four days to force them to sign the parole form. The results of this can well be imagined. Some prisoners in Hong Kong who, similarly, refused to sign a parole were confined in a prison without food and forced to kneel all day. If they moved they were beaten. The same thing happened in almost every camp, and sometimes prisoners were threatened with death to induce them to sign.

These regulations, issued and enforced by the Japanese Government to compel prisoners of war and civilian internees to give an oath under duress, violated the laws and customs of war.

There were several distinguished officers and civil officials in Kwarenko camp, British, American and Dutch. They included the Governors of Hong Kong, the Malay States and

Guam, a number of Chief Justices, General Percival, General Sir Louis Heath and General Wainwright, an American. There were also some Red Cross representatives who were treated as ordinary prisoners of war.

The discipline was extremely harsh and was enforced by brutal methods. Prisoners of war were severely beaten for the most trivial offences, and often for no reason at all. Offences were invented in order to provide an excuse for chastising the prisoners. They discovered, by the fact that they were continually being stopped in the camp grounds and having their finger nails inspected, that it was a disciplinary offence to have any dirt under the nails. The punishment was a beating, and General Percival was severely beaten up on the allegation that he had a speck of dirt under one of his nails.[1]

The excuse given by the Japanese for inflicting such severe punishment for this offence, in the circumstances very venial, was that it was unhygienic and tended to spread dysentery which was already rife in the camp. This was somewhat ironical, for the insanitary condition of this camp, described below, was appalling and the sole cause of these epidemics.

Another serious offence was to have even a single clothing button undone, and the sentries would suddenly burst into the huts after dark and inspect the prisoners for unfastened buttons. Anyone found with a button undone was immediately beaten. The blows varied in severity and in method, but they were usually administered with the fist, the foot, a rifle butt or a heavy stick.

Compliments had to be paid to all Japanese private soldiers and civilians on the camp staff irrespective of the prisoner's rank. A favourite sport of the Japanese sentries was to hide in the bushes and other dark places on the route from the sleeping quarters to the latrines. If a prisoner passed any of the hidden sentries without saluting and bowing he was at once beaten up although, of course, he had not been able to see the sentry.

[1] See Brigadier Blackburn's evidence, IMT, Far East, proceedings, pages 11,547-8-9, where the details are given.

[167]

Another little Japanese jest was to force an officer prisoner, who had left his quarters during the night to go to the latrines, to hold a bucket full of water at arm's length for about a quarter of an hour. Other sentries were then called to the spot so that they could make fun of the prisoner's humiliation. This happened to a number of British, Australian and American colonels.

Owing to an old war injury General Sir Louis Heath, had a slightly withered arm which he was unable to keep straight down to his side. For not doing this, on one occasion, he was severely beaten by a Japanese soldier.

Frequent complaints were made to the Camp Commandant, Imamura, about the ill-treatment of officers in this camp. With one exception, the only effect which these complaints had was to cause an outbreak of still worse brutality throughout the camp, and when any senior prisoner of war officer intended to make a complaint he used to warn his comrades so that they could remain on their best behaviour during the next few days.

The exception mentioned was after Sir Louis Heath had been assaulted. The attack on Sir Louis had been so brutal that it had ruptured the blood vessels of one eye and it was feared that he might lose his sight. After a protest had been made about this, the General was taken by the orderly officer over to the Japanese guardroom where the sergeant of the guard was sitting in a chair. Sir Louis was made to stand to attention in front of the sergeant who then spoke to him in Japanese. When the sergeant had finished, the orderly officer turned to the General and said, 'You have now received an apology', and marched him back to his quarters.

Everything was done in this camp to humiliate the Allied officers and senior officials. Twelve of the oldest or most senior prisoners were employed as goatherds. Among them were the Governor of Hong Kong, the Governor of Singapore, the Governor of the Malay States, General Sir Louis Heath, General Percival, General Wainwright, and three

American colonels over sixty years of age. If any of the goats escaped or got out of hand and were found in the vicinity of the guardroom or, as was more usual, in one of the vegetable allotments, the goatherds were beaten for having allowed the animals to stray.

In April 1943 all officers above the rank of colonel and all Governors were moved to Tamasata camp. They were told that this move was made so as to give the prisoners better accommodation. The living quarters were undoubtedly an improvement on Kwarenko, but the food was much worse.

Two months later the prisoners were told that a Red Cross representative would be coming to visit the camp. He walked through it, inspected the accommodation and was allowed to talk to a few officers, but only in the presence of a Japanese. Half an hour after he left all the prisoners, except those of the rank of major-general and above, were informed that they would, on the following day, be returned to Kwarenko. This they were, but a few days later they were moved to yet another camp at Shirakawa.

SHIRAKAWA

The journey from Kwarenko to Shirakawa was made in open trucks, and at every village, level-crossing, or station through which the train passed the civilian population, including all the school children, were lined up to watch it go through. At each such place the train slowed down so as to give the spectators an opportunity to laugh and jeer at the prisoners.

Shirakawa was no better than Kwarenko. The officers were beaten on the slightest pretext. General Cox was beaten on the legs with a rifle butt, because a Japanese sentry complained that when the General should have been standing to attention his legs were not close enough together. While the sentry was doing this the Japanese orderly officer was standing only five yards away enjoying the fun.

The sanitation in Shirakawa camp was extremely bad.

Within a month of the prisoners arriving there the latrines had begun to overflow into open drains which ran right through the camp, alongside the sleeping quarters and within a few yards of the kitchen. Frequent complaints were made about this and the answer to them was typical. The British and American colonels were given the job of emptying the latrines with open buckets. This unpleasant fatigue entailed getting the contents of the latrines out by hand, putting them into a bucket and walking out of the camp, in full view of the amused civilian population, to empty the bucket outside. About sixty colonels were employed on this duty, after a complaint had been made about the sewerage system in October 1944, but subsequently, as the Japanese doubtless anticipated, very few similar complaints were made.

In June 1944 another Red Cross representative paid a visit to the camp and interviewed a number of officers, specially selected by the Japanese commandant, who were forbidden to mention the subject of work. Nevertheless, one of the officers did tell the Red Cross official that the prisoners were forced to do work much beyond their strength. The sole result of this report was that the camp discipline was tightened up even more than before.

The colonel in charge of the administration of all prisoner of war camps in Formosa, Colonel Suzawa, also paid infrequent visits to the camps under his command, but it was useless to complain to him for nothing ever came of it, other than harder work and severer punishments.

In May 1945 there was a further move, this time to Manchuria, where the prisoners from Shirakawa were taken to the main camp on the outskirts of Mukden where they remained until the end of the war, overcrowded, underfed, and always ill-used.

THE INDIAN ARMY PRISON CAMPS

An account of the ill-treatment of prisoners of war by the Japanese would be incomplete without some mention of those who belonged to the Indian Army. They were early subjected to particularly harsh ill-treatment in order to 'persuade' them to join the Indian National Army which, they were told, was to liberate India from 'British Imperialism' and give her independence.

Immediately after the fall of Singapore the Indian prisoners of war were collected at Farrior's Park, where they were kept apart from the British and Australians, who had been taken to Changi Gaol. They were told that an Indian, Captain Mohan Singh of the 1/14 Punjab Regiment, had been appointed GOC the Indians and that they must obey his orders. Every kind of pressure, both moral and physical, was put upon these unfortunate Indian soldiers, and they were sent to concentration camps where they were beaten, tortured and even beheaded for refusing to join the renegade army. Many died of their ill-treatment. Deprived of the moral support of their British officers, in whom they placed such trust, they doubtless felt their position very keenly, and it is to their undying credit that so many of them resisted all the efforts of the Japanese to sway them from allegiance to their King-Emperor.

By the end of 1942, however, Mohan Singh had resigned from his appointment, for he had begun to mistrust the sincerity of the Japanese Government's intention to give independence to India, and simultaneously the Japanese policy of attempting to press Indian prisoners of war into the INA came to an end. Nevertheless, those who had not joined it were told that they had forfeited the status of prisoner of war and would in future be regarded as auxiliaries (heiho), voluntary collaborators, and subject, therefore, to Japanese military law.

Early in 1943 parties of Indian prisoners were moved from Singapore to a number of different prisoner of war camps in widely separated parts of Japanese occupied territory. One such party, consisting of five hundred and twenty-two all ranks of the 2/12 Frontier Force Regiment and the 1st Battalion of the Hyderabad Regiment, Indian State Forces, left

Singapore in May for the Palau Islands, which are situated about six hundred miles north of New Guinea.

The trip was made, in the usual horrible conditions, aboard the *Thames Maru* and, after a voyage of just over a month, the contingent arrived at their destination, which was the island of Babel Thuap. There they remained until liberated by the American forces in September 1945. On the ship with them and in charge of them was the 7th Special Service Company of the Japanese Army, commonly called the 'Gozawa Butai' from the name of their OC, Captain Gozawa.

During their stay in Babel Thuap the Indian prisoners of war remained under Gozawa's command and were at all times treated with the utmost brutality. The story of their ill-treatment was told to the world at the trial of Gozawa and nine officers and NCOs of his company in Singapore in January 1946, a trial which excited much interest for it was the first war crimes trial to be held in the Far East.

Another of these Indian POW camps was at Tijku, where Lieutenant Kobuta was the Japanese officer in charge. Although there were other NCOs senior to him, Lance-Corporal Tanaka appeared, in fact, to act as second-in-command, for all orders were discussed between him and Kobuta, and Tanaka himself gave orders to members of the Japanese staff and to Indian prisoners of war.

Captain S. N. Paul of the Indian Medical Service was told by Tanaka, in February 1945, that all the Indians were no longer prisoners of war. They were, he said, by order of the Japanese High Command, part of the Nipponese Army. Captain Paul protested that this order was in contravention of the laws and customs of war and that he and his comrades did not want to be part of the Japanese Army.

Parades were started to teach the Indians Japanese Army procedure and customs. The Japanese custom of 'slapping as a means of training', which Tojo explained so speciously during his interrogation,[1] was one of the earliest lessons

[1] See page 160.

which the Indians learnt, for Tanaka was no mean exponent of what was known in the Japanese Army as a 'corrective measure'.

As Captain Paul has testified, 'when Tanaka slapped with his hand it was severe enough to knock men to the ground. I often heard him say to a prisoner, "your brain is not all right so I am going to fix it" '.[1] When Tanaka's hand was tired he beat his new 'recruits' about the head and body with a stick. About twenty of them would be beaten daily during the so-called training period.

In March 1945 three Indian prisoners of war were reported by Tanaka for not working properly. The doctor examined them and told the Japanese lance-corporal that all three men were greatly debilitated through beri-beri. Tanaka's reaction to this information was to beat them unmercifully. He slapped them until they fell down, then got them to their feet again and beat them with a stick on their heads, their knuckles and their knees until they became unconscious. This went on for half an hour. One of the three Indians, Ali Haider, needed medical attention but Tanaka, in spite of Ali's condition, continued to keep him on fatigues until, about ten days later, he died. His death, according to Captain Paul, was the direct result of the beatings that he received.

One Indian officer, Jamadar Mohan Singh[2] was suffering badly with dropsy from which he died in the camp in August 1945, a few days before the Japanese surrender. Captain Paul was looking after him. In April, the doctor realized that Mohan Singh was in great pain as his abdomen was swollen with dropsical fluid. This interfered with his breathing and it was important that it should be drawn away from the stomach to ease the pain. Captain Paul had no proper instruments and asked both Tanaka and Kobuta

[1] Comparable with Dorothea Binz, the head wardress at Ravensbrück Concentration Camp of whom it was said by one who had suffered, 'a slap from Binz was no light matter'. See *The Scourge of the Swastika*, Chapter VI.
[2] Not to be confused with the captain of that name.

to supply him with an instrument for the purpose of removing the water. They refused to help and would not even allow the patient to be admitted into hospital. Captain Paul managed, however, to obtain a small hypodermic syringe needle and, using it for eight or nine hours, he was able to drain away some of the water, though not without causing great pain to the wretched patient. Captain Paul has testified that had he been able to give Mohan Singh proper treatment and medicine, his life might well have been saved.

There were in this camp, not surprisingly, a few cases of food pilfering, for which the punishment was usually a severe beating. From March 1945 a more serious view was taken of these misdemeanours and several prisoners of war were beheaded for petty theft.

Mahomed Din confessed to stealing a tin of fish from the camp store. He was tied to a tree in the compound and beaten all afternoon. At dusk he managed to give the guards the slip, but was caught by the Military Police and beheaded.

After the Japanese surrender, Tanaka approached Captain Paul with a request. He wanted the doctor to sign a statement to the effect that Mahomed Din had died from natural causes. The official camp records contained an entry that Din had been 'beheaded following a conviction for stealing', and Tanaka wanted to erase that entry and substitute a false one, for, he said, it would be better for Mahomed Din's family that they should not know that he was a thief as that would bring 'shame and dishonour on them'.

The camp staff stole a large proportion of the prisoners' rations. When these were drawn each month they were put into the same store as the staff's rations, but many of the items such as biscuits and vegetables never reached the prisoners' table. This deprivation of their proper rations led to an increase in the incidence of beri-beri from which eventually more than half the camp were suffering, of whom large numbers became paralysed and a substantial proportion died.

When the prisoners of both these camps were eventually liberated, they were nearly all in need of hospital treatment. There was evidence of multiple vitamin deficiencies and marked weakness due to semi-starvation. Their clothing was in rags and few had shoes of any kind. Those were the conditions observed and recorded by the Americans who looked after them after their liberation. In these circumstances Gozawa's speech to the Court in mitigation of sentence, which refers to the prisoners in his charge at Babel Thuap, makes strange reading:

When we sent the Indians to the American ship they were all wearing shoes. We had given each of them new clothes. We always did everything to please them, and when we bade them farewell by the side of the ship we did so just as if we were parting from our own children. They wept, and we wept. The regret at the separation was mutual.

The captain of the ship was much impressed with the scene and called us on board the ship and gave us lunch. He said on that occasion that from what appeared he could easily imagine how well we must have treated them, and he thanked us for that. Now we have been told that the Indians have complained of our treatment of them. We cannot understand this. How is it that they were not wearing any sort of footwear when they were found by the American forces? How is it that their clothing was shabby? In our treatment of them we never made any distinction between them and the Japanese soldiers. We did everything for them that we could. . . . Why must they now complain, after having departed with gratitude? However, I do not reproach them with that for they must have reasons of their own. I thank them for having worked for me, and I hope that they will lead a happy life in their home country.[1]

LAWE SEGALAGALA—*Forced enlistment*

A number of Dutch prisoners of war who were captured

[1] *The Trial of Gozawa Sadaichi*, 'War Crimes Trials Series', edited by Colin Sleeman, B.A. William Hodge and Company Ltd.

at Padang on 17th March 1942 were taken, three months later, to Lawe Segalagala Camp at Kota Thare, in Sumatra.

Early in May of the following year the Japanese camp commandant, Myasaki, told them that they would shortly have to enlist in the Japanese Army as *heiho*. On 29th May a Japanese Army officer, accompanied by an officer of the Kempei Tai, arrived in camp, and the prisoners were ordered on parade.

When they had all assembled the camp interpreter told them that they had exactly five minutes in which to decide whether or not they would enlist in the Japanese Army. At the end of the parade the prisoners were divided into three groups: A, those who were rejected as medically unfit; B, the volunteers; C, those who refused to enlist. Among those who had refused were three sergeants, Croes, Stolz and Voss, also a private soldier named Wolff.

The prisoners in Group C were then taken by the police to Kota Thare and locked up in the gaol. Two hours later Wolff and the three sergeants were bound hand and foot, taken to the village square and exhibited to the local inhabitants whom the Japanese, by proclamation, had summoned to attend. They were publicly executed at 11 p.m.

A brief description of the execution has been given by another Dutch prisoner of war, who was acting that day as Myasaki's driver, and who has admitted that he was one of the 'volunteers' in Group B. He was made to stand in the 'front line', as he called it, to witness the killing of his comrades.

Voss was asked his last wish. He answered that he wanted to die with the Dutch national flag wrapped round his body. His request was granted. He then addressed the unwilling spectators in Malay, giving his opinion of the Japanese and abusing them. When he had finished the Japs wanted to blindfold him but he declined, saying, 'I am a Dutchman and not afraid to die.'

The Kempei Tai officer then pointed his rifle at Voss and fired twice. Voss was not killed and shouted 'Long live the

Queen'. The officer then put the rifle to Voss's head and shot him dead. The same officer then tried to behead Sergeant Croes with his sword, but he missed and hit hi n on the shoulder so he drew his revolver and shot Croes in the head.

Sergeant Stolz and Wolff were then killed in the same way.

MACASSAR

The conditions in all the prisoner of war camps in this area were the same as everywhere else, and conformed to the well-known Japanese pattern of neglect and brutality.

At the camp at Macassar itself the accommodation was very bad. The camp was grossly overcrowded and the prisoners had no furniture, no bedding, and no issue of clothing.

They were overworked and employed on prohibited tasks. The old and the infirm were also made to work.

The sanitary conditions were appalling and the medical supplies quite inadequate, and it is small wonder that dysentery and malaria were rampant. The death rate from deficiency diseases, due to malnutrition, was also high.

No Red Cross parcels were distributed, no recreation was provided, even singing was forbidden, and the prisoners received no mail.

Discipline was maintained, in the usual way, by a system of terrorization with severe and frequent corporal punishments.

The prisoners were made to climb up trees which were full of red ants, and had to remain there; they were beaten into unconsciousness resulting in bruises and cracked ribs. The commandant himself took part in the beatings. The prisoners also underwent some of the standard Kempei Tai tortures.[1]

While on a working party a Dutch prisoner of war named Sergeant Smit was spoken to by a Japanese who commented on what he was doing. Smit, in accordance with the regulations which required prisoners of war to pay military com-

---

[1] These are described in detail in Chapter XIV.

pliments to all Japanese, jumped up from the ground where he had been sitting and sprang to attention, a shovel in his hand. The Japanese soldier was apparently startled by the sudden movement and accused Smit of having threatened him. The sergeant was then made to do the 'lizard',[1] and was then beaten thirty times with a pick handle.

When the working party returned to camp the matter was reported to the camp commandant, Yoshida, who gave Smit fifty strokes. As by that time he could no longer stand on his legs he was held up against a tree by other prisoners who were forced by Yoshida to do so. Then these prisoners, in their turn, were also beaten.

Smit's beating was so severe that the blood soaked through his shirt and ran down his legs. He had to be admitted to hospital where he remained for some considerable time until he was again able to walk.

One morning a medical orderly named Lewis was walking along the hospital veranda, near which Yoshida was inspecting some repairs being done to a wire fence. The commandant called out something to Lewis who, being unaware that the shouting was directed at him, took no notice. Yoshida ran after him, knocked him down and thrashed him. A Dr Nanning, who was medical officer on duty, attracted by the noise, appeared in the doorway and was called by the commandant. A misunderstanding arose, through the doctor's inability to understand Yoshida's mixture of Japanese and bad Malay, which resulted in both Nanning and Lewis being badly beaten up, revived with buckets of water being poured over them, and then made to stand to attention for four hours.

Another Dutchman, who was one of the working party leaders, was given twenty strokes with a wooden club and was then made the object of a one-sided demonstration of wrestling. During the demonstration he was kicked on the head and in the fork. Partial strangulation was followed up by the water treatment and the whole performance was

[1] A punishment which involved crawling about like a lizard.

[178]

rounded off with forty more strokes. The same punishment was administered to three other working party leaders, and when it was all over the victims were ordered to stand to attention. Two of them, however, were by this time lying unconscious on the ground.

On 4th August 1944 one English prisoner was given seventy strokes by Yoshida personally because he had not given 'eyes right' to the commandant's satisfaction.

On the following day a stoker of the Royal Navy, named Wilkinson, failed to obey some order which resulted in a working party leaving camp short of one man. Yoshida decided that Wilkinson should receive a beating. The stoker's endurance maddened the commandant, and Wilkinson had been given more than two hundred strokes before the punishment ended. Even then, though he was weak and unsteady, the stoker managed to stand to attention immediately afterwards for two hours.

On 20th February 1945, Marine Dodds, of the Royal Marines, was caught with a bag of eggs. These he had smuggled in from outside for prisoners who were ill and needed special food.

The entire camp was paraded to witness Dodds suffer tortures which are beyond description. The entire working party to which Dodds belonged was also tortured after being made to do the 'lizard' for an hour. All the British officers and the chaplain were included in this collective punishment.

Dodds was then condemned to death by Yoshida and the chaplain was ordered to say prayers for the dead. After the prayers had been said, however, the parade was dismissed. Dodds was not, in fact, executed but he was kept in solitary confinement for a long period though he was, at the time, suffering from a bad attack of dysentery.

On another occasion, in February 1945, a Japanese doctor was making an inspection of the camp hospital when he discovered some remains of food in a dustbin. The senior Dutch medical officer and his two assistants were then made to stand for a considerable time, their heads bent down over the dustbin, while all the other doctors and orderlies were fallen in at the hospital gate and given a severe beating. Many of them were beaten senseless, and were then given the water treatment.

Day in and day out this terrible round of tortures and beatings went on unceasingly, and by this time the physique of the prisoners was deteriorating rapidly and their ability to endure such ill-treatment was diminishing. The prime mover of it all was Yoshida, who clearly enjoyed himself, for he was never absent from these torture sessions and was, more often than not, an active participant.

On 14th March 1945, however, his sadism reached, perhaps, its peak. He ordered all the patients in the Q, P, O, and 'No work' blocks of what were known as the 'sick barracks' to parade outside. Q Block contained all the diagnosed cases of dysentery and beri-beri. In P Block were suspected cases of dysentery and other infectious or contagious diseases, O was the convalescent block for patients who had been in blocks Q and P, and the 'No work' block was for those who were temporarily incapacitated from working on account of injuries or bouts of malaria. Many of the patients in these blocks were, of course, unable to stand, let alone walk.

Nevertheless, although it was pouring with rain all the patients without exception were taken outside. Captain Dieudonné, a Dutch officer who was the senior prisoner of war in the camp, tried to prevent some of the more seriously ill patients being lifted from their beds, and was beaten.

All the patients were then marched to the camp gate, those unable to walk being carried by their friends. The distance to the gate was about one hundred and fifty yards and the rain was pouring down in torrents. Most of them had nothing on but the clothing they wore in bed and were soaked through in no time. Yoshida kept the parade waiting in the rain, after it had reached the gate, for at least a quarter of an hour, after which he dismissed it. As a result of their exposure a number of prisoners died, and the conditions of many others were aggravated.

PALAMBANG

There were three prisoner of war camps in the Palambang area: Chungwa Camp, Mulo School and Soengei Geru Camp. From March 1942 until March 1944 the Allied prisoners of war lived in Chungwa and Mulo, but were then transferred to Soengei Geru. There they remained until the end of the war. In the school the prisoners were mostly British officers and Dutch officers and men. In Chungwa were the British and Australian troops, a few Malay troops and about eighty British and Dominion officers to look after them.

These three camps were little different from the others. There was the continuous brutal ill-treatment, mass and individual beatings by the Korean and Japanese guards with every kind of weapon. Punishment parades were held at night when inadequately clothed prisoners were kept out in the open for several hours, often standing to attention.

The basic ration was twice reduced, and by May 1945 it was cut to three hundred grams of rice per man. Due to the shortage of weight in each rice sack, only about two hundred and eighty grams were actually issued, and this amount was insufficient to maintain the health of the prisoners. Hunger was so great that the prisoners ate anything they could get hold of, snakes, lizards, dogs, cats and even worms and insects.[1] When the supply of these unusual dishes ran out, the prisoners went to unmentionable lengths to find other food.

Red Cross parcels seldom reached these camps, but when they did their contents were invariably stolen by the commandant and two members of his staff.

Air-raid trenches were dug by the prisoners, on the orders of the commandant, but they were not allowed to use them.

[1] Mr Russell Braddon who has had personal experience of this diet wrote in his book, *The Naked Island*:
For the information of the shrinking reader snake tastes like gritty chicken mixed with fish; dog tastes like rather coarse beef, cat like rabbit, only better.

When there was an air-raid the prisoners were locked up in their huts where they remained until it was over.

An instruction was issued by the commandant that all British officers must give orders to their men in the Japanese language. Protests were made against what was clearly intended to humiliate the prisoners, but they were of no avail. The order inevitably led to many misunderstandings and provided the Japanese NCOs and the Korean guards with additional pretexts for beating up the prisoners.

The medical officer, Lieutenant Nakai, was weak and inefficient, utterly indifferent to the misery and suffering of those whom it was his duty to care for, and caused many deaths through criminal negligence.

The conditions in which the sick were housed were disgraceful. There was practically no nursing staff, very little equipment, and there were no mattresses, blankets, or mosquito nets. The sanitary conditions were the same as those already described as prevailing in all the other camps.

If any prisoner made a complaint which Nakai considered unnecessary, and that meant every one, he got one of the Korean guards to come in and beat the prisoner so that he would be unlikely to complain again.

In May 1944 a number of prisoners who were suffering from dysentery were brought into Soengei Geru Camp. A British naval surgeon, through the camp interpreter, told Nakai that this would be bound to lead to an epidemic of the disease unless isolation wards were built immediately to house these patients. Nakai refused to listen and an epidemic of dysentery did in fact occur, resulting in the deaths of many prisoners. Previously there had been surprisingly little dysentery in Soengei Geru, but from then on it became endemic.

A naval rating named Usher broke his back while on a working party and Surgeon Lieutenant Reed asked Nakai for some plaster of Paris. The Japanese doctor gave him a roll of elasticized sticking plaster. Usher will never be able to walk again.

In September 1944 one of the camp inmates saw Nakai

remove all the containers of M and B 693 from a number of Red Cross parcels, and then send the rest of the contents over to the camp store.

The head ration storeman, Sergeant Ito, was a despicable character and exercised considerably more authority than his rank and appointment would suggest.

In June 1945 he ordered, on his own authority, a parade of the whole camp late at night; sick men were forced to attend and the parade lasted for over four hours. It was a cold night and a few of the prisoners died of exposure.

Ito had expensive tastes which the meagre pay of a sergeant in the Japanese Army could not satisfy. He had mistresses in Palambang and gave drink parties nearly every night. He stole from the Red Cross parcels and sold the prisoners' rations to the brothels in the town. He was fond of saying that the sooner the prisoners died, the sooner the Japanese and Koreans would be able to go home. Nor was any clothing issued to the prisoners from Ito's store after 1944, and they had to go about without boots, shirts and hats, clad only in the most diminutive shorts which were colloquially known as 'Tojo's step-ins'.

That the prisoners were not issued with mosquito nets, bedding, and clothes was not due, as Japanese counsel have so often argued at war crime trials, to a general short-age. After the Japanese surrender the prisoners in the Palambang camps were provided with more of these things than they needed and the commandant of one camp appealed to all the British and Dominion prisoners to wear the clothing supplied because, as he told them, 'Great Britain is an honourable nation and it is not good for the local natives to see the members of so great an Empire walking about with-out clothes'.

All the prisoners were employed on prohibited work, that is to say, work in direct connection with the prosecution of the war. They constructed airfields, and anti-aircraft and searchlight positions, they unloaded ammunition, and some, who had the necessary skill, worked in precision instrument factories repairing range-finders and aeroplane components.

Sick men continued to work until they dropped, for once they stopped working they were put on half rations, and half a prisoner's ration in those last twelve months was near to starvation. The working parties were kept hard at work for very long hours, frequently from 8 a.m. until 1 a.m. the following morning.

The work was supervised, as usual, by the camp guards who beat the prisoners unmercifully at every opportunity, and as a punishment for what they called laziness, which included even a momentary pause to take breath, they made prisoners stand for several hours in the sun holding logs of wood over their heads at arms' length.

There was also a very unpleasant form of confinement in the camp at Soengei Geru which one of the ex-prisoners who saw it in operation has described in these words:

> In our camp a barbed wire cage was built with dimensions of six feet by four. It had a flat atap roof, no protection at all at the sides, and was situated on top of a red ants' nest. On one occasion there were nine prisoners confined in it at the same time. There was no room for them to move in any direction. They had to stand to attention all day and all night. Two of the nine were supposed to be undergoing a sentence of ninety-six days' confinement, but after sixteen days they were so covered with tropical ulcers that they were taken out and admitted to hospital.

In this camp also, the fairly common collective punishment parades were sometimes held. On one occasion the whole camp, including all the patients in hospital, was paraded at 10 p.m. and kept there on a very cold night until 4 a.m. Four of the hospital patients died within twenty-four hours.

Those who escaped from the camp and were recaptured were generally beheaded without trial.[1] Three Australians

---

[1] A trial and conviction, however, would not have made these executions legal.

met their deaths in this way in 1942, very shortly after they had been taken prisoner.

A Dutch soldier, who had become a mental case while in camp, was found out of bounds one day, severely beaten by the Kempei Tai and brought back to camp. The Japanese commandant then put him in a cell without food or water until he died.

When the Sumatran camps were eventually liberated hundreds of prisoners had died of malnutrition and disease and in one camp alone, out of a strength of 1,050, during the last three months of the war there were two hundred and seventy-six deaths.

THE PHILIPPINE ISLANDS

On 6th May 1942 between nine and ten thousand American and Filipino troops surrendered at Corregidor. These prisoners of war were split up amongst many different camps and many of them were frequently transferred from one camp to another in one of the prison hulks which form the subject of Chapter VII.

The first camp to which the majority of the prisoners were taken after the fall of Corregidor was known as the 92nd Garage. Like many others it was terribly overcrowded and sleeping had to be organized in shifts. There was no protection from the sun during the day, nor from the rain at any time, save for a few improvised shacks roofed with tarred paper which some of the prisoners found.

As usual the sanitary arrangements were almost non-existent, and certainly inadequate for the large numbers who required them, and the camp area was, therefore, swarming with flies. One tap which provided a small trickle of salty, unpalatable water was the sole source of drinking water. The food was scarce and no medical supplies were available.

There was no excuse for not feeding the prisoners properly because Corregidor had been prepared for a long siege and was well stocked with stores of all kinds. The Japanese used working parties of as many as two thousand prisoners daily to load these stores on to Japanese transports and cargo ships which then sailed for the China Seas.

When the prisoners were moved out of Corregidor on 24th May they were put on board three Japanese transports which landed them, after a two-hour trip, at Paranque. There they were taken ashore in barges, dumped into the water up to their shoulders and assembled on the beaches.

They remained there all day in the hot sun without food or drink and later marched through the main streets of Manila, which were lined with thousands of Filipinos who had been brought out to witness the procession. Many of the Filipino spectators tried to give the prisoners food and water, but they were beaten back by the Japanese guards.

This march was a distance of seven miles, and it is abundantly clear that the Japanese deliberately arranged for the prisoners to pass through the centre of Manila in order to humiliate them and to attempt, as they did in Fusan and Seoul for a similar purpose, to lower their prestige in the eyes of the Filipinos. There was a pier, reputed to be the longest in the world, situated within one mile of Bilibid Prison where the march, in fact, ended. Had the prisoners been landed at this pier, instead of on the beach at Paranque, as they could well have been for it had not been damaged, a march through the principal streets of Manila would have been unnecessary.

From Manila they were transported by sea to the Davao Penal Colony, which before the war held about two thousand Filipino convicts. Here the sanitary conditions were much better and there was plenty of drinking water but the food was scarce.

Mass punishments, however, were common and on one occasion six hundred Americans were punished for the escape of ten men. This took the form of solitary confinement in cages made of wood and wire five feet six inches long, three feet wide and three feet high in which it was impossible for a tall man to lie full length. The confinement on that occasion lasted two months during which time the rations, already meagre, were considerably reduced.

While these prisoners were at the Davao Penal Colony six hundred men were detailed to make a military airfield at Lasang. The senior American officer protested to the commandant on the grounds that it was forbidden by international law to put prisoners of war to work on projects connected with military operations or the prosecution of the war. An attempt was then made to get the prisoners to sign forms agreeing to do the work voluntarily. Each of the six hundred was given such a form but all refused to sign it.

In June 1944 the prisoners were moved from Davao. They were taken to the docks in trucks having first been blindfolded and roped together. They were packed in so tightly that they lay piled on top of one another. Many prisoners were already ill, and during the four-hour trip many lost consciousness.

When at last they arrived at the dockside the bandages were removed from their eyes and they were unbound. A Japanese General who was watching them embark appeared to be amused at their plight.

The commandant of the prison camp, however, apologized to the senior American officer on parade for the treatment being meted out to the prisoners and, in particular, for the means of transport. He said that he was merely obeying the orders of his superiors. The prisoners then embarked on a ship and returned to the same area from which they had come to Davao two years earlier. After a couple of months there, they returned to Manila where they were kept in the Bilibid Prison until December 1944, when once again, they were on the move, and by ship, for their destination this time was Japan.

On 13th December approximately 1650 prisoners embarked on the *Oryoku Maru*.[1] She carried no distinguishing marks and she was heavily armed. The conditions on board

[1] So as not to take it out of its context the voyage of this ship is described here instead of in Chapter VII.

this ship were much the same as on all the other prisoner of war transports.

At a war crimes trial, Lieutenant-Colonel A. J. Montgomery of the United States Army gave this testimony:

> To one hold, the one I was in, seven hundred had been allotted—and those seven hundred just had to get down there even though they had to walk on somebody's back to do it. Down below it was terribly hot, and this was made worse when the Japanese battened down the hatches, as they did on several occasions. I would estimate that it got as high as a hundred and twenty degrees in that hold. During the two days we were on the ship before she sank we got one issue of rice and one very small issue of water.

During those short forty-eight hours forty prisoners died. Only one canteen of water had been issued for each thirty-five men, and the combination of heat, dehydration, and the smell from the lack of sanitation drove many of the prisoners out of their minds.

Some drank urine to try and assuage their thirst, some even cut themselves so as to drink the blood—anything to be able to wet the tongue or moisten the lips. The scene below was like bedlam. Those who had gone mad were screaming, and those who still retained a vestige of sanity were trying to quieten them. Curses filled the air. To deaden the noise the Japanese then battened down the hatches.

The *Oryoku Maru* was spotted by American aeroplanes on the morning of her second day out and was bombed and strafed during most of that day. Some damage was done and it was apparent that she would not be able to complete the voyage and, indeed, some civilians who were on board were taken off during the night of the 14th–15th. On the morning of the 15th, however, a bomb hit the ship right alongside the after hold and badly holed her.

The story of what happened then is told by Lieutenant-Colonel Montgomery:

> In the hold I was in we were informed by a Japanese inter-

preter that we should make for the shore, and that we would probably have to swim. We were ordered not to take any shoes with us, and to strip down as much as possible, as it was a fairly long swim.

We climbed the ladders leading to the hatchway and some people were allowed to go to one of the lower decks and jump overboard, others were made to jump in from where they were, a distance of about eighteen feet. The Japanese guards were trigger-happy and several prisoners were shot while they were still on board. Machine guns, which had been set up on the beaches, opened fire on many of the prisoners, who were on improvised little rafts or clinging to driftwood, apparently not too confident of their swimming ability to make the shore.

As I was swimming in I passed a raft with five officers on it whom I knew, Colonels Maverick, Humber and Dencker, Major Nerdlinger and Chaplain Cleveland. The Japanese machine-guns opened fire on them killing Dencker, Nerdlinger and Cleveland. The other two officers managed to get ashore but they subsequently died of wounds.

A roll call was held as soon as all the survivors had been collected on shore, and only a few over thirteen hundred answered their names out of an original 1650. Many had died on the ship before she was abandoned, but the others were killed by the indiscriminate shooting of the guards.

At least sixty of those who reached the shore were either wounded or injured, but the Japanese gave them no medical treatment. One United States Marine, named Speck, had a bullet wound in the arm and because it had received no attention, gangrene set in. The American doctors repeatedly asked the OC Troops, through the interpreter, for permission to send the Marine and many other seriously wounded men to some place where they could be given medical treatment but all such requests were refused. At last, one of the United States Army medical officers decided to amputate Speck's arm without any anæsthetic and with only the crudest substitutes for surgical instruments and appliances. The operation was performed, but the patient died three days later.

When the thirteen hundred survivors had all been rounded

[189]

up they were marched to a tennis court enclosed by wire netting. The prisoners were put inside and kept there for six days waiting for another ship to take them further on their journey.

There was no shade and sleeping was, as so often happened, arranged in reliefs. For the first two days on the tennis court no food at all was issued to the prisoners, and on the third and succeeding days they received one large spoonful of uncooked rice per man and nothing more.

On the third day a Japanese officer, named Lieutenant Uki, who had been at the penal colony at Davao and knew many of the prisoners, came to visit them. He had recently been given an appointment in the office of General Kuo who commanded all the prisoner of war camps in the Philippines.

Uki sent for Lieutenant-Colonel Montgomery and another senior American officer to come and see him. They then told him all about the conditions which had existed aboard the *Oryoku Maru*, not that this was necessary, for the Japanese had visible evidence of the Americans' pitiable state and the condition under which all the prisoners were at present living.

The officers also told Uki, among other things, that they had had no cooked food since 13th December, that is to say for six whole days, and asked him whether he would bring all this to the attention of higher authority in Manila. Uki promised to do this, but nothing resulted before the convoy left on the second leg of its journey four days later.

The prisoners' destination was a prisoner of war camp at Fukuoka on Kyushu, the southernmost island of Japan. This second ship, the *Brazil Maru*, took them as far as Takao in Formosa, where they were transferred on board a third transport, the *Enoura Maru*, which was bombed while still in Takao Harbour with great loss of life.

Eventually the prisoners, or what were left of them, arrived in Japan, but of the 1650 who had left Manila in December 1944, a mere four hundred and fifty reached the port of Moj whence they were sent to their new camp.

SANDAKAN and RANAU

A few months after the general surrender in Malaya in February 1942, large parties of prisoners of war left Changi to go to various camps in Malaya itself and in other territories occupied by the Japanese. One such party went to Sandakan in North Borneo. It was known as 'B' Force, and had a strength of 1496.

After landing at Sandakan on 18th July 1942 and spending one night in the Catholic school, the prisoners were marched out to Eight Mile Camp, which was situated at the Agricultural Station.

The accommodation was quite inadequate and the water supply insufficient and polluted. The water was pumped up from a filthy creek about three-quarters of a mile from the camp into a reservoir, which held only 2700 gallons; the water, in any event, was muddy and full of bacteria.

Early in September, a few prisoners of war managed to escape from the camp, and the first collective punishment was then imposed. No food was given to the remaining prisoners for nearly a week.

On 12th September all the prisoners were called on parade to be addressed by the camp commandant. The parade ground was surrounded by a large number of armed guards who had been brought in from outside. They were armed with machine guns, as well as rifles with fixed bayonets.

The commandant, Lieutenant Hoshigima, then mounted a platform and read out a document that he held in his hand. It was to the effect that the prisoners would have to sign an undertaking not to escape and to obey all the orders issued by the Imperial Japanese Army. In the event of any of the prisoners attempting to escape, all would be shot.

Colonel Walsh, the senior Allied officer in the camp, was then taken up on to the platform, shown the document, made to read it and then told to sign it. He said, in a loud voice so that all the other prisoners could hear, 'I certainly won't sign it.'

He was at once dragged down off the platform, on Hoshigima's orders, taken outside the camp and bound with his hands behind his back. A firing party was then called up by Hoshigima and formed up facing the colonel. The other prisoners, realizing what was about to happen and considering that a signature under duress would not be morally binding, called out: 'Don't shoot the colonel, we will sign.' Colonel Walsh's life was spared and, after a slight alteration, the document was signed.

It was not until they had been at Sandakan for a week that the prisoners realized that, like their comrades who had been transferred from Sourabaya to Haroekoe, they had been brought to Borneo to make an aerodrome.

As soon as they knew this a protest was made to the commandant on the grounds that it was contrary to international law to put prisoners of war to work on a military project. They were told by Hoshigima, however, that it was ordered by the Imperial Japanese Army, that it had to be finished within three years and that, if necessary, the prisoners would work on it until they died.

Some weeks later, when a Colonel Suga, who was in charge of the administration of all prisoner of war affairs in Borneo, visited Eight Mile Camp, a similar protest was made to him. His reply was that it was a civilian airport, entirely unconnected with military operations and that the work must go on. This was, of course, untrue. From September 1943 until December 1944 the airfield was used continually by all types of military aeroplanes.

After Suga's visit, camp discipline was tightened up, and the already frequent assaults on the prisoners forming the working parties greatly increased. A new set of camp guards took over control of the camp. They belonged to a unit called the 'Prisoner of War Guard Unit' but the guards themselves were known to the prisoners as 'Kitchies', because they were little men. Their treatment of the prisoners was twice as bad as that of the former guards, and they slapped and beat them without rhyme or reason.

At the same time the Army Construction Unit, under an

officer named Okahara, which had been responsible for work on the aerodrome, was also relieved and a special gang of old soldiers took their place. The new arrivals, for obvious reasons, soon earned the nickname of 'The Bashers'.

The Bashers appear to have been brought to the camp, not for the purpose of getting more work out of the prisoners, but for the specific object of maltreating them. This account of one of the Bashers' exploits supports this view.

A party of prisoners were digging an artesian drain. One of these special gangs of Bashers, about eight in all, came on the scene. They ordered the prisoners out of the drain, lined them up and stood them to attention with their arms stretched out in front of them. Armed with pick handles, bamboo canes and other suitable implements, the Bashers walked up and down the line of prisoners belting them under the arms, over the shoulders, anywhere. They were not particular where they hit a prisoner, or what they hit him with. This went on for about twenty minutes. The whole party of prisoners were beaten, and if anyone showed signs of pain, he got more.

The only result of this senseless brutality was that on the following day there were eight men less working on the airfield. This was not an isolated occurrence which this eyewitness was describing. It happened frequently and when it did, to use the same witness's words, 'the result would be that a number of prisoners would be taken back each night to camp, either carried back on stretchers, unconscious, or with a broken arm or leg or in a badly beaten up condition, for the men were already so weak.'[1]

Prisoners who were brought before the commandant for trivial disciplinary offences received outrageous punishments, the worst of which was, perhaps, what the prisoners knew as the 'cage treatment'. The cage was a heavy wooden construction about four feet six inches wide, six feet long and three feet high. The floor and ceiling were made of heavy

[1] Proceedings of the IMT, Far East, page 13,354. Evidence of Warrant Officer Sticpewich of the Australian Imperial Forces.

planks and the sides consisted of two-inch bars about two inches apart. There was a small door, measuring two feet by one foot six inches, through which the prisoner had to crawl. The Japanese called it 'Esau'.

Describing one of at least forty occasions on which he had seen the 'cage treatment' in operation, the same witness said:

> Private Hinchcliffe was apprehended at the airport for being away from his working party. His reason for absenting himself was to look for fallen coconuts to supplement his food. He had, on this occasion, found some on the ground and picked them up. He was caught only a short distance away from where he should have been, but he had the meat of the coconut in his possession. He was taken back to the camp and placed in front of the guardroom, first standing to attention. While he stood there he was subjected intermittently to beatings from the guard, as many as four at a time. He was beaten with a stick, a replica of a Samurai sword which one of the guards had, another guard had a board, and the others used their feet. The second-in-command of the Guard Unit, Lieutenant Morotiki, then came along and ordered him to be put in the cage. Daily, at frequent intervals, I saw Hinchcliffe taken out of the cage and beaten by the guards. During daylight he had to remain in the cage sitting to attention, and if he relaxed at all he was brought out and beaten.[1]

This witness himself went through the 'cage treatment' and while he was in it with two other soldiers, four more prisoners were put in—three officers and another private soldier. All seven remained in the cage for three days and four nights, being let out for a few moments only twice a day, at 7 a.m. and 5 p.m.

In October 1942 some of the officers decided that the prisoners should have a wireless set. A lieutenant of the Australian Military Forces, A. G. Weynton, obtained materials from natives outside the camp and built the set with which he listened regularly to the B.B.C. news and dis-

---

[1] Proceedings of the IMT, Far East, pages 13,355-7.

seminated it round the camp. When not in use the set was hidden.

While this was going on, other officers were engaged in smuggling medical supplies into the camp, and a message on this subject, sent by radio to the British camp near by, was intercepted by the Japanese.

Weynton was arrested and taken before Captain Hoshigima who, having assaulted him, made him stand to attention outside the guardroom all night.

Next morning he was sentenced to fourteen days' imprisonment in Esau. Five others had been sentenced to periods of imprisonment in the cage and all six were put in together. They were given the normal camp rations but they had no bedding, and there was only room for one to lie down at a time. It rained very heavily, and for two whole days they were all wet through, and when Weynton was released he was admitted to hospital. There he remained until July when he was once again confined in the cage until 12th August.

After this preliminary 'softening up', Weynton was called before the commandant a second time and questioned about the radio set. 'Where was it?'

As Weynton denied all knowledge of its existence the commandant told him, in excellent English, that he would be sent to some place where he would be made to talk. Weynton can have had little doubt what that threat meant. He was to be handed over to the tender mercies of the Kempei Tai.[1]

For two days Weynton remained in the cage to which he had been returned after his interview with the commandant, waiting in suspense for the moment when he would be dragged away to the torture chamber, as many an innocent civilian in the territories occupied by the Japanese had done from the 'Bishop of Singapore to the humblest coolie', as the Editors of *The Double Tenth Trial* wrote in their Introduction,

[1] The Kempei Tai combined the functions of the military and security police, and though not the exact counterpart of the Nazi Geheime Staatspolizei, commonly known as the Gestapo, the two organizations were similar.

'for none could be sure that the next knock would not arouse his household from its early morning sleep to provide another victim for the torturers of the Kempei Tai. For it was by such melodramatic methods that the Japanese military police achieved the dread in which they were universally held in the occupied territories. The darkness of the night, the sudden swoop, the atmosphere of terror were their agents to impose submissiveness upon a reluctant people'.[1]

Weynton did not have long to wait, for on the 14th August, he was bound hand and foot, thrown into a lorry, and taken to the Kempei Tai Headquarters in Sandakan. There he was put into a room and made to sit cross-legged to attention. In the same room were about twenty-five others, Australian soldiers, English internees and natives, and all were made to sit in the same way throughout the day, and although they were allowed to lie down at night the lights were kept on the whole time.

For five minutes each day they did PT exercises and if these were not performed to the satisfaction of the guards, and they never were, the offender was either beaten or forced to remain in one of the PT positions, without moving, for ten minutes.

Never once did Weynton leave that room between 14th August and 26th October except for visits to the latrines or interrogations. What happened to him during that period is best told by himself.

I was first taken out for interrogation at about 9 a.m. on 16th August. I was taken to another room where I was again compelled to sit cross-legged at attention on the floor. An interpreter and six or seven members of the Kempei Tai were in the room with me. I was asked what I knew of a radio set in the camp and the activities of Captain L. C. Matthews and Lieutenant R. G. Wells. I denied all knowledge of these matters.

I was immediately beaten about the head and shoulders with a riding whip. I was again asked the same questions and again

[1] 'War Crimes Trials Series', edited by Colin Sleeman, B.A., and S. C. Silkin. William Hodge and Company Ltd.
Cf. *The Scourge of the Swastika*, Chapter VII.

denied all knowledge. The Kempei Tai then held me down, tore my shirt off and burnt me underneath the arms with lighted cigarettes. I was then sent back to the main room to sit at attention again.

Three days later I was again taken out for interrogation. I was asked the same questions, but still denied all knowledge of the radio set or the activities of the other officers. I was once again beaten and burnt as previously. In addition they applied ju-jitsu holds to me, throwing me round the room and causing me great pain by twisting my arms, neck, legs and feet. After that I was again returned to the main room.

On 28th August I was taken by the Kempei Tai to another building for interrogation and treated once more in the same way. After this treatment they placed before me statements which they had obtained from the natives. These showed that I had been outside the camp compound at night securing radio parts.

They also showed me a diary which had been kept by an officer in our camp. This contained information as to the activities of myself and my two assistants, Corporals Mills and Small. They then brought Mills and Small into the room, and we all then admitted that we had a radio set in camp but denied all knowledge of the activities of the other officers. The Japanese continued to interrogate the three of us until 3 a.m. when we returned again to the main room in the other building.

Later the same day Mills and Small were interrogated separately. When their evidence differed in any detail from the evidence that I had given on the previous day, we were all beaten up together and made to agree on the points on which the Japanese considered that we differed. This went on until the interrogation was completed, a period of approximately four and a half days.

Having completed the interrogation with regard to the radio set I was then subjected to further interrogation with regard to my association with Matthews and Wells, and because of the denials I made I was further tortured with cigarette butts, tacks were put down my finger nails and hammered so that they entered the quick, and I was tied by the wrists to a beam and forced to kneel on the ground with my legs out behind me.

A beam was placed over my ankles and two Kempei Tai officers see-sawed on the beam in such a way that the arch caused by the natural bending of the foot was subject to extreme pressure. After about two and a half minutes of that torture I became unconscious and came to only after a bucket of water had been thrown over me. I was unable to walk for approximately four days.

I saw Matthews, Wells, Dr Taylor and Mr Mavor subjected to the same kind of treatment, but in addition Wells was subjected to the rice torture,[1] and although I did not see it administered I saw Wells within three hours after it had been administered.

I was not further interrogated at Sandakan.

Shortly afterwards Weynton was taken to Kuching, tried, convicted and sentenced to ten years' imprisonment, but he was never at any time informed of the nature of the charge. The trial took place on 29th February 1944, and by the same court, presided over by Lieutenant-General Baba,[2] were tried Captain Matthews, Lieutenant Wells and a number of other prisoners of war.

None of them was given a defending officer or told what charge was preferred against him. All the accused had previously been forced to sign certain statements written in Japanese, the contents of which they did not understand. No evidence was given. The accused were merely questioned on the statements which they were supposed to have made and half an hour after the court had opened, all the accused with the exception of Matthews, Wells, and three other ranks had been sentenced.

Two days later Matthews and Wells were also sentenced, the latter to twelve years' imprisonment with hard labour and the former to death. A firing squad was waiting for Matthews as he left the court, and about ten minutes later Wells heard the sound of a rifle volley coming from the direction of the Roman Catholic Cathedral.

[1] This was a variation of the water treatment, for which see page 276.
[2] See Appendix, page 320.

[198]

The conditions in Eight Mile Camp gradually deteriorated during 1943 and 1944, and by the beginning of 1945 the daily ration of each prisoner had been reduced to a small quantity of tapioca and sweet potatoes, a few greens and four ounces of rice. Yet the demand for working parties was ever increasing.

The prisoner of war strength at Sandakan had been augmented since the first batch of Australians had arrived there in July 1942. About seven hundred English prisoners had been brought to Sandakan in March 1943 and after spending a couple of months at the airfield they were moved to another camp alongside the Australians. A month later five hundred more Australians, known as 'E' Force, started up a third camp adjacent to the other two.[1]

When a further demand was made, at the end of January 1945, for another working party of five hundred Australian prisoners of war from all the three camps, only four hundred and seventy fit men could be mustered. Of those who were left behind 90 per cent were unfit, and the other 10 per cent were employed on essential camp duties.

Attempts were continually being made to find more workers, and from time to time special selection parades were held. The inspections were taken by an ordinary Japanese private soldier who walked round the assembled ranks. If a prisoner had his leg bandaged the inspecting 'officer' would kick it to see whether or not its owner was malingering. If one of the Australian or British doctors objected to a prisoner being selected he would himself be given a belting for interfering.

During March 1945 there were two hundred and thirty-one deaths in the three camps, and the following month, as the total strength had fallen so low, the British prisoners were moved into a wired-off enclosure in No. 1 Australian Camp.

On the morning of 29th May, at about 9 a.m., Captain Takakura, who was then camp commandant, accompanied

---

[1] Nos. 1 and 3 Camps held Australian prisoners of war. No. 2 Camp was entirely British.

by his lieutenant and the quartermaster, inspected No. 1 Camp, the only one then occupied. About fifteen minutes after they left, Camps 2 and 3 were seen to be on fire. They and the ammunition dumps near them were completely burnt out.

At 10.30 a.m. orders were received to clear the camp within ten minutes, clearly an impossibility, but the time limit was then extended by twenty minutes. By 11 a.m. the last sick man had been carried out, and the camp was then set on fire.

At 5 p.m. that evening a parade of every prisoner able to walk was ordered for 6 p.m., in the garden area of No. 2 Camp, the huts of which had been destroyed by fire. This was in the open where there was no protection for those who were ill.

The prisoners were then formed up in column of fours and marched out of the camp gate where they were halted on the road. A party of armed Japanese soldiers was ordered by Captain Takakura to take up positions in front, on both flanks and at the rear of the prisoners' column, with instructions not to allow anyone to fall out or escape.

The column of prisoners numbered five hundred and thirty-six and they were divided into platoons of about fifty each. Late that night they began to march, but not one of them knew where he was going. For twenty-six days they went on marching and eventually arrived at Ranau.[1]

When the party of prisoners which left Sandakan on 29th May reached Ranau they numbered only one hundred and eighty-three. Three hundred and fifty-three had lost their lives on the way. These survivors were joined by six other prisoners who had also marched from Sandakan to Ranau only three months earlier. They were the only survivors of that first party. When it had left Sandakan it was four hundred and seventy strong. When it reached Ranau it numbered two hundred and forty, and by 24th June there were only six left alive.

[1] The journey from Sandakan to Ranau was described in Chapter VII.

Within four days of the arrival of this second party, weak and exhausted as they were, working parties were requisitioned for many heavy tasks which involved amongst other things having to walk eighteen miles a day. During the next few days many more prisoners died from the exertion.

There was one Japanese guard, however, who did not approve of the camp staff. On 1st July Warrant Officer Sticpewich, with nine other prisoners, was detailed as carrying party to accompany the Japanese on a hunting trip to kill cattle. The guard in charge of the prisoners became very talkative and told Sticpewich that he had just been punished by Captain Takakura and was 'very sad'.

He also informed the Australian warrant officer that 'all the prisoners were going to die,' all be killed off, and that afterwards the Formosan guards would have to take the place of the prisoners.

He mentioned, too, that on the recent march from Sandakan Takakura had killed off all the prisoners of war who fell out on the line of march, that Takakura was 'no good and would die'.

Next evening Sticpewich was in the cookhouse preparing a meal at about 5 p.m. when the same guard came in and said good-bye. A few minutes later four rifle shots rang out in quick succession, followed by a short interval, and then a fifth shot. After saying good-bye to Sticpewich the guard had walked over to the officers' quarters and shot Captain Takakura, Lieutenant Suzuki, Sergeant Fugita and a batman, wounding all except Suzuki who fell down dead. Having shot them he then threw a hand grenade in amongst them, but this did not explode. Meanwhile the guard had put the muzzle in his mouth and blown off the top of his head.

By 20th July only seventy-six prisoners of war were still alive, the rest of those who had survived the march had since died from starvation, overwork and exposure, except for one, a staff sergeant, who had been kicked to death by two Japanese guards.

But whatever the cause of death, the death certificates

were always the same. Warrant Officer Sticpewich, whilst at Ranau, made out these certificates under Japanese direction. The only causes of death ever allowed to be entered on these documents were 'dysentery' or 'malaria', irrespective of what the doctor's opinion might be.

On 26th July a medical orderly, who supervised the burial of the dead, told Sticpewich that he had seen an order that all the prisoners were to be killed. He had seen it in the *Hombu*, the officers' quarters. He told Sticpewich to keep the information to himself. That night the camp guards were doubled, and it looked as though the medical orderly's information had not been far wrong.

Having been warned two days later, on 28th July, by a friendly guard, that if he wanted to get away he had better do so quickly, Sticpewich escaped that night together with a Driver Reither. When these two left Ranau there were only thirty-eight prisoners still alive, and eight of these were at the point of death. Ten days later Driver Reither was dead.

The total number of prisoners who were in the camps at Sandakan between April 1942 and May 1945 was 2736. Before the first march to Ranau began in January 1945 two hundred and forty prisoners had been transferred to Kuching, and one hundred to Labuan, leaving 2396.

When the war ended only six of that number were living. The three camps had been practically exterminated.

Many of those who survived captivity will carry its marks upon them for the rest of their lives, and for many more the expectation of life has been considerably shortened.

That so many were able to come through their terrible ordeal, sound in mind, if not in body, was apparently due to two things : religion, and a sense of humour.

In times of adversity man finds comfort in religion, and the long years spent in Japanese hands were no exception. As Lieutenant-General A. E. Percival, formerly C-in-C Malaya, has written :

In Malaya very soon churches began to appear. In some cases the ruined remains of existing buildings were adapted for this purpose; in others new buildings were erected with such material as could be found. . . .

Under the direction of the chaplains they were built by the willing hands of voluntary workers—and there was never any lack of volunteers. But the churches were but the visible sign of the religious revival which was taking place. In those dark days, when news of the outside world was scarce, and when most of what there was came from enemy sources, there could be in those prison camps little of that national fervour which impels the peoples of belligerent countries in times of stress. Something else was needed to take its place. It was found in the development of an implicit faith in the ultimate triumph of right over the forces of evil which were threatening the very existence of peace-loving and God-fearing people. Every Sunday the churches were filled, and where there were no churches and no chaplains, services were held in ordinary buildings or in the open air, and were conducted by the prisoners themselves. . . .

Inspired by faith, the British soldiers in these camps displayed some of the finest qualities of their race. Courageous under repression and starvation, patient through the long years of waiting, and cheerful and dignified in face of adversity, they steadfastly resisted all the efforts of the Japanese to break their spirit and finally conquered.

The imperturbability and the indefatigable sense of humour of many of the prisoners made no small contribution to the maintenance of morale in conditions which might otherwise have sapped it.

As their captors were humourless and gullible, Allied prisoners of war lost no opportunity of taking advantage of these characteristic traits.

In every camp there was a permanent shortage of food and medical supplies, and without money it was difficult to take advantage of the black market which often flourished across the barbed wire. Anything that could be bartered was as valuable as precious stones, and petrol was pure gold.

During the first year of their captivity a working party

from the Royal Army Ordnance Corps and the Indian Army Ordnance Corps[1] was employed building a road near the Singapore docks, and its members were supplied by the Japanese, on indent, with the tools, equipment, transport and materials required. Amongst these was a steamroller, and the British party succeeded for a whole year in drawing from the Japanese twenty gallons of petrol a week for this machine. The petrol was sold across the wire to the great benefit of the camp invalids.

Another opportunity to obtain amusement at the expense of the prison camp authorities occurred, also at Singapore, a year later, and it is here described in Major-General Morphy's own words:

We were informed that the Japanese C-in-C Far East, Count Terauchi, was coming to Singapore to inspect the POW camps and we were ordered to manufacture and erect ornamental gates at the entrance of each camp for the delectation of the Great Man. This was too good an opportunity to miss, and our particular outfit rose to the occasion by building quite an attractive portal with the following words inscribed upon it: 'Optime qui ultime ridet'.

You do not have to be a great scholar of the classics to know that the translation of this motto is 'He laughs best who laughs last'. Fortunately for everyone concerned, and rather to everyone's surprise, as the Japanese were always on the look-out for propaganda against themselves, suffering as they did from a great inferiority complex, the jest succeeded and the inscription remained for all to see until the camp was disbanded when we moved on elsewhere.[2]

[1] In command of this party was Major-General (then Lieutenant-Colonel) E. C. O. Morphy, IAOC, who supplied this information

[2] A drawing of the ornamental gate was made by one of the Allied POWs and used as a camp Christmas card. See illustration facing page 273.

CHAPTER X

THE CIVILIAN INTERNMENT CAMPS

THE conditions in many of the civilian internment camps were just as bad as in the prisoner of war camps. In Sumatra alone some thirteen thousand civilians, of whom the majority were Dutch, were interned in such camps which were located at one time in three main areas, in north, south and central Sumatra.

One of these camps, situated at Brastagi, in northern Sumatra, was exclusively for women and children. By November 1944 the daily ration issued was only one hundred and forty grammes of vegetables per person.[1] The physical condition of the internees had become so poor that hundreds of half-starved women were determined to break camp in order to find additional food outside, regardless of the severe punishment which they well knew would follow such drastic action.

The two women camp leaders, Mrs Prins and Mrs Eikens, protested to the Japanese camp commandant on many occasions about the inadequacy of the rations being issued, but without any result. When more women threatened to break out, these two women staged a hunger demonstration at which some of the thinnest internees were produced in front of the commandant so that he could see for himself, if in fact he was not already aware of it, the effects which this starvation diet was having on the women in his charge.

He promised to visit headquarters in Medan to see what could be done about it, but bluntly refused a request by the camp leaders that they should be allowed to obtain extra food from outside the camp by means of barter.

[1] The official scale of rations at this date was 200 grammes per adult, 100 grammes per child, and 50 grammes of vegetables for each internee; but in practice the lower amounts mentioned were issued.

No improvement having been brought out by 20th November, the date by which the commandant had promised to increase the rations, the internees could be restrained by their leaders no longer, and at 3 p.m. on 27th November three hundred and eighty-six women left the camp. The Japanese military police in the neighbouring village were called out and by 9 p.m. all the women were back in camp.

The camp leaders were then arrested and a preliminary investigation took place. An attempt was made to obtain the names of all those who had broken bounds but this proved unsuccessful. The following morning, therefore, all the block leaders were taken one by one into separate rooms and interrogated, in the usual method, by the Kempei Tai.

A hospital nurse, named Sister Schuddeboom, who was fifty years old, was brutally beaten with a curtain rod about an inch thick. Mrs Prins heard the nurse's screams and when she protested to one of the guards she was told that the beating would stop if all the women concerned would plead guilty of their own accord.

What happened then is described in her own words:

> I retorted sharply that the Japanese were themselves guilty, which so outraged the Kempei Tai NCO that he struck me with the same curtain rod, on my back, shoulders and neck about six times and with such force that it broke in two. That evening I was summoned again for questioning, but I sent a message that I was unable to walk and could not come. The following morning I was ordered to attend at the commandant's office with the other camp leader and six other women.
>
> On arrival we were all driven to the Penitentiary at Katon Djahl, where, on our arrival, our coats and hairpins, if any, were taken from us and we were locked up. Mrs Eikens and I were each thrown into a small cell and the six other women were put together in a larger one. My cell was without light or ventilation, the floor was wet with urine, and excreta was smeared all over the walls. I learnt later that these cells were used to house lunatics who were *en route* for the asylum. There was no bed in the cell and no lavatory receptacle.
>
> I remained there all night, and in the morning was taken by

the warder to a room in an outbuilding at the rear of the prison. Two members of the Kempei Tai were there. I saw lying on a table a selection of weapons, cudgels, belts and whips and in the centre of the floor was a lighted brazier with irons heating in it. I realized that I was in the torture chamber, although very little light came in through the small window.

I was then put through the same interrogation as before. Pointing to the instruments, one of the Kempei Tai threatened me with torture unless I pleaded guilty. When he found that I refused to do so he made me stand on a chair, after he had tied my wrists tightly together behind my back. He tied a rope, which ran over a pulley right over my head, to the cord around my wrists and pulled the other end until I could hardly reach the seat of the chair with the points of my toes . . . he kept on raising and lowering me until my arms were nearly pulled out of their sockets. Each time he lowered me he said, 'Do you plead guilty?' to which I replied, 'Nippon salah,'[1] and each time I gave that answer he beat me on my back with a rubber truncheon. After about ten minutes I said to him, 'White officers do not behave like this,' and he suddenly let go of the rope and the sudden jerk caused me excruciating pain, and my nose started to bleed profusely.

Two Indonesian policemen were then called in to take me back to my cell. They helped me along, and showed clearly that they disapproved of my ill-treatment and were sorry for me. When I reached my cell door, however, the Japanese warder pushed me into the cell with such force that I fell flat on my face on the filthy floor and lay there for a long time completely stunned.[2]

In the evening Mrs Prins was taken back to the torture chamber and the same performance was repeated, though for a shorter period and without any beating. When it was over the local chief of the Kempei Tai entered the room and asked her whether she had anything more to say about Japanese officers. When Mrs Prins told him that what she had said was about Netherlands officers he slapped her face

[1] 'The Japanese are wrong.'
[2] Mrs Prins learned next day that Mrs Eikens had received similar ill-treatment.

and ordered her to follow him to his office. There she was again asked to name the women who had broken out of camp, but all she did was to give him the names of all the women who lived in the camp, so far as she could remember them.

Next morning both the camp leaders were told that they had been condemned to death, and an hour later all the eight women were taken back to Brastagi Camp, where a mock execution was staged.

Mrs Prins described it when she gave evidence at the trial of major Japanese war criminals in Tokyo:

> About one hour later Mrs Eikens, Mrs ten Bloemendaal and myself were taken to a large room where we expected to be shot. We were placed with our faces to the wall and our hands crossed behind our backs. . . . We then heard some Japanese soldiers enter the room behind us and heard the noise of rifle bolts being opened and closed. Another Japanese entered the room and gave a word of command in a loud voice which we thought was the order to fire. We waited for the end to come but nothing happened. Mrs ten Bloemendaal could not control her curiosity and peeped behind her. 'They cannot fire, because the dust covers are still on their rifles,' she whispered. The Japanese officer gave a second command, whereupon we were struck once by one of the soldiers, and led out of the room.

Both Mrs Prins and Mrs Eikens carried the marks of their torture for over a month. For at least ten days Mrs Prins had to be washed by friends for she could not move her arms or use her hands.

These two gallant women might well have been forgiven had they broken down under such savage brutality, but they never wavered and set such an example of cool courage that it appears to have impressed even the Japanese soldiery who were as merciless as they were cruel.

The above description of some aspects of life in a civilian

internment camp is a very fair sample of them all. Some were better than others, and some were worse than Brastagi, particularly those in Java. Many of them were little better than Hitler's concentration camps, minus the gas chambers.

A true picture of the horrible conditions prevailing in the Japanese camps and the effect which they had on those who had to live and suffer in them, can best be given by someone who inspected a number of camps within a few days of the Japanese surrender.

Lieutenant-Colonel Read-Collins was sent to Batavia, where he arrived on 18th September 1945, to organize emergency air supplies to prisoner of war and civilian internment camps in Java and Sumatra. In Batavia itself he was responsible for feeding sixty-five thousand prisoners of war and women internees.

His first reaction on visiting the camps was that he was in another world and talking to people who had already died. It is hardly a coincidence that it closely resembles Sylvia Salvesen's impressions when she was thrown into Ravensbrück Concentration Camp in 1942, and saw for the first time the women who were to be her companions until the liberation of the camp in 1945. Giving evidence at the Ravensbrück Trial in Hamburg in 1946, she said:

> This for me was like looking at a picture of Hell—not because I saw anything terrible happen but because I then saw, for the first time in my life, human beings whom I could not distinguish whether they were men or women. Their hair was shaved and they looked thin, filthy and unhappy. But that was not what struck me most; it was the expression of their eyes. They had what I can only describe as 'dead eyes'.[1]

Read-Collins was all the more shocked and revolted by what he saw because it came as a surprise. He had expected, so he told the Tokyo Tribunal, to find the conditions in these camps the same as those enjoyed by the Japanese who were interned in India at Gwalior and Delhi. He had been im-

---

[1] *The Scourge of the Swastika.* Chapter VI.

P

pressed, so he said, in the past by the Japanese conception of moral and social behaviour 'as indicated in the ethereal Bushido'. It must have surprised him to find that the 'Knights of Bushido' had sunk so low.

He did not know, as anyone who reads these pages will know, that many of the worst crimes perpetrated by the Japanese were committed in the sacred name of Bushido.

The visible effect which their camp experiences had had on these unfortunate women in the camps which Read-Collins first visited at Tjideng, Kramat and Struisweg was enough to shock anyone. Their entire existence appeared to revolve round hunger and starvation. They were so conditioned to hunger by September 1945 that when adequate supplies of food arrived the women camp leaders could hardly be persuaded to issue them. They felt that it would be rash not to hoard them against some future shortage. They could not quite realize that those days were over.

Another abnormality that Read-Collins noticed was the urge to acquire and possess trivial things: a piece of string, an old cigarette packet, a piece of cellophane paper. He was in touch with the women and children from these camps while superintending their evacuation, which took several months, and he found that they always carried about with them a collection of useless material, such as old tins and pieces of cloth, things that they had found so useful during their internment. When the ex-internees travelled from Padang in Sumatra to Batavia, *en route* for Holland, they took with them the old tins which they had used as drinking vessels and their makeshift cooking utensils. On board the ship, the mothers brushed the crumbs off the tables after each meal and took them away. All these scraps they kept in tins, so ingrained was the habit of hoarding every morsel.

Most of the women appeared quite listless and showed little or no emotion. Some children appeared more affected by their terrible experience than others, but as they had nearly all suffered at one time from dysentery they had an unhealthy pallor and their little bodies were very emaciated.

The worst camp that Read-Collins saw was the women's camp at Tjideng where there were over ten thousand internees. They were confined in a space about a thousand yards square. The Japanese had taken over one of the poorer residential quarters of Batavia and sealed it off for this purpose.

Most of the houses were without doors and windows, which had been removed by the Japanese for firewood. They had little ventilation, and, without fans, the heat was stifling in the hot weather. The whole area was very overcrowded and it was quite normal for not less than fifteen people to be housed in a small garage big enough to take a ten horsepower car. In one house there were eighty-four people living, and there was no room for them all to lie down at the same time.

There were no amenities of any kind, no place for the children to play, and they could only take exercise in the narrow streets which, during the rainy season, were ankle deep in sewage from the septic tanks which had overflowed.

Most of the women internees had managed to keep one dress and some of them wore this every day. The others, however, kept their dresses for better times, and the clothing usually worn by the women in camp on ordinary days consisted of a pair of shorts and a brassière, and nothing more.

The most common diseases were deficiency diseases like œdema and beri-beri. Dysentery and malaria were also rampant, the first for obvious reasons, the second because the internees had no mosquito nets. At Tjideng every woman and every child had had several bouts of malaria during their internment.

The food was meagre and the diet monotonous. The principal item was an insufficient quantity of rice, sometimes a little meat, sour black bread made from tapioca flour, and a small quantity of obi leaves, the only vegetable. Immediately after the Japanese surrender the internees' rations were doubled. There had been no shortage of food in Batavia prior to the return of the Allies, and Read-Collins saw no signs of malnutrition amongst the local native population.

On 18th September there were already twelve hundred patients in the camp hospital. There were many others who also should have been in hospital but who had carried on for the sake of their children. When those were all admitted the number of patients rose to two thousand, and every available building in Batavia was converted into a convalescent home. Many of the worst cases were evacuated to Singapore.

As and when they were fit to travel and transport became available, the women and children were returned to their homes and, in many cases, back to Holland. And so their three years of misery came to an end, but not its effects. They had been half starved and brutally ill-treated, and their Japanese masters had never ceased to humiliate them whenever opportunity offered.

Many thousands of civilian internees died during captivity, and many others have prematurely died since, wasted by disease. There are some who will never recover from their experiences of Japanese occupation, and will remain, until their dying day, broken in body or warped in mind.

All this they owe to the 'Knights of Bushido'.

CHAPTER XI

WAR CRIMES ON THE HIGH SEAS

ARTICLE 22 of the London Naval Treaty of 1930 between the United States of America, Great Britain, France, Italy and Japan provided that:

(I) In action against merchant ships submarines must conform to the rules of International Law to which surface vessels are subject.

(II) In particular, except in the case of persistent refusal to stop on being duly summoned, or of active resistance to visit and search, warships, whether surface vessel or submarine may not sink or render incapable of navigation a merchant vessel without having first placed passengers, crew and ship's papers in a place of safety. For this purpose the ship's boats are *not* regarded as a place of safety, unless the safety of the passengers and crew is assured in the existing sea and weather conditions, by the proximity of land, or the presence of another vessel which is in a position to take them on board.

Although this Treaty was allowed to expire on 31st December 1936, Article 22 remained binding on the parties by virtue of Article 23, which laid down that Part IV of the expiring Treaty relating to submarines should remain in force without time limit. In any event, Japan would have been under an obligation to observe those provisions for she signed a Protocol in London on 6th November 1936, with the United States, Great Britain (including the Dominions and India), France and Italy, which 'incorporated verbatim the provisions of Part IV relating to submarines'.[1]

---

[1] *Oppenheim's International Law*, edited by H. L. Lauterpacht. Seventh Edition, 1952, page 491.

These provisions were consistently disregarded by the Japanese Navy during 1943 and 1944, for the survivors of passengers and crews of torpedoed merchant ships were murdered in large numbers.

This was largely the result of talks which took place between Hitler and the Japanese Ambassador to Germany, Oshima, on 3rd January 1942, less than a month after the United States of America entered the war, and Germany was forced to face the fact that there would now be a large increase in tonnage available for the use of the Allies and an almost inexhaustible ship-building capacity. More drastic orders than already existed were then given, and U-boat commanders were instructed not merely to abstain from rescuing crews but to exterminate them.[1]

At his conference with Oshima, Hitler explained these new developments. He said that no matter how many ships the Americans built, lack of suitable crews would be their main problem, and that it was his intention that all merchant ships would be sunk without warning. Germany was fighting for her very existence and humane feelings could not enter into it. He would give the order that U-boats were to surface after torpedoing and shoot up the lifeboats.

According to the shorthand note which was taken of this exchange of views, 'Ambassador Oshima heartily agreed with the Führer's observations and said that the Japanese too would have to adopt these methods'.

An order issued by the Commander of the Japanese First Submarine Force at Truk on 20th March 1943 contained the following:

All submarines will act together in order to concentrate their attacks against enemy convoys and totally destroy them. Do not stop at the sinking of enemy ships and cargoes. At the same time carry out the complete destruction of the crews of the enemy's ships; if possible seize part of the crew and endeavour to secure information about the enemy.

[1] See *The Scourge of the Swastika.* Chapter III.

This order was faithfully carried out by the Japanese submarine commanders to whom it was issued, and between 13th December 1943 and 29th October 1944, eight British, American and Dutch merchant vessels were sunk by Japanese submarines in the Indian Ocean, and one American vessel in the Pacific Ocean.[1]

In each case the submarine, after firing her torpedoes, surfaced, and her commander took the master of the torpedoed ship on board, together with a few of the passengers and crew selected for interrogation. That having been done, the submarine proceeded to destroy all the lifeboats and rafts, and murder the remaining survivors.

A protest from the British to the Japanese Government about these crimes was forwarded by the Swiss Minister in Tokyo to the Japanese Foreign Minister, Shigemitsu, on 5th June 1944.

It began by stating that HM Government had received numerous reports from survivors of torpedoed merchant ships which made it plain that the commanders and crews of certain Japanese submarines in the Indian Ocean were acting in complete disregard of international law and of the humanitarian principles recognized by all civilized states.

It then gave brief particulars of six of these war crimes:

(1) SS *Daisy Moller* was torpedoed and sunk at 2100 hours GMT on 13th December 1943 in position 16° 21′ N, 82° 13′ E. Ship's boats containing survivors were rammed by a submarine identified as Japanese. Survivors were afterwards fired on in boats and machine-gunned in the water.

(2) SS *British Chivalry* was torpedoed and sunk at 0530 hours GMT on 22nd February 1944 in position 0° 56′ S, 68° E.

[1] These nine ships, with the dates of their sinkings, were: SS *Daisy Moller*, 13th December 1943; SS *British Chivalry*, 22nd February 1944; MV *Sutley*, 26th February 1944; SS *Ascot*, 29th February 1944; MV *Behar*, 9th March 1944; SS *Nancy Moller*, 18th March 1944; SS *Tjisolak*, 26th March 1944; SS *Jean Nicolet*, 2nd July 1944; SS *John A. Johnson*, 29th October 1944.

Two boats and four rafts containing survivors were subjected to deliberate machine-gun fire by a submarine identified as Japanese. Many were killed and one of the boats was sunk. The master of the ship was taken prisoner and compelled to watch the machine-gunning of his crew from the submarine.

(3) MV *Sutlej* was torpedoed and sunk at 1835 GMT on 26th February 1944 in position 8° S, 70° E. A submarine identified as Japanese fired with small arms upon survivors clinging to rafts and to wreckage.[1]

(4) SS *Ascot* was torpedoed and sunk on 29th February 1944 approximately 800 miles 72° from Diego-Suarez. Ship's lifeboat was subsequently machine-gunned by a submarine identified as Japanese and forty-four out of fifty-two survivors were killed.

(5) SS *Nancy Moller* was torpedoed and sunk at 0800 hours GMT on 18th March 1944 in position 2° 14' N, 78° 25' E. A submarine identified as Japanese fired repeatedly on survivors killing a large number.

The British protest also mentioned an incident involving a Dutch ship, SS *Tjisalak*, about which a protest had been made by the Royal Netherlands Government. Survivors from SS *Tjisalak* had been treated with the utmost brutality after she had been torpedoed by a Japanese submarine, and as a number of British subjects were killed in a massacre committed by the crew of this submarine, the British Government associated itself with the Dutch protest.

This document concluded by making a 'most emphatic protest against inhuman and criminal actions of the Japanese submarine commanders and crews involved in the above incidents', and the British Government demanded that the Japanese Government should issue 'most immediate' instructions to prevent any repetition of such atrocities, and take disciplinary action against those responsible. The number and circumstances of these incidents, it was stressed, indicated

---

[1] Cf. the case of the SS *Peleus*, sunk by German submarine U-852 in the Atlantic Ocean on 13th March 1944. See *The Scourge of the Swastika*. Chapter III.

that not one but several Japanese submarine commanders had flagrantly violated the elementary humanitarian principles of maritime warfare.

As no reply had been received to the above Note or to a supplementary Note sent on 20th June, the Swiss Minister despatched a polite reminder to Shigemitsu on 15th September 1944, to which, two months later, he received the following unsatisfactory reply from Japan's Foreign Minister:

28th November 1944.

My dear Minister,

I have the honour to acknowledge the receipt of Your Excellency's letters . . . concerning a protest by the British Government which pretends that in the Indian Ocean some Japanese submarines torpedoed British merchant vessels and unlawfully attacked the survivors of the vessels.

Concerning this matter I have caused the competent authorities to make strict investigations in each case indicated, and it is clear that Japanese submarines had nothing to do with the facts alleged in the protests.

I have the honour to ask Your Excellency to forward this reply to the British Government.

I take this opportunity,

[etc., etc]

[Signed] Mamoru Shigemitsu
Minister for Foreign Affairs

This blank denial of all the allegations set out in the British protests was quite unacceptable, for the British Government already had knowledge of the operation order issued by the Admiral commanding the First Japanese Submarine Force on 20th March 1943,[1] authorizing submarine commanders not to stop at the sinking of the Allies' ships but to carry out complete destruction of their crews except for those whom it was considered desirable to take prisoners with a view to obtaining intelligence about ship movements.

That order made it abundantly clear, and Shigemitsu

___

[1] See page 214 above.

must have known it when he sent the above reply, that the inhuman practices described in the British Government's protest were officially sanctioned and prescribed by high-ranking officers in the Japanese Navy.[1]

The particulars of the unlawful killing of Allied survivors set out in the British protest of 5th June 1944 gave only the bare bones of these atrocities. The details of these massacres did not become public knowledge until after the war, when evidence was given by eye-witnesses of these events at the trials of Japanese war criminals in Tokyo, Singapore and Hong Kong.

The master of the *Daisy Moller* described how his ship was hit by a torpedo between Nos. 1 and 2 holds, and immediately began to list and sink by the head. All boats were lowered, but as the starboard forward boat was smashed in during the process, the Captain took the complement of both boats with him in the port forward boat. All on board got safely away and within three minutes of abandoning her the *Daisy Moller* sank.

As the vessel sank the submarine appeared about one hundred yards to the north of where she had just gone down and approached my boat after firing a tracer bullet at us. No words were passed and the sub turned away, but three minutes later came straight at us and rammed us at an approximate speed of sixteen knots, opening fire with machine-guns directly after. I swam to a raft about one and a half miles away. The submarine then rammed the other two boats and machine-gunned the water over a large area. . . .

The total number on board the *Daisy Moller*, when she was hit by the torpedo, was sixty-nine. Only sixteen survived.

The sinking of the *British Chivalry* on 22nd February 1944

[1]Having regard to the terms of Shigemitsu's letter of 28th November 1944 the Author's comment at page 300 of Chapter XV upon the widely held opinion that the Tokyo Tribunal was, perhaps, unjust to the Japanese Foreign Minister, can scarcely be regarded as without foundation.

and the subsequent experiences of some of the survivors is described in these extracts from the ship's log.

After sinking the vessel the submarine then opened fire on the two lifeboats with light machine-guns. A white flag of truce was displayed from the Master's boat, and the machine-gunning ceased. The submarine closed the boats and waved us alongside. It was noticed that she was manned by Japanese. They intimated that they required the Master to board her, which he did. The boats were then ordered to carry on, and the submarine moved off.

About five minutes later

. . . the submarine suddenly altered course, and steered towards the boats heavily machine-gunning them. Most of the crew dived into the water, and a few lay down inside the boats.

The machine-gunning lasted for quite a time, and one boat containing the radio equipment was sunk, and another left in a sinking condition. The sub then made off in a south-westerly direction. . . . At 1130 on 23rd February Able Seaman Morris lost his life by drowning. His wounds were of such a character that he had been rendered insane and efforts were made by the survivors on the raft to restrain him. He proved to be too violent to hold, and during the struggling he managed to jump overboard and disappeared from view before rescue could be effected.

The survivors of this vessel, numbering thirty-eight, subsequently suffered great hardship for they were cast adrift in an overcrowded boat for thirty-seven days before being picked up by another ship.

The *Ascot* left Colombo on 19th February 1944, bound for Diego Suarez. At about 1205 (ship's time) the gunners on watch sighted a torpedo close on the starboard beam, but before warning could be given, it struck the ship on the starboard side in the fore part of the engine room. Her two starboard lifeboats were blown away, and as she appeared at first to be settling fast, the two port boats and a raft were got away.

Four of the engine and boiler room staff were killed by the first explosion, but the remainder of the crew, fifty-two strong, got away.

By this time the *Ascot* had begun to settle, and ten minutes after abandoning ship, a submarine was seen to surface about a mile away on the starboard quarter. She circled the *Ascot* and began to shell her.

The submarine then approached the boats, and although she carried no distinguishing marks the survivors were able to identify her class by means of silhouettes, shown to them when they were later interrogated. They also stated that all the sailors on her deck were Japanese, dressed in khaki shirts and slacks and the soft Japanese type peaked caps. There was a European in the conning tower, wearing a European type of naval officer's cap, with yellow or gold wings just above the peak.

A Japanese, in broken English, asked for the captain, chief engineer and radio operator and, as no reply was forthcoming, a burst of machine-gun fire opened from the submarine. The *Ascot's* captain then disclosed his identity and was ordered on board.

The Japanese, who had first called out for him, took away the despatch case which the captain was carrying, saying, 'So you don't speak English, you English swine'. He then slashed the Captain's palms with a knife and pushed him into the water, where he was picked up by a lifeboat.

Machine-gun fire was then opened from the submarine on the two boats, and the rafts, and all the survivors jumped into the sea to avoid being hit. Ten of them were killed while swimming around.

The machine-gun fire then ceased, and about thirty shells were fired at the *Ascot* which by then was blazing from stem to stern. Those of the *Ascot's* crew who were still alive clambered back into the boats and on to the raft, but after about half an hour the submarine came back and re-opened fire with her machine-guns.

The survivors on the raft again took to the water with the exception of one badly wounded man, Richardson, who was delirious, and a Gunner Walker of the Maritime Regiment who bravely stayed behind to look after him.

Gunner Walker, with great courage, attempted to shield Richardson, and at the same time informed those who were swimming about in the sea where the submarine was, to enable them to shelter behind the raft. The wounded sailor was hit a second time and killed, and Walker was wounded twice, once in the leg and once in the thigh, but he told nobody about his wounds until the following morning and, though in considerable pain, behaved with great fortitude until picked up.

The submarine machine-gunned the survivors intermittently until dusk, when she made off and was not seen again. When she did not re-appear five of the survivors, who were still in the water, climbed back on to the raft and hoisted sail.

The next morning, 1st March, a lifeboat was seen in the distance but was soon lost to sight; on 2nd March it was again sighted and at noon came alongside the raft on which there were still seven of the crew. In this lifeboat was another member of the crew, named Hughson, and as it was badly damaged he, and the boat's provisions, were transferred to the raft.

Hughson had a terrible story to tell. When the machine-gun fire opened a second time, he had been in a boat with the master and other members of the crew, the other lifeboat having been rammed and sunk by the submarine, which then made for their boat with the apparent intention of doing the same.

All the occupants, except Hughson, had taken to the water where they were killed by machine-gun fire.

Hughson, meanwhile, had lain in the bottom of his lifeboat which the submarine had then taken in tow alongside, presumably to ensure that no more survivors reboarded her. He had remained quite still, feigning death, and nothing had happened to him. After being in tow for about ten minutes, his boat had been cut adrift, and then rammed by the submarine in the port quarter causing considerable damage.

Hughson had stayed quiet all night and the following morning, as the submarine was no longer in sight, he had hoisted the foresail and, though she was by then waterlogged, he had sailed his boat throughout the day in a freshening wind and sea, until at last, on the morning of 2nd March, he had sighted the raft and sailed towards her.[1]

At 1325 on 3rd March, the raft was sighted by MV *Straat Soenda*, and its crew of eight, after their three days' hell, were taken off and landed at Aden. Of the fifty-two who had abandoned ship on 29th February they were the sole survivors.

The SS *Jean Nicolet* was an American ship and had sailed from Fremantle about 22nd June 1944 for Calcutta via Colombo where she was to put in for orders. Her passengers and crew numbered one hundred.

About five minutes past seven on the evening of 2nd July, the first torpedo struck the ship between the Nos. 2 and 3 holds, and she lurched hard to port and then listed back to starboard. When the torpedo struck, it blew the No. 3 hatch covers off and started a fire. Very shortly afterwards a second torpedo struck her on the starboard side by No. 5 hold, and the captain gave orders to abandon ship.

The crew began to lower the lifeboats, and all were successfully launched and got safely away with all but six of the passengers and crew. Only one man was injured, an Army lieutenant who fell into one of the boats and broke an arm. The six who remained behind on deck were the captain, a naval gunnery officer, Lieutenant Deal, USNR, two naval

---

[1] This account was contained in a report on the sinking of SS *Ascot* made by Lieutenant-Commander L. A. Seward, RNR, a staff officer of the Naval Intelligence.

gunners and two able bodied seamen of the US Merchant Marine, Hess and McDougall.

The captain decided that they should leave the ship by the No. 2 forward raft and McDougall went down, checked the sea painter and let the raft go. McDougall was first on the raft and then came the two gunners. The captain and lieutenant decided to make a final round of the ship to make certain that there was no one left on board. When they had done so the lieutenant and AB Hess boarded the raft. The last to leave the ship was, of course, the captain, and when he had joined his men on board the raft they cut the sea painter and drifted astern.

While the raft was still drifting away one of the motor lifeboats, with the chief mate in charge, came alongside. The captain went aboard her and took command for he had seen a light on the *Jean Nicolet*, which was still afloat, and he wanted to go back and check once more to make quite certain that no one had been left behind.

The captain's boat made off in the direction of the *Jean Nicolet* when suddenly, on the starboard side, the Japanese submarine surfaced, and at once trained her deck gun on the sinking ship. The *Jean Nicolet's* captain quickly cut out the engine so as not to give away their position and silently rowed back to the raft on which Lieutenant Deal and the other four men had remained when the captain left them. The Japanese crew, meanwhile, had sighted the two American boats, and the submarine put about and cruised slowly towards them.

Able Seaman McDougall has thus described what then happened:

> When the submarine came alongside our raft, we slipped into the water on the far side and clung on. For a time we could not see exactly what was happening, but we did see the submarine go astern and heard machine-gun fire . . . later she came back in our direction and put a light on us. We then climbed back on to the raft and the submarine came alongside and threw a line to us.
>
> Hess was the first man on board and I was the second. They

would only let us come on board one at a time, amidships on the port side by the conning-tower. When I climbed on to the deck I was told to remove my life jacket and to put up my hands. . . . While my hands were raised one of the Japanese sailors spotted my watch. He pulled my hand down and took the watch off my wrist. Then he saw my ring and tried to get it off my finger, but it was too tight. He drew his knife and as he appeared to be about to cut my finger off I managed to get the ring off and handed it to him.

All but three of the survivors were taken on board the submarine. The Japanese tried to shoot them while they were still swimming about, but they were never hit, and managed to reach one of the few rafts which the Japanese had not sunk by gunfire. Then, with the survivors on board, the submarine returned to within about eight hundred yards of the *Jean Nicolet*, and fired three shots into her. The survivors, meanwhile, had all been bound and made to sit together on the submarine's foredeck with their legs crossed and their chins on their chests. They were told that if anybody moved, there would be trouble.

They did not have to wait long, however, for something to happen. One by one they were led by Japanese sailors past the conning-tower to the after deck. One by one they disappeared from view, but none returned. A ship's carpenter, who was able to take a quick look behind the conning-tower, saw what happened to one of them, an ordinary seaman, named King, aged eighteen. He was bayoneted a couple of times in the stomach and then pushed overboard.

All but three of about sixty men who were taken to the stern of the submarine met with the same fate; the others were never seen again. Two of the three, Pyle the first assistant-engineer and Butler, one of the naval gunners, have told graphic stories of their experiences after they had abandoned ship.

Shortly after Pyle had got into his lifeboat, the submarine made her appearance, and someone on board her asked in good English for the name of the torpedoed ship and the whereabouts of her captain and officers. Pyle gave the ship's name, *Jean Nicolet*, but said that the skipper and all the ship's officers were still on board.

The lifeboat's occupants were then ordered to come aboard the submarine and a line was thrown to them. After all the survivors had boarded, their boats were sunk by machine-gun fire. Like McDougall and the others, Pyle was first robbed of all his possessions, tied up, and made to sit on the forward deck.

The rest of the story is in his own words.

Somewhere around midnight I was picked out and led aft, at which time I noticed that the deck guns were being secured and that thirty-five survivors of our vessel were still sitting on the submarine's deck.

I then found out that the Japanese crew were employing a tactic somewhat similar to the old Indian practice of running the gauntlet, and were forcing the survivors to pass between two lines of Japanese sailors, armed with clubs, iron bars and other blunt instruments, and when the victims reached the end, pushing or knocking them into the sea.

Apparently this process had been going on for some time before I was called out to take my turn, and I estimated that the gauntlet consisted of about thirteen to fourteen men. When I stopped for a second to take stock of the situation I was struck a terrific blow at the base of my head which caused me to feel a sensation similar to a bouncing ball. From there on, I was pushed along through two lines of Japanese sailors who rained blows upon my head and body with various objects, which I was too stunned or dazed to identify, although I was later told by my doctor that I had been cut with a bayonet or sword in the process.[1] When I reached the end of the gauntlet I fell into what appeared to be a white foamy sea.

Butler too had to run the gauntlet and this is how he has described it:

After we were all sitting on the deck of the sub they started

---

[1] When McDougall saw Pyle on HMS *Hoxa*, his 'head was split open from ear to ear'.

picking out men and taking them aft. I did not know what they were doing to them as I was sitting pretty far forward and could not hear anything that went on at the stern, and was afraid to look back.

Soon they came and got me, and took me aft where eight or ten Japs were lined up abaft the conning-tower holding sabres, clubs, and lengths of lead piping. One Jap stopped me and tried to kick me in the stomach. Another hit me over the head with an iron pipe. Another cut me over the eye with a sabre. I managed to break away, after I had gotten past the second one, and jumped overboard, and although I did not lose consciousness the sub was gone when I came up, but was still in sight. . . . I started to drift towards my ship, but the submarine opened fire on her again, and as I was afraid that they might machine-gun me if they spotted me, I turned and swam the other way.

While this massacre was taking place the submarine was cruising slowly round the *Jean Nicolet*. McDougall, Hess and a few others sat waiting their turn to be led aft to what they now knew would be a certain and unpleasant death.

Suddenly a klaxon sounded, and the Japanese crew left what they were doing, ran towards the conning-tower and disappeared below. The submarine was about to submerge.

The American sailors also knew what the klaxon meant and, now that the guards had gone, they wasted no time. Hess had been usefully employed during the past two hours fraying the rope which bound him, by sawing it with his finger nails, and he had worn it so thin that he was able to break it. But there was more good fortune to come. He discovered that he still had a knife in his pocket which the Japanese had overlooked when they searched all the survivors as they came on board. With this it took only a few moments to free about half a dozen others, but by that time the submarine's bows were almost under water and within seconds McDougall and his companions had jumped or been washed overboard.

After swimming about until dawn McDougall, Hess and

sixteen others reached the *Jean Nicolet*, which had been burning all night and would obviously not be afloat much longer.
A few hours later she sank, but as she went under, a raft
which had earlier become jammed in the rigging and had
never been launched, miraculously came adrift and rose to
the surface. McDougall and the others scrambled on to her,
and remained there until the afternoon of the following day,
when they were taken aboard HMS *Hoxa*, which had come
to search for survivors.[1]

Of the *Jean Nicolet's* complement of one hundred passengers and crew there were only twenty-two left to tell the
tale.

During February 1944, the Japanese South-West Area
Fleet, under the command of Admiral Takasu, embarked on
an operation in the Indian Ocean for the disruption of
Allied lines of communication and the capture of Allied
shipping.

During the operation the MV *Behar* was sunk and several
days later seventy-two of her survivors, who had been taken
on board the Japanese cruiser *Tone*, were massacred on the
orders of Vice-Admiral Sakonju, commanding the 16th
Squadron.

In September 1947 Vice Admiral Sakonju and Captain
Mayuzumi, commanding the *Tone*, who carried out his
superior's orders, were brought to trial before a British
military court at Hong Kong upon the following charge:

Committing a war crime, in that on the High Seas at or
about midnight of 18th–19th March 1944, the accused Vice-
Admiral Sakonju Naomosa, as Commanding Officer of the
16th Squadron, South-West Area Fleet, and the accused
Captain Mayuzumi Harus, as officer-in-command of HIJMS
Tone, were, in violation of the laws and usages of war, together

---

[1] The survivors had been sighted by an aircraft of the Royal Canadian Air
Force which gave the information that led to the arrival on the scene of
HMS *Hoxa*.

concerned in the killing of approximately sixty-five[1] survivors from the sinking of the British MV *Behar*, being members of the crew or passengers on the said vessel.

The ships taking part in the operation were three heavy cruisers: *Aoba*, the flagship; *Chikuma*; and *Tone*, commanded by Mayuzumi, on which the massacre of survivors took place.

The advance order for the operation was received by Captain Shimanuchi, who was Chief-of-Staff, 16th Squadron, in January 1944 and its objective was stated to be 'to proceed to the line of communication of the Allies in the Indian Ocean, to capture Allied shipping and disrupt Allied communications', and in February a conference was held at Penang where the HQ of the South-West Area Fleet was located. At the conference it was explained that whenever possible Allied ships were to be captured, not sunk, and that prisoners were to be taken. If it became necessary to sink a ship, only the minimum number of prisoners considered necessary were to be brought back. As a result of this conference orders on these lines were issued to all ships of the 16th Squadron about the middle of February.

The Japanese task force sailed from the Banka Straits on 28th February, and for about a week cruised south-west of the Cocos Islands without meeting any Allied shipping. Course was then changed to northward, and on 9th March, about 1100 hours, *Tone* sighted a British ship which proved to be MV *Behar*, with one hundred and eleven passengers and crew on board. *Tone* signalled the *Behar* but as no reply was received she sheered off to a parallel course and immediately opened fire. As she opened fire the Japanese flag was broken. The first salvo fell about a hundred feet short, but

[1] Although the charge alleged that only sixty-five survivors were murdered, the official figures given by the *Behar's* owners are seventy-two, as stated above, made up as follows:

On board: Europeans, forty-four; Indians, sixty-seven. Saved: Europeans, fifteen; Indians, seventeen. Killed by enemy action: Europeans, two; Indians, one. Died during internment: Indians, four. Murdered by Japanese on or about 19th March 1944: Europeans, twenty-seven; Indians, forty-five.

ricocheted on the foredeck and burst there. Three or four more salvos were fired, and it soon became necessary to abandon the *Behar*. Twenty minutes later she sank. All the passengers and crew, except for two Europeans and one Indian who had been killed in the shelling, got away safely in the boats and were later all taken aboard the Japanese cruiser.

What happened to them when they got on board was told by Captain P. J. Green, a master in the Merchant Navy who was on board the *Behar* as a passenger bound for Bombay.

> Arriving on deck I found myself facing six to eight men with their rifles ready to shoot. Other Japanese sailors removed most of our clothes, leaving us only in shirts and trousers. My hands were then tied tightly behind my back with marline. My arms were forced up behind my back and the rope put round my throat.

The same was done to the other passengers and crew as they came on board, including two women, but an officer had them released a few minutes later. They were then all formed up in lines, and made to sit on deck in the same way as survivors from submarine attacks were forced to do, as has already been described earlier in this chapter.

Meanwhile *Tone*'s captain, Mayuzumi, signalled the flag-ship that he had just sunk a British ship, and gave her name. On being asked from the flagship why he had sunk the *Behar* and not captured her, Mayuzumi replied that she was too far away to take back and he had therefore sunk her. *Tone*'s signal had also given particulars of the number of survivors who had been taken on board.

Later that day, or on 10th March, the exact date was never clearly established at the trial, Vice-Admiral Sakonju person-ally dictated a signal to a staff officer on the bridge of *Aoba* stating that only the minimum number of prisoners were to be kept, and Captain Mayuzumi was to 'dispose' of the others.

During World War II there were many euphemisms used by the Germans and the Japanese for plain murder. Opposition in the occupied territories was 'rendered harmless', the Jews were 'resettled' or 'liquidated'.

No one at either the sending or receiving end of Admiral Sakonju's signal had any doubt of what was meant by the words 'dispose of the others' nor, to do them justice, did any of the Japanese accused or witnesses at this trial pretend that they were not perfectly aware that Admiral Sakonju was ordering Captain Mayuzumi to kill all but a few of the Behar's survivors.

The Chief-of-Staff, and who should know better, said in evidence that he 'took the words to mean "to execute" '. The chief paymaster on board *Tone*, Nagai, 'understood that except for a few survivors the remainder should be killed', and so did all the *Tone*'s officers who discussed the order in the wardroom. Commander Mii, second-in-command of *Tone*, who was on the bridge when the signal was received, had no doubt of its true meaning for he referred to it throughout his evidence as 'the signal for the execution'. Captain Mayuzumi not only understood the order perfectly but objected strongly to carrying it out, and after discussing it with Mii, sent the following signal to the flagship, 'Please save survivors and take steps to have them landed', which brought the reply, 'dispose of prisoners immediately'.

Meanwhile the three cruisers were making for Batavia where they arrived on 15th March. On the 13th Captain Mayuzumi, who had still not obeyed the second signal from his admiral, decided that the only thing left to do was to go and see him immediately after their arrival in port, and beseech him, on hands and knees,[1] if necessary, to withdraw the order.

The interview met with no success, however, and when he returned to his ship, the captain told his commander that it was 'hopeless'. The admiral had rebuked him for not having obeyed the disposal order promptly, and made it very clear

[1] Captain Mayuzumi himself used the expression 'by bowing'.

that as soon as they left Java the execution must be carried out without further delay. This, of course, the admiral denied in evidence at his trial. Before *Tone* left Batavia, however, thirty-two survivors were landed, fifteen European and seventeen Indian, leaving seventy-two still on board when the cruiser sailed.

The closing stages of this sordid crime are described by the *Tone*'s commander who gave evidence at the trial of his admiral and his captain.

> On the evening of 18th March I was told by Captain Mayu-zumi that the execution of the prisoners still remaining on board must be carried out that night at sea. I refused to be associated with the execution, so the captain issued orders direct to Lieutenant Ishihara. I cannot now remember the names of the members of the execution party, but learnt that most of them were gunroom officers, although Lieutenant Tani and a few other wardroom officers were in the party. I later heard Sub-Lieutenant Tanaka and Otsuka boasting of their participa-tion in the execution. As I was not an eyewitness I could not describe the exact method used, but I did hear that the prisoners were knocked down by a jab in the stomach and a kick in the testicles and then beheaded.

Both Vice-Admiral Sakonju and Captain Mayuzumi pleaded that they had only obeyed the orders received from higher authority. There was considerable doubt whether, in the case of Sakonju, any such orders had been received, and according to the evidence of Shimanuchi, the 16th Squadron's Chief of Staff, the 'disposal' of the survivors in this way appears to have been the admiral's own idea. Nor was this defence accepted by the Court, who followed the recognized and well established international law concerning the plea of superior orders.[1] The Court convicted Sakonju and sentenced him to death.

There was, however, some sympathy for Mayuzumi who tried hard to get the order withdrawn before finally obeying

[1] This is discussed in the Appendix, at pages 313–19.

it. Why did he finally succumb? There was little danger that anything drastic would have happened to him had he refused point blank to kill the prisoners. His second-in-command, Mii, would not be associated with the execution in any way, as he stated in his evidence, yet no disciplinary action was ever taken against him by the Japanese. Nevertheless, there was something to be said in mitigation of punishment on behalf of Mayuzumi and the Court 'after very carefully considering the extenuating circumstances', thought it consistent with their duty to send him to prison for seven years.

CHAPTER XII

CANNIBALISM, VIVISECTION AND MUTILATION

THERE are not many categories of war crimes which have not already been described in the previous chapters of this book, but it would not be complete without a short account of a particularly disgusting aspect of Japanese savagery.

That the Japanese behaved with the utmost brutality to prisoners of war and civilian internees, that they massacred many thousands of civilians, that they murdered captured aviators is well known. Nevertheless, it will, doubtless, surprise many to learn that vivisection by the Japanese medical authorities was practised upon prisoners of war, that the mutilation of dead and living bodies was not uncommon, and that cannibalism was sufficiently prevalent in the Japanese Army to have been the subject of more than one Army Order.

There is evidence that at Khandok a prisoner of war, who was described by an eye-witness of the incident as unwounded and in perfect health, was treated as follows:

> . . . the prisoner was tied to a tree outside the Hiari Kikan office. A Japanese doctor and four Japanese medical students stood round him. They first removed his finger nails and then cut open his chest and removed his heart with which the doctor then proceeded to give a practical demonstration.

The following extract from the diary of a Japanese officer prisoner of war tells of another similar incident.

> Discovered and captured the two prisoners who escaped last night in the jungle. To prevent their escaping a second time pistols were fired at their feet, but it was difficult to hit them.

The two prisoners were later dissected while still alive by Medical Officer Yamaji and their livers taken out, and for the first time I saw the internal organs of a human being. *It was very informative.*

A case of mutilation of a living captive is known to have occurred at Canangay, in the Philippines. The following is an eye-witness account of the atrocity.

A young woman, about twenty years of age, was caught hiding in the grass. The officer in command of the Japanese patrol which discovered her tore off all her clothes whilst two soldiers held her. She was then taken to a small shelter without walls where the officer with his sabre cut off her breasts and cut open her womb. Soldiers held her while the officer did this. At first the girl screamed but finally lay silent and still. . . . the Japanese then set fire to the shelter.

Another eye-witness has described how in Manila his house boy was tied to a pillar. While still alive the Japanese cut off his genitals and thrust his severed penis into his mouth.

Yet another instance of the mutilation of live prisoners of war was related by an eye-witness. This occurred at Balik-papan in Borneo.

I saw a district officer and a police inspector, both in uniform, in conversation with a Japanese Army officer. During the interview the officer had been continually ill-treating the district officer [a Dutchman], slapping his face and hitting him all over the body with the scabbard of his sword. Suddenly the officer drew his sword and hacked off both the Dutchman's arms just above the elbows, and then both his legs above the knees. The trunk of his body was then tied to a coconut tree and bayoneted until life was extinct. The Japanese officer then turned his attention to the Dutch policeman, who had his arms and legs hewed off in like manner. The policeman struggled on to the stumps of his legs and managed to shout 'God save the Queen', he then fell dead, a bayonet through his heart.

The mutilation of the bodies of Russian soldiers on Russian territory as early as 1938, during the Lake Hasan incident, was quite common. A young lieutenant was wounded and taken prisoner by the Japanese during an attack on the Russian lines one evening. On the following morning, after a successful Russian counter-attack, the young officer's body was found. Five stars had been carved on his back. A large star, with the hammer and sickle, was carved on his chest. Cartridges had been hammered into his eyes, the skull was fractured in many places, and both wrists and ankles had been smashed. His penis had been cut off and an anti-tank shell driven into his stomach. The soles of his feet were scorched, his finger nails torn off, his tongue cut out and his ears cut off. No detail of mutilation had been omitted.

The above is but one incident of many. At the Tokyo trial evidence was given that mutilation of Russian corpses was carried out on a large scale and in some cases it was apparent that mutilation had been done while the victim was still alive.

During the last year or so of the Pacific War the Japanese Army and Navy even sank so low as to practise cannibalism, and they ate parts of the bodies of Allied prisoners of war whom they had murdered contrary to the laws and usages of war.

One instance of this disgusting practice, seemingly foreign to a nation so proud of its historical antecedents, its civilization and its Bushido code of chivalry, was deposed to by Havildar Chandgi Ram, formerly of the Indian Army, who must have wondered, when he saw it, whether he was awake or dreaming.

On 12th November 1944 I was digging a trench for the Japanese in the Totabil area of New Britain. About 1600 hours a single-engined United States fighter plane made a forced landing about a hundred yards away from where I was working. The Japanese belonging to Go Butai Kendebo Camp rushed to the spot and seized the pilot, who could not have been more than twenty years old, and had managed to scramble out of the plane before the Japs could reach him.

About half an hour from the time of the forced landing, the Kempei Tai beheaded the pilot. I saw this from behind a tree and watched some of the Japanese cut flesh from his arms, legs, hips and buttocks and carry it off to their quarters. I was so shocked at the scene and followed the Japanese just to find out what they would do with the flesh.

They cut it in small pieces and fried it.

Later that evening a senior Japanese officer, of the rank of major-general, addressed a large number of officers. At the conclusion of his speech a piece of fried flesh was given to all present who ate it on the spot.

There are quite a few people who refuse to believe unpalatable facts even upon the most reliable evidence. Lest the above statement of Havildar Chandgi Ram should be considered unworthy of belief, there follows the text of a captured Japanese order on the subject of cannibalism and some extracts from the interrogation of a Japanese officer, Major Matoba, who was questioned about the practice of cannibalism by a military commission convened in August 1946 by the United States Navy commander of Guam and the Marianna Islands.

ORDER REGARDING EATING FLESH OF AMERICAN FLYERS

I. The battalion wants to eat the flesh of the American aviator, Lieutenant (Junior Grade) Hall.

II. First Lieutenant Kanamuri will see to the rationing of this flesh.

III. Cadet Sakabe (Medical Corps) will attend the execution and have the liver and gall bladder removed.

Battalion Commander : Major Matoba.

Date : 9th March 1945.

Time : 9 a.m.

Place : Mikazuki Hill Headquarters.

Method of issuing orders : Called to my presence First Lieutenant Kanamuri and Cadet Sakabe and gave verbal order.

Place to report after completion of order : Brigade Commander : Major-General Tachibana.

Also informed : Divisional HQ Detachment, Major Horie, 308 Independent Infantry Battalion.

When asked by the US military commission to relate the circumstances of the first case of cannibalism of which he had personal knowledge, Major Matoba gave the following answer:

> The first case of cannibalism occurred between 23rd and 25th February 1945. On that day I went to Divisional HQ and personally reported to General Tachibana that an American flyer would be executed at the Suycyoshi Tai. While I was there *sake* was served, and the conversation turned to the Japanese forces stationed on Bougainville and New Guinea, and it was mentioned that the troops had been on very short rations and had had to eat human flesh. While I was still at the Divisional HQ a telephone call came through from 207 Infantry Battalion HQ asking us both to come over to a party which Colonel Kato had prepared for General Tachibana and myself. We walked to Colonel Kato's quarters and when we arrived found that he did not have enough 'eats' to go with the drinks. The General was annoyed, and a discussion took place as to where some meat and more *sake* could be obtained. The General then asked me about the execution, and the possibility of getting some meat in that way. I therefore telephoned to my own headquarters and ordered them to send over some meat and sugar cane rum at once to 307 Battalion. The meat arrived and was cooked in Colonel Kato's room. It was human flesh. Everyone ate some but nobody relished the taste.

Although the experiment does not appear, from Major Matoba's statement, to have been a gastronomic success it was, nevertheless, repeated on a number of occasions. General Tachibana decided that in future the procedure should be adopted after every prisoner of war execution, and made these views known at one of his conferences. Supplies would diminish and ammunition run short, he said, and in the end the men would have to fight 'even with rocks and would be forced to eat even their own comrades killed in combat and the flesh of the enemy'.

The General emphasized this at more than one conference. On one occasion, when all the battalion commanders were present, he told them that the invasion of the island was imminent and that it would probably be the last battle before the invasion of Japan. He then went on to say once more that even when ammunition and food had run out they must still go on fighting, and live on the flesh of their comrades and that of the enemy.

In any event, he told them, the enemy were only beasts. When using this expression General Tachibana was merely repeating what his masters had continually been saying. The word '*Kichibu*', meaning 'beastly', was commonly used in orders emanating from Imperial Headquarters to describe the Allies, and in the speeches of most of Japan's military leaders. Suzuki and Tojo frequently used the word in that context, but it is doubtful whether they intended that it should be so literally interpreted as it was by General Tachibana and his officers.

But Tachibana was not alone in his opinions, for he had the full agreement of his opposite number in the Japanese Navy, Admiral Mori.

Admiral Mori on his way back from the first party given by 307 Battalion, at which human flesh was served and eaten, discussed the matter with Major Matoba, and asked him whether he would be so kind as to bring along a little liver next time an enemy pilot was executed by 308 Battalion, which was under Matoba's command. It was, doubtless, pursuant to the admiral's request that Cadet Sakabe, in the Battalion Order quoted above, had been instructed to remove the liver from Flight-Lieutenant Hall's body after execution, although in fact it was removed by a medical officer, named Teraki, as Sakabe was not sufficiently experienced.

A full account was given by Major Matoba during his interrogation.

> I ordered Surgeon Teraki to hurry up and remove the liver because I wanted to take it to the admiral's headquarters. The doctor later told me that he had left it in my room, but as there was an air-raid in progress I was unable to take the liver to Naval headquarters so I had it sliced and dried . . . later on we

all ate the liver at a party at 308 Battalion's headquarters. While we were eating it Admiral Mori mentioned that during the Sino-Japanese war human flesh and liver was eaten as a medicine by the Japanese troops. The medicine made from this liver was called *Seirogan*. . . . All the other officers agreed that liver was good medicine for the stomach. . . . Altogether I ate human flesh on three occasions, at my own Battalion HQ, at 307 Battalion HQ, and at the Naval base.

Cannibalism was also practised by the Japanese troops in New Guinea and the Solomon Islands. As this happened in a country where some of the native tribes were formerly cannibalistic great care was taken, when atrocities on these islands were being investigated by the Australian judge, Mr Justice Webb, to sift the evidence very carefully. Evidence was taken from several persons who had long experience of the natives regarding their habits and tendencies. Among these witnesses were district officers of many years' standing. After hearing the evidence, Mr Justice Webb formed the conclusion that some of the native carriers who were brought by the Japanese from Rabaul might have resorted to cannibalism had the need and opportunity arisen, but it was established by other evidence that these natives were nowhere near the fighting area where the bodies had been found with slices cut off them.

In his report to the Commonwealth Government Mr Justice Webb summed up the evidence in these words:

However, any lingering doubt as to the guilt of the Japanese forces has been removed, (1) by the admission of at least three prisoners of war that Japanese soldiers ate flesh of their own, and from Australian and American dead, and (2) by other authentic enemy sources that as early as October 1942, during the Japanese retreat some of them began eating Australian soldiers. . . . One Japanese prisoner admitted that on the 10th January 1943 at Buna he ate human flesh for the first time, and said that it tasted comparatively good. . . . On the evidence of numerous witnesses, including an Australian major-general, a brigadier-general of the United States Army and several other responsible officers I find that Australian, American and Japanese dead were cut up, and in many cases eaten, by members of the Japanese armed forces. Not only were Japanese soldiers seen cutting up their own dead and putting the flesh into dixies, but they actually admitted that they were eating one another. However it is worthy of note that the majority of Japanese private soldiers who were left without food preferred to starve to death rather than resort to cannibalism.

The practice of eating each other did not have official approval, for an order was issued on 10th December 1944 from 18th Army HQ to the effect that while troops were permitted to eat the flesh of Allied dead, they must not eat their own. Furthermore a memorandum on 'Discipline' found in the possession of a Japanese major-general contained this passage: '. . . although it is not prescribed in the criminal code, those who eat human flesh (except that of the enemy), knowing it to be so, shall be sentenced to death as the worst kind of criminal against mankind.'

The consumption of enemy flesh, however, was not considered a crime. Indeed, it was sometimes made into something of a festive occasion in the officers' mess. As has already been described even admirals and generals took part in these festivities, and the flesh of murdered prisoners, or soup made from such flesh, was served to the other ranks.

The evidence available indicates clearly that cannibalism was frequently practised when there was other food available, that is to say, from choice and not of necessity.

CHAPTER XIII

ATROCITIES AGAINST THE CIVILIAN POPULATION UNDER JAPANESE OCCUPATION

BETWEEN 1942 and 1945, in the territories occupied by the Japanese armed forces, many thousands of innocent civilians were murdered, often in circumstances of the utmost cruelty, in a series of widespread massacres, some of which are described in this chapter.

One of the earliest of these occurred at Balikpapan in Borneo on 20th January 1942, little more than six weeks after the attack on Pearl Harbour. On that date two Dutch officer prisoners of war were sent to Balikpapan by the Japanese to convey an ultimatum to the Dutch commandant demanding the surrender of Balikpapan intact. The ultimatum was read, in the presence of a Japanese major-general and five other Japanese officers, to the two officers who were to deliver it to the garrison commander of Balikpapan. When it had been delivered, the Dutch commander replied to the effect that he had received orders from his superiors to carry out certain demolitions and had no alternative but to comply with them.

On the approach of the Japanese the oilfields were, accordingly, set on fire. The enraged Japanese then proceeded to massacre the entire white population of Balikpapan by driving them into the sea and there shooting them. Some had previously been killed by having their arms and legs lopped off with swords.

Nevertheless, the massacre was not committed spontaneously in a moment of rage and frustration at the sight of the precious oilfields going up in flames. It was strictly in accordance with the preliminary draft of a Japanese Foreign

Office top secret memorandum, issued on 4th October 1940, on the subject of 'Japan's policies towards the Southern Regions'.

Dealing with the Dutch East Indies, this memorandum stated that 'were any of the important natural resources destroyed, all the persons connected with the raw material, and the Government officials concerned, would be severely punished as being the responsible persons'.

It was of paramount importance that Japan should capture the NEI (Netherlands East Indies) oilfields intact. The supply of oil was a decisive element in the move southwards and the Japanese Government was apprehensive lest, in the event of war, the oilfields would be set on fire. Matsuoka, when Foreign Minister, had expressed this fear to von Ribbentrop in March 1941 when he said that if at all avoidable he would not touch the Netherlands East Indies as he was afraid that in the event of a Japanese attack on that area the oilfields would be set on fire. They could then only be got back into production after an interval of one or two years.

Owing to the action taken by the Japanese at the end of the war to destroy all 'harmful documents', the final memorandum was never discovered. However, when Yamamoti, a former high official in the Foreign Office, was asked why most of the contents of the draft memorandum, which he said had been prepared by a junior secretary, were, in fact, carried out he cynically replied that 'these secretaries were very good students'.

There is no reason to doubt that this atrocity was according to plan, for a similar massacre of men occurred in Blora in connection with the demolition of the oilfields at Tjepu in Java. On this occasion only the male population was killed. The women's lives were spared but they were all raped several times in the presence of the Japanese commander. Between December 1941 and April 1942, massacres of this kind occurred at no less than twenty-six different places under Japanese occupation and in many different countries such as

Hong Kong, Malaya, Borneo, Sumatra, Java, the Moluccas, New Guinea, New Britain and the Philippines.

When Singapore capitulated on 15th February 1942 it was not long before the advanced Japanese formations of General Yamashita's Army arrived on the island and became the occupation force.

Different parts of the island were allocated to the various formations under Yamashita's command. The Imperial Guard Division, commanded by Lieutenant-General Nishimura,[1] was given the task of garrisoning and administering the eastern half of the island. The town of Singapore itself and the area immediately surrounding it were occupied by a force commanded by Major-General Kawamura, consisting of No. 2 Field Kempei Tai, two battalions of infantry and five independent companies for guard duties. The northern and western sectors of the island came under the command of Lieutenant-General Matsui and Lieutenant-General Mutaguchi respectively.

When the occupation of the island was completed, a general order was issued by General Yamashita to his four commanders, Nishimura, Matsui, Mutaguchi and Kawamura to the effect that all Chinese residents in Singapore were to be assembled in concentration areas and screened. Undesirable elements, such as those with anti-Japanese sentiments and government employees were to be taken away and killed.

The order stipulated that the screening should be finished by 23rd February but it was found impossible to do it in the time and it was not until 3rd March that the operation was completed.

The selection of the victims and the time, place and method of killing were all left to the discretion of the sector

---

[1] In March 1947 Lieutenant-General Nishimura, Major-General Kawamura and five other Japanese officers were tried by a British Military Court upon a charge of being concerned in the massacre of several thousand Chinese civilian residents of Singapore between 18th February and 3rd March 1942. All seven officers were convicted, Major-General Kawamura and one other were sentenced to death by hanging and the remainder were sentenced to life imprisonment. See Illustration following page 272.

commanders, who had been appointed by the four generals. To assist them in the execution of this order a number of Hojo Kempeis were allotted to them for guard duties. The massacres themselves, and they were many in number, were carried out under the supervision of the Kempei Tai, the Hojo Kempei being employed to do the actual shooting under the orders of a Kempei Tai officer.

These terrible massacres, which have long been known collectively as 'The Chinese Massacres', took place all over the island and were not confined to the area occupied by the Field Kempei Tai. The total number of innocent civilians who lost their lives is not accurately known, but on the Japanese own figures, there were not less than five thousand victims.[1]

The first series of massacres to take place began with the seizure of Tanjong Pagar Police Station on 16th February when it was occupied by a detachment of Kempei Tai and a hundred attached troops allotted for guard duties. The officer in command, Lieutenant Hisamatsu, set up his head-quarters in the police station and assembled all the Chinese civilians in his district at three concentration points, Tiong Bahru, the junction of the Cantonment and Neil Roads and the Harbour Board coolie lines.

The interrogation and subsequent detention of those judged to be 'undesirable' were personally supervised by Hisamatsu who had previously lectured to the civilian police staff of 'D' Division of the Singapore Police, who had just surrendered, on the necessity for purging all anti-Japanese elements.

After interrogation, large groups of Chinese were driven away every day to the Tanjong Pagar wharf to be beheaded. Many headless bodies were subsequently seen on the Yacht Club beach. During the period of screening motor launches were daily seen coming from Singapore Harbour. They were

[1] This figure was given in evidence by Colonel Sugita at the Chinese Massacre trial.

packed with Chinese civilians. When the launches reached a point about a mile from Blakan Mati Island, the Chinese were pushed overboard and shot by the Japanese guards. At least one hundred and fifty bodies were subsequently washed ashore on the island, some still wearing armlets which proclaimed them to be dock labourers employed by the Singapore Harbour Board.

The details of this atrocity were given in evidence at the Chinese Massacre trial by two inspectors of the Malayan Police Force, Arthur John and Thomas Isaac, who were stationed at the Tanjong Pagar Police Station when the massacres took place.

Inspector John was given orders that all Chinese civilians living in the area were to be concentrated at certain points, and rewards were offered for the arrest of prominent members of the Chinese community in Singapore.

Between 17th and 24th February more than seven hundred male Chinese, after they had been screened at the concentration points, were brought to the police station and locked up. They were then removed by lorry, in batches of about thirty at a time, to a destination unknown to Inspector John, but a few days later, near the Tanjong Pagar wharves, John saw several headless bodies. They were all Chinese, their hands had been tied behind their backs, and their heads appeared to have been severed from their bodies by a sword cut.

The so-called screening was in name only. None of the victims was asked any questions except to give his name and sometimes his address. Some were picked out for execution merely because they were known to the police for their criminal records, and many were chosen because they had tattoo marks on their bodies. The Japanese pretended that these marks indicated that their possessors were members of some secret society, but it was well known that the Chinese were in the habit of being tattoed purely for decorative purposes and that the marks on their bodies had no political significance whatsoever.

Another massacre, involving about fifty innocent Chinese

civilians, took place on the beach near Amber Road on 23rd February. An eye-witness of this was Lee Siew Kow who lived in a house very near the beach in question.

On the afternoon of 23rd February he saw three lorries containing Chinese civilians and Japanese guards driving past his house. When they stopped close by and got out of the lorry he noticed that the Chinese had their hands bound behind their backs. The Japanese guards then tied them together in batches of three and marched them down a lane past the Chinese Swimming Club to the beach. Lee Siew Kow, following at a discreet distance, saw the Chinese kneel down on the beach facing the sea and the Japanese guards take up positions behind them. A Japanese NCO waved a red flag and upon this signal the Chinese victims were all killed by rifle fire or sword thrusts.

Another massacre took place on 23rd February near the seventh milepost on the East Coast Road. This followed a concentration and screening of all the Chinese residents in the Geylong district who were rounded up between 18th and 20th February and taken to the Teluk Kuran English School.

A graphic eyewitness account was given by Khoo Ah Ling at the Chinese Massacre trial. This witness was ordered to proceed to the school on 20th February and stated that there were at least three thousand other Chinese there, ranging from sixteen years of age up to fifty.

When the interrogation began, all those who owned property valued at fifty thousand dollars or upwards were told to put up their hands. Those who did were taken on one side and put into an adjacent field. The next categories to be separated from the others were the schoolteachers, the Hainanese, and those who had been in Malaya for less than five years. All these categories were taken into the school and confined there. Khoo Ah Ling did not know the exact number who were locked up in the school but there were not less than two hundred in the same room with him.

On the following day all the occupants of the school were taken out in couples and put into lorries in which they were driven to the seven-and-a-half milestone on the Siglap Road. The victims were then ordered down from the lorries and bound together in one long chain of about forty to fifty. Still bound together, they were dragged up a slope from the road towards a hill from which rifle fire would not be heard. Those who were reluctant to move were goaded on by bayonet pricks.

When they reached the top of the hill Khoo Ah Ling managed to slip his bonds and escape into the jungle. Shots were fired but no one pursued him, and after running several miles he finally reached a friend's house near the Changi Road. Of the Chinese in his own group who were personally known to him none was ever seen again.

The victims of the massacre near the East Coast Road were buried where they fell. A Chinese woman named Ang Ah Mui had been made to dig trenches near the hill on the morning of the very day on which the massacre had taken place. When all the Chinese had been killed the Japanese set fire to every house in the district, including Mrs Ang's, but when she returned a few days later there were still obvious signs of the massacre. On the ground there lay rice, spectacles, shoes, odd pieces of clothing and personal documents. The trenches had been filled in and when the dogs began scratching round a few days later they revealed further evidence of the carnage.

Between 18th and 20th February all the Chinese civilians living in the Jalan Besar district were driven from their homes and assembled on the playing ground of Victoria School. The usual pretence of screening was carried out by the troops attached to the Kempei Tai and about eight hundred 'undesirables' were picked out from the others.

During the next three or four days these unfortunate people were taken away in batches and massacred. The first of these massacres took place a mile away from the village of Mata Ikan when about one hundred and twenty lost their lives, and the second was carried out at Changi Beach near Tana Marsh involving the death of six hundred.

Wong Peng Yin was one of those ordered to parade at the Victoria School, and as he stated that he was an employee in the government service he was detained with a large number of others. They were taken from the school in lorries to a point about half a mile past Changi Prison where they were made to get out and walk along a lane leading to the seashore. What happened after his party left their lorry was thus described in his evidence.

> When we got off the lorries the Japs tied us in fives and we were then marched down to the beach. When we got there I noticed some dead bodies lying there. They were all Chinese. As soon as I got into the water my rope loosened and we were then driven about two hundred yards from the shore. The Japanese guards remained on the beach. When we were two hundred yards out the Japanese opened fire on us with machine-guns and rifles. I had managed to struggle out of my ropes and swam away in the direction of Mata Ikan where I waded ashore and spent a night in a squatter's house. As far as I know only one other in my group escaped, and he was wounded.

Another victim, who yet lived to tell the tale, had an even worse experience. Chua Choon Guan was driven down to the same beach in a convoy of about eleven lorries each containing some thirty-five to forty Chinese. When they arrived there they were tied up eleven in a row and led down to the water's edge. The Japanese then opened fire with machine-guns. As far as he could see all the others in his group were killed. He described his experience in these words:

> They were all machine-gunned and I presume they died for I have never seen them again. I was in the fifth row to be machine-gunned. They hit me but I was not killed. I fell down and the others who were shot dead fell on top of me. I was in a state of almost unconsciousness and then I received a hard knock on the head which made me completely unconscious.

[248]

When I regained consciousness it was dark. I had come to because the tide had come in a little and lapped against my face. I was still bound but I found a sharp rock near the beach and was able to cut the cords by rubbing them against it. I then crawled away and escaped.[1]

The next sector to be 'mopped up' was the Fort Canning Area. After establishing his headquarters in Ord Road, the sector commander, Captain Goshi, sent out his Kempei Tai subordinates and attached troops, on 19th February, to round up all the Chinese residents in that district of Singapore.

Within forty-eight hours several thousand had been mustered at the junction of River Valley Road and Ord Road and a screening lasting for three days began.

Between three and four hundred 'undesirables' were finally picked out for 'disposal' and were handed over to the Hojo Kempei Company commander who took them away in batches on three consecutive days and had them shot on the Changi beaches.

On 28th February a round-up took place of all the Chinese living in the Imperial Guards Divisional area under the command of Nishimura.

About one thousand of them were assembled near Oehler's Lodge and squeezed into a tennis court. There they were asked whether any of them were tattooed and what were their occupations. As usual these questions appear to have been asked merely to give the impression that some sort of screening was being carried out. Irrespective of the answers to the questions, and quite arbitrarily, about three hundred were detained and the remainder dismissed.

One of the three hundred has described their fate in these words:

[1] Privates Pooley and O'Callaghan escaped in a somewhat similar way after the massacre of a hundred men of the Norfolk Regiment at Le Paradis by the 2nd SS Totenkopf Regiment on 26th May 1940. See *The Scourge of the Swastika*. Chapter II.

My younger brother was released but I and my two other brothers were detained. We were then taken in a lorry to a place about nine miles away where we were stripped and inspected for tattoo marks. From there we were driven, again in a lorry, to the eleventh milepost on the Ponggol Road. When we reached it we saw eleven trucks full of more Chinese guarded by about a hundred Japanese soldiers. . . . After being made to kneel down for twenty minutes in the garden of a bungalow near the seashore, eighteen of us, including myself, were marched by the Japanese guards over the road into a field near a rubber plantation. The leader of the Japanese escort wrote in the sand that he was our saviour . . . we thought that he was giving us an opportunity to escape and ran quickly up a small hill into the plantation. Shots were fired at us on the way but all save two of us got safely away.

But the others were not so lucky. Nearly three hundred are known to have been shot on the seashore at the end of the Ponggol Road. An inspection of the scene of the massacre, three days later, revealed many corpses strewn about the foreshore, and floating in the sea. One hundred bodies were buried by a working party from the Public Health Department.

The last of the principal Chinese massacres on Singapore Island took place on 1st March. A few days before the end of February, notices had been posted up in the Chinese coffee houses of the Mata Ikan district ordering all the local residents to assemble at the eight-and-a-half milepost on the Changi Road for registration.

On 1st March, after the usual selection had been made, about three hundred Chinese were removed under escort in lorries to the vicinity of Samba Ikat, a village near the tenth milepost on the Changi Road.

A Chinaman, who was then living in Samba Ikat, was an eye-witness of the massacre of these three hundred, and described it in these words when giving evidence at the trial of Nishimura.

In the early afternoon I saw two cars pass my house, one with a red flag and the other with a blue. Some Japanese soldiers got out of them and examined the air-raid shelters which were at the end of a lane at the rear of my property. Then they left.

Two hours later six or seven lorries full of Chinese civilians, guarded by Japanese sentries, came past the house from the same direction and halted by the air-raid shelters. The occupants were made to get out of the lorries and kneel down in front of the air-raid shelters. I saw all this for I was hiding behind a mango tree and was never noticed. They were then mowed down by machine-gun fire. I saw them fall as they were hit and I heard the moaning of those who had not been killed outright. Shortly afterwards the lorries all returned empty whence they had come.

I visited the place some days afterwards when the bodies had been covered over lightly with earth. It had not been done properly, however, and as the smell of rotting bodies was so bad, we farmers reburied the dead.

By 2nd March, therefore, General Yamashita's orders had been executed. The Japanese have since tried to justify these massacres on the grounds of security. No such excuse can be accepted and the real reason is not hard to find.

When the invasion of Malaya began on 8th December 1941, the Chinese residents unanimously decided to co-operate with the British war effort. The authorities in Chung-king told the British Ambassador that the Chinese Government was ready to instruct Chinese overseas to stage 'an anti-Japanese movement in co-operation with Britain, if the British Government found it necessary'. Japan had been at war with China, although they had consistently refused to call it by that name, ever since the Mukden Incident and the Chinese and Japanese had become sworn enemies.

The Chinese massacres on Singapore Island were clearly carried out as a vengeful measure against the Chinese residents of Malaya for daring to espouse the British cause.

After the Japanese forces had occupied the territory and all fighting had ceased, massacres were freely committed as a means of terrorizing the civilian population and subjecting them to Japanese domination. Massacres of this type were committed in no less than twenty-nine different places.

Many other civilians, principally conscripted labourers, were massacred during the Japanese occupation because they had become unfit to carry on working for the Greater East Asia Co-Prosperity Sphere by reason of disease or starvation. They had ceased to be an asset and had become a liability. There are no less than fifteen places where such massacres occurred, and in the labour camps along the working site of the Burma–Siam Railway they were quite common.

Other massacres had as their object the discouragement of prevalent breaches of Japanese regulations, such as that at the labour camp on Hainan Island, in an attempt to prevent smuggling; at Saigon, in French Indo-China, intended to prevent the prohibited use of radio; and on the island of Amboina, where civilians were killed for giving food to prisoners of war.

The murder of a large number of citizens of the USSR took place in Manchuria in August 1945. This was done at the instance of the commander of the Kwantung Army. The victims had not been charged with any offence, and the reason given for killing them was that they might carry on espionage or sabotage against the Japanese occupying force.

Massacres of many civilians took place in anticipation of a Japanese withdrawal, or an Allied attack or invasion, in order to prevent their liberation.

When it became apparent that Manila would be liberated, massacres of this nature were committed all over the city together with wholesale rape and arson. Nor was this a spontaneous outburst of Japanese savagery, as at Nanking in 1938. There is indisputable evidence that it was planned, for orders were captured which put the matter beyond doubt.

The following extracts are taken from a file of 'Manila Navy Defence Force and South-Western Area Fleet Operation Orders', dated from 23rd December 1944 to 14th February 1945.

4. Be careful to make no mistakes in the time of exploding and burning when the enemy invades.

6. When killing Filipinos, assemble them together in one place, as far as possible, thereby saving ammunition and labour. The disposal of dead bodies will be troublesome, so either collect them in houses scheduled to be burned or throw them into the river.

Extracts from the captured diary of a Japanese warrant officer, named Yamaguchi, confirm the other evidence that these atrocities were carried out in pursuance of orders.

> *We are ordered* to kill all the males we find. Mopping up the bandits[1] from now on will be a sight indeed . . Our aim is to kill or wound all the men and collect information. Women who attempt to escape are to be killed. All in all, our aim is extermination.

As the American troops were closing in on Manila the bombing and shelling became continuous. Fire had broken out, water and food had become extremely difficult to obtain, and safe shelter was sought by countless numbers of refugees throughout the city.

During the afternoon of 9th February Japanese patrols scoured the Ermita district turning everybody out of their houses and places of business, and bringing them to the Plaza Ferguson. Most of these went voluntarily and unsuspectingly for they had been told by the Japanese that they were only being moved for their better safety.

By 5 p.m. about two thousand men, women and children, of mixed nationalities, had been assembled in the Plaza, and a Japanese officer, who appeared to be in charge, gave orders

---

[1] From his use of the word 'bandits' to describe the enemy it would appear that Warrant-Officer Yamaguchi had served with the Japanese forces in China. See Chapter II.

for the men, youths and older boys to be separated from the women and children. The former were taken to the Manila Hotel, the latter to the Bay View Hotel, save for a small group of about twenty girls who were taken to a nearby restaurant called 'The Coffee Pot', which was a club for Japanese officers. There they were given food and drink and then taken to one of the upper floors in the Bay View. During the night any doubt which these unfortunate women in the Bay View Hotel may still have entertained as to the reason for their being there was quickly dispelled. In twos and threes, officers and other ranks came to the various rooms where the women were quartered, selected whom they wished, took them to other rooms and raped them.[1]

Throughout Manila, during the last few terrible days before its capture the slaughter went on relentlessly.

Between January 1942 and February 1945 many hundreds of civilians had been taken to Fort Santiago and detained there for questioning. During the whole of that period the Japanese meted out the most appallingly brutal treatment to all the prisoners there.

In February 1945, just before Manila fell, the cells were packed tight with all the civilians who lived within the Walled City. The doors were barricaded, petrol was sprinkled everywhere, the buildings set on fire and many hundreds were burned to death. Others were executed. Hundreds of bodies were discovered by the American troops when Fort Santiago was taken.

Many of these civilians succeeded in escaping from the burning buildings only to be shot by the Japanese guards as they ran out of the flames or while they were attempting to swim the river.

Some, however, survived and lived to tell the tale, and it is from them that this description was obtained.

At the German Club in Manila yet another atrocity was

---

[1] The details of this orgy which went on without cessation for four days are contained in a report made by the Judge Advocate General's Department of the United States Army, and evidence of it was given before the Tokyo Tribunal.

committed. During the first few days of that same February a large number of civilians had taken shelter, under the club buildings, from shell fire and air bombardment. While they were there Japanese soldiers surrounded it with a barricade of inflammable material, poured petrol over it and lit it. The civilians, who were sheltering underneath the building, then ran out and tried to climb the barricade, but most of them were shot or bayoneted by soldiers who were lying in wait. Some of the women were caught and raped by the Japanese who then poured petrol over their hair and ignited it. Other women who were carrying infants had them bayoneted in their arms.

Another massacre took place at St. Paul's College in the following circumstances. About two hundred and fifty civilians were collected and placed in one of the buildings and the door and windows were then shut and barred. While so confined it was noticed that three chandeliers, which hung from the ceiling, had been wrapped in blackout paper and that strings or light wires ran from inside the wrappings through the windows to the outside of the building.

About an hour later the Japanese brought in some biscuits and sweetmeats, and put them on a table in the centre of the room, telling the people inside that they would be quite safe there and could help themselves.

A few minutes after the Japanese had left, and while the occupants of the building were helping themselves to the food, three loud explosions occurred. The covered chandeliers had contained explosives. Men, women and children were thrown to the ground, many were injured, and panic ensued. The explosion had blown out the windows and a large hole in the wall, and through these all those who were able to move tried to make their escape. As they did so they were mown down by rifle and machine-gun fire.

The headquarters of the Filipino Red Cross in Manila, the scene of another outrage, was situated in a large building at the junction of Isaac Peral and General Luna Streets, and was clearly marked with the Red Cross sign. About six o'clock one evening the Japanese troops arrived. There were over seventy civilians in the building including seven patients and five members of the permanent staff. The remaining sixty odd were local residents who had taken refuge there, trusting in the protection of the Geneva emblem.

Miss Andaya, who was a trained nurse, together with a few others, was at the rear of the building preparing the evening meal when she heard shots near the back gate. At that moment an unknown woman ran screaming into the building carrying a child who had been shot. Close behind came four Japanese marines and an officer who began firing his pistol at the children in the building. Nurse Andaya ordered everyone to lie flat on the floor and all obeyed save one, a young child who was frightened and ran wildly about the room screaming, but not for long, for he soon fell dead with three bullets in his head. When the firing momentarily stopped the Japanese officer was informed by Miss Andaya, through the Red Cross interpreter, that she was a Red Cross nurse, that he and his men were in a Red Cross building, and was asked what it was he wanted. The only answer she received was a shot in the chest. She fell, but before she lost consciousness she saw other troops enter the ward and shoot and bayonet the patients in their beds.

Next door, the manager, Mr Farolan, was talking to a doctor who was preparing for an operation. As the marines entered his room he was able to slip down under the desk, behind which he was sitting, and was thus hidden from view. A young woman, a volunteer member of the staff, tried to protect the doctor by saying, 'he is our doctor, please spare him', but it was of no avail. The doctor fell dead, a bullet through his heart. The marine who shot the doctor then went round the ward bayoneting everyone in it, some of whom were in the beds and others hiding underneath them. Amongst the victims were a grandmother, her daughter and baby granddaughter ten days old. When the father of the baby found the bodies two days later, that of his wife showed that she had been bayoneted in the face and stomach and

[256]

shot through the chest, while the condition and position of the baby's body indicated that she had been bayoneted in the right arm only, and had been suffocated under the mother's body.

A film actress who had also taken refuge in the Red Cross headquarters was in a corridor on the ground floor when the Japanese arrived. She tried to hide behind a medicine cupboard but was caught in the act and shot through the elbow, falling to the ground with her child still in her arms. She lay still and feigned death, but the marine who had fired the shot stabbed her with his bayonet nine times, as she lay there, to make sure that she was dead.

The slaughter went on for nearly half an hour, after which the Japanese left the building. An examination of the premises by Mr Farolan after the marines had left revealed numerous dead bodies. After the building was burnt down two days later ashes, bones and bodies were found piled up in odd corners, along the corridors and even in the latrines, in many cases only identifiable because some of the survivors knew who had been hiding in those places. All the Society's records and files were destroyed in the fire so that the exact number of victims is unknown. The estimates have varied between eighty and thirty, but the most reliable is, doubtless, that of Mr Farolan, who has given the number as not less than fifty.

Nothing in Manila was spared. Even the cathedral was entered by Japanese troops who dragged young girls outside and raped them in the west porch just before they set fire to the building.[1]

Captured diaries of Japanese soldiers covering the period December 1944 to March 1945 confirm all the other available evidence.

I cannot remember the date, but we received information from the Lipa military police detachment that approximately

---

[1] This was given in evidence by an eye-witness, Rosa Calalong, at the trial of General Yamashita.

T

thirty guerrillas had attacked the Lipa Air Depot with hand grenades and other explosives and eleven of them had been captured. We were asked by the military police to 'dispose of' the captives. During the night we dug holes here and there in the coconut grove near the graveyard and bayoneted them to death. They had no strength left as they had eaten nothing for the last three days since their capture. Their hands were tied behind their backs and they were made to stand in front of the holes with their heads slightly bent downwards. It seemed that their minds were clearly made up that they would be killed, for they said nothing. Their hair was very bushy. I was irritated. Later, one by one the members of our section bayoneted them. The first one was bayoneted by Suzuki. *My turn* came next. The moment I bayoneted him the victim cried 'Ah' and fell into the hole behind him. He was suffering but I had no emotion at all, that may be because I was so excited. After bayoneting them we covered the bodies with soil and laid coconut leaves on top.

We then returned to the company at 2200 hours singing a marching song.

The following extracts are from the diary of another Japanese soldier.

7 Feb. 45.   150 guerrillas were disposed of tonight. I stabbed 10.

9 Feb. 45.   Burned 1,000 guerrillas tonight.

13 Feb. 45.   Enemy tanks are lurking in the vicinity of Banzai Bridge. Our attack preparation has been completed. I am now on guard duty at the Guerrilla Internment Camp. While I was on duty 10 guerrillas tried to escape. They were all recaptured and bayoneted. Later. At 1600 hours all guerrillas were burned to death.[1]

The following is an extract from a battle report made in April 1945, by the commanding officer of the Ijichi Unit.

4. Number of rounds of ammunition expended, 28. (For killing natives.)

[1] See Appendix, pages 321-6.

5. At 1200 hours today, 22 natives passed in the vicinity of our company positions. All were either stabbed or shot to death by the remnants of a squad under Superior Private Hayashi which had just returned from a suicide assault mission.

In another diary, kept by a member of the Fujita Force, the following entries appeared:

13 Feb. For security reasons, all inhabitants of the town were killed and all their possessions confiscated.

17 Feb. Because 90% of the Filipinos are not pro-Japanese, Army Headquarters issued orders on 10th inst. to punish them. In various sectors we have killed several thousands (including young, old, men and women and Chinese). Their homes have been burned and their valuables confiscated.

Two entries found in other captured diaries indicate that there were at least some members of the Japanese forces who did not approve of such barbarism. The first is from the diary of a member of a military police unit.

On 10th July, the Japanese troops gathered all the men and boys at the church and questioned them in connection with the guerrilla operations. They made them drink water, and slapped them on the cheeks. It was pitiful and I couldn't watch. They then shot them or speared them to death with bamboo lances. Indeed the Japanese Army does extreme things.

The second extract is from the diary of a Japanese soldier who was engaged during the month of February 1945 in rounding up Filipino guerrillas, and unarmed civilians.

Feb. 45. Every day is spent in hunting guerrillas and natives. I have already killed well over 100. The innocence I possessed at the time of leaving the homeland has long since disappeared. Now I am a hardened sinner and my sword is always stained with blood.

Although it is for my country's sake, it is sheer brutality. May God forgive me. May my mother forgive me.

[259]

Throughout the entire occupation of the Philippines the most terrible atrocities were committed by the Japanese forces against the civilian population, mass murders, brutal torturing and wholesale rape.

As early as August 1942 most of the inhabitants of a barrio in the province of Lanao were murdered and all the houses burnt to the ground. Early one morning, just after dawn, about a hundred Japanese soldiers from the garrison of Dansalan City arrived under the command of four officers. One of the few villagers to escape has given the following account of what happened.

Our barrio had a population of two thousand five hundred. We were taken by surprise. When the Japanese arrived they immediately began bayoneting all the inhabitants, many of whom were fishing in the lake. Afterwards they set fire to the houses. In the commotion that ensued four Japanese soldiers got killed. The soldiers then withdrew from the village taking me and three others with them as prisoners.

A year later twenty-four men and three women were tied together like cattle and beheaded in Iloilo province. The Japanese troops swooped down on the village and seized a number of the inhabitants for interrogation. When it was over the twenty-seven referred to above were tied with their hands behind their backs. Later, they were all strung together on a larger piece of rope and pulled along like cattle into a thicket twenty-five yards away where they were beheaded. During the round-up a baby, just three months old, was thrown into the air by some of the soldiers and impaled on a bayonet. This was witnessed by a villager named José Tupaz who afterwards made a statement.[1]

A month later, in the same province, one of the inhabitants was crucified by a Japanese soldier during a raid on Ajuv.

[1] This incident is reminiscent of Obersturmführer Wilhaus, once Commandant of Yanov extermination camp, who used young children for clay pigeon practice. See *The Scourge of the Swastika*. Chapter IV.

After describing the bayoneting and shooting of a large number of the villagers an eye-witness stated:

> ... on this same day I saw other Filipino civilians killed by the same group of Japanese soldiers, Aurelio Artacho aged thirty-eight and Lucas Doctolero aged forty. The former was chopped in the neck with a sword and thrown into a house which was later set on fire. The latter was crucified to the ground with three six-inch nails, one through each wrist and the third driven through the base of the skull.[1] I was standing only two metres away.

On 19th October 1943 a revolt broke out in Jesselton, seaport and capital of North Borneo, then under Japanese occupation. About forty Japanese were killed. The Japanese retaliated by sending over aircraft to bomb and machine-gun all the villages north of the capital, razing to the ground every building in Kota Bolud and causing much damage and loss of life in Tuaran, Mengatal, Inanam and the surrounding country.

This suppressed the revolt but it did not satisfy the Japanese who decided to carry out terrible reprisals.[2] A number of Kempei Tai were drafted to Jesselton from Kuching and during the following months this detachment established a reign of terror among the civilian population, arresting hundreds of men and women on suspicion and torturing them to extract information about the guerrillas.

Forced confessions were followed by mass summary executions and on one occasion, admitted by the Japanese themselves, one hundred and eighty-nine suspects were put to death without trial. In addition to this several hundred others died in prison from torture, disease or starvation.

The revolt was predominantly a Chinese uprising, but the Japanese made it a pretext for a determined effort to exterminate a whole race of people, the Suluks, who inhabit a

[1] The Germans behaved similarly in France. See *The Scourge of the Swastika*, Chapter IV.
[2] See Appendix, page 324.

number of islands off the west coast of North Borneo. The Suluks had really very little to do with the rebellion, and it would appear from the evidence available that only a few of them participated in it on the first night.

In February 1944 a Japanese force was sent to one of the Suluk group of islands, Mantanani. Its main objective appears to have been to search for a Chinese guerrilla who was supposed to be in hiding there, and was suspected of taking a prominent part in the revolt.

Shortly after the arrival of the force in Mantanani, however, a Chinaman, named Dr Lou Lai, who had been arrested on suspicion by the Kempei Tai, broke down under repeated torture and gave the names of a number of people who were in the anti-Japanese resistance movement. These names included those of some of the Suluk leaders.

It was as a result of that information that reprisal action against the Suluks was then taken, details of which were given in a report made by a British Army officer, Captain M. J. Dickson, who was later appointed to carry out an investigation.

When the Japanese force commander on Mantanani was unable to find the Chinese guerrillas for whom he was searching, he arrested fifty-eight Suluk males and took them back to Jesselton. During the next few weeks each one of these men died of torture or starvation at the Kempei Tai headquarters or in Jesselton Prison. Not a soul survived.

Two days after the Japanese force had left Mantanani with the arrested Suluks, it returned. Eight eye-witnesses of what happened on the return visit, Chinese, Malay, Suluk and Japanese, have established that two atrocities were committed. Firstly, the machine-gunning of Suluk men and women, and the subsequent killing of all the wounded, after an encounter between a Japanese search party and a group of Suluks. Secondly, immediately after this incident, the massacre of twenty-five women and four children.

All these eye-witnesses have testified that the Suluks had no firearms, and that such resistance as they offered was with spears and parangs, either in reply to Japanese fire or in an effort to protect their women and children.

The Japanese then burned the village and destroyed the islanders' boats, thus depriving them at one and the same time of their homes and their livelihood.

Lieutenant Shimizu, who was in command of this force, made a statement admitting that he ordered the killing of the women.[1] In it he stated that all the members of his little force collected, near the mosque which was their headquarters, as many of the Suluk women and children as could be found. They were ordered to remove their jewellery and this and any other valuables, including money, in their possession were taken by the Japanese soldiers. The victims then had their hands tied behind their backs and were strung together on a rope which was then made fast to the pillars of the mosque. When a machine-gun had been set up, Shimizu gave the order to fire. When the firing ceased other ranks of the Kempei Tai finished off with their revolvers those who still showed any signs of life.

A few weeks later the Japanese paid the island a third visit and found it deserted. A month later, eight or nine Suluks were caught on the mainland opposite Mantanani and were detained at Kota Bolud. Two of them were men, and the remainder women and children, the youngest a baby in arms. All were survivors from the February massacres. After being kept in custody by the Kempei Tai for six weeks they were executed. Being given the choice of shooting or beheading they chose the former.

The population of Mantanani was reduced by the Japanese action from four hundred and thirty to one hundred and twenty-five, of whom not more than twenty were adult males.

None of the Suluks who lived on the island of Dinawan took any part in the rising, yet they suffered a similar attempt at extermination. The island's population was reduced from

---

[1] Lieutenant Shimizu was tried in 1946 at Singapore by a British Military Court which sentenced him to death.

one hundred and twenty, before the arrival of the Japanese, to fifty-four after their departure, all of whom were either women or children under sixteen years of age. Of the original population not a single adult male survived.

In February 1944 all the males on Dinawan over twelve years of age, numbering thirty-seven, were arrested and taken to Jesselton Prison. Precisely what happened to all of them is not known but there are no survivors.

The same thing happened on three other islands inhabited by the Suluks—Mangolum, Sulug and Udar. An experienced colonial administrator, who knew the Suluks in peace and war, has given it as his opinion that the loss of the adult male population will have a serious effect on the race. A sufficient number of Suluk children of both sexes survived to carry on the race and prevent its extinction, but 'their health is poor and there is almost certain to be an assimilation of a large element of Bajar blood. In any event some of their hereditary skill in fishing, their chief means of livelihood, and other traditional occupations may be lost for lack of adult men to hand down the traditions of the race'.

In Dutch Borneo between October 1943 and June 1944 murder occurred systematically on a huge scale. The Japanese Naval Military Police, called the Tokei Tai, pretended that there was a vast anti-Japanese resistance movement in the country, and supported the myth of its existence by obtaining a large number of confessions by means of torture. By these means they secured the execution of sixty-three innocent civilians after staging a number of spy trials. After a time, however, they dispensed with even the semblance of legal procedure and summarily executed many more.

Altogether a thousand were put to death at Mandor, two hundred and forty at Sunggei Durian, a hundred at Katapang, and an unknown number at Pontianak, a large seaport on the west coast of Dutch Borneo. Among these victims were several of the native rulers of West Borneo, including the Sultan of Pontianak and his two sons, many well-to-do Chinese and Indonesians and some Dutch officials.

This action was taken on orders from Japanese Navy Headquarters at Sourabaya and the interrogation reports of Lieutenant Yamamoto, an officer of the Tokei Tai detachment concerned, give all the relevant details. They confirm that only sixty-three of the total number executed were brought before a court-martial and that, in any event, the trials were a farce. The remaining 1340 were not tried because 'it would have taken two or three years perhaps and there was no time'.[1]

Later, in the month of August 1944, the Tokei Tai continued its campaign of repression by executing a further hundred and twenty civilians, all Chinese, at Singkawang, West Borneo, of whom only seventeen went through a form of trial after confessions had been obtained by the usual method of torture.

According to the Japanese interpreter, Hayashi, who was concerned in the investigation of this so-called 'Second Plot', it had no existence in fact, and the only motive for the murders appears to have been greed.

In August 1944 I discovered that some Chinese were holding a meeting in Singkawang. I reported this to my superior, Okajima, who gave me a list of fifty people to arrest. After arresting them I interrogated them. After the electric and water treatments had been applied they admitted conspiring to overthrow the Japanese Military Government. I took part in the torturing. In my opinion all these hundred and twenty people had committed no crime and had been involved in no conspiracy. They were arrested on account of their wealth. The whole affair was a plot executed by three members of the Tokei Tai and myself. The confessions purporting to have been made by the suspects during interrogation were, in reality, drawn up by the Tokei Tai beforehand, and were only signed by their supposed authors after torture. We anticipated that the death sentence would be given on the strength of these reports. They were most wealthy and important people and it was, therefore,

[1] See Appendix, page 324.

better to kill them. Their money and valuables were confiscated by the Tokei Tai.

In September 1944 a reprisal was ordered by General Tanaka against the inhabitants of Loeang and Sermata, two small islands east of Timor, because two or three members of the Kempei Tai had been murdered by the native population upon whom they had imposed a veritable reign of terror.

The Japanese military police operating in this area had been applying their usual methods of interrogation, torture and punishment. Burning with cigarettes, the water test, hanging, kneeling on sharp stones, and, in many cases, summary execution without trial.

The Rajah of Loeang was ordered by the Japanese to find the leader of the so-called 'rebels'; as he failed to do so, he was executed. Eventually no less than ninety-six islanders were executed as part of this reprisal. These were all innocent victims as the real murderers were never discovered.

Describing the killing of some of these natives on the island of Moa, a Japanese lieutenant has given this description. 'The natives were killed by bayoneting, three at a time, by twenty-one Japanese soldiers. After the execution I organized a brothel in which I forced native girls to act as prostitutes *as a punishment for the deeds of their fathers.*'[1]

In Portuguese Timor the Japanese behaved in the same fashion. Most of the inhabitants were interned and conditions in the camps were deplorable. In December 1942, at Atsabe, during a Japanese attack on the Australian troops, who were defending the island, between fifty and sixty natives were used as a screen, many of whom were killed. In several villages in the vicinity of Mount Katrai the Japanese troops set the native huts on fire and shot down the women and children as they ran out.

Neither New Guinea nor even the remote Solomon Islands escaped the Japanese terror.

[1] Author's italics.

Within a few hours of their landing at Milne Bay in the south-east corner of Papua (New Guinea) the Japanese troops attacked the unarmed natives, including women and children, near the villages of Lilihoa and Wandala West, where they committed murder and rape on an extensive scale.

They lay in wait underneath the native houses, captured the occupants as they came out and killed them on the spot. Others they led away for questioning. If no satisfactory information was obtained from them, they too were killed.

In this district the Japanese troops killed, without any justification whatsoever, fifty-nine male and female natives, in addition to murdering thirty-six Australian prisoners of war, as already described in Chapter VI. Many of the natives, including women, were shockingly mutilated and some were used for bayonet fighting practice while still alive.[1]

In his report on these atrocities Mr Justice Webb found that

> . . . each of the killings of these natives constituted a breach by the Japanese armed forces of the rules of warfare and was an atrocity, seeing that in every case the killing was carried out with savage brutality. . . . Japan's reasons for her reserve of Article 44 of the Hague Rules are apparent from her conduct towards the unfortunate natives who refused to act as guides to her troops at Milne Bay. Even had she a right to their services in that way, there is no evidence that they refused them, and no justification for bayoneting and shooting them without trial.

In July 1942 the Japanese made another landing, this time in the Buna area, and advanced southwards into central New Guinea. A party of five Australian airmen, one of whom was wounded, and twenty-five native soldiers were on the march when they were joined by three missionaries, two of whom

[1] The shocking details of this massacre are given in the text of Mr Justice Webb's report to the Australian Commonwealth Government on Japanese atrocities in New Guinea, the Solomons and adjacent islands.

THE KNIGHTS OF BUSHIDO

were women. Later during the march, near a place called Dobadura, the party was fired upon by the Japanese and dispersed in different directions. What happened to the two women is set out in Mr Justice Webb's report in these words:

> After wandering in the jungle throughout that day and night they found themselves back at Dobadura soon after daybreak. At first they met friendly natives but later, hostile natives handed them over to the Japanese at Popindetta. The Japanese retained them for one night, and next day took them to the Haruru coffee plantation where they dug a hole about three feet deep. When the hole was almost finished a Japanese soldier escorting one of the women seized and hugged her. She struggled and almost got out of his grip when he thrust his bayonet deep into her side. She screamed and fell. At that moment the other missionary hid her face in a cloth or towel and the Japanese escorting her drove his bayonet through her neck. The Japanese then picked up the two bodies and threw them into the hole. On 25th February 1943 the bodies were disinterred in the presence of two doctors.

War crimes were committed, also, by the Japanese troops on the isolated island of Guadalcanal at the southern end of the Solomons group.

A native boy was questioned by a Japanese officer for information about the American troops, but without any satisfactory result as the boy refused to say anything. The officer then had the boy's hands tied with fish lines and bayoneted him eight times. One of the bayonet thrusts pierced his neck and severed his tongue. He was left for dead, but was picked up later by other natives and taken to the American lines. He partially regained his power of speech and was awarded the George Medal.

A month later, in the same district, other atrocities were committed in contravention of Article 46 of the Hague Rules[1] and these are also described in Mr Justice Webb's report.

[1] Article 46 provided that 'family honour and rights, the lives of persons and private property, as well as religious convictions and practices must be respected'.

I find that about August 1942 two Roman Catholic priests, a Dutchman, an American and two Roman Catholic nuns, aged twenty-five and thirty-five, were bayoneted in the village of Tasimboko by the Japanese armed forces. The bodies of the two nuns were naked when found. A third nun about sixty years old, had been allowed to escape. . . . As the young nuns were stripped naked and the elderly nun allowed to escape I am satisfied that the two nuns bayoneted were also raped.

By June 1945 the position of the Japanese forces in Burma had become precarious. For some months British paratroops had been operating with guerrillas behind the Japanese lines at Tenasserim in the area between Moulmein and the Dali Forest, and the commander of the Japanese 33rd Division decided to send an expedition to the area.

On its arrival a preliminary sweep was made by 3rd Battalion of 215 Regiment. Very little information, however, was obtained about the guerrilla forces and the regimental commander mounted an operation against Kalagon in order to destroy the paratroopers and dacoits in the area who, it was suspected, were receiving assistance from the local inhabitants.

At a conference held before the start of the operation he told the commanding officer of 3rd Battalion that if necessary he had authority to 'kill the inhabitants of Kalagon'.[1] Before the expedition left its base it was joined by the OC Moulmein detachment of Kempei Tai, and four NCOs from his unit.

On the following morning the battalion moved off, and arriving at Kalagon on 7th July occupied the village. By 4 p.m. all the inhabitants had been rounded up, the men being confined in the mosque and the women and children locked up in the adjoining buildings.

Several villagers were then interrogated by the Kempei Tai to the accompaniment of some of their usual methods of torture. The so-called investigation was carried on throughout the night during which men and women were beaten and

[1] See Appendix, page 326.

brutally ill-treated in other ways. Eight were taken off by the Kempei Tai to their own headquarters for further 'treatment'.

The next morning the battalion commander held an officers' conference and gave orders that the village should be destroyed and the inhabitants, men, women and children massacred.

That same afternoon they were tied together in batches of from five to ten and taken out to nearby wells. There they were loosed, tied up individually, blindfolded, bayoneted and thrown into the wells irrespective of whether they were alive or dead. The Japanese troops then pounded the bodies in the wells with bamboo poles. In this way 3rd Battalion 'disposed' of over six hundred villagers.

Miraculously, two victims who had been thrown into one of the wells managed to escape, and they gave evidence when the battalion commander and thirteen others were subsequently brought to trial before a British Military Court held in Burma.

On 9th July the Japanese force left Kalagon to search the Dali forest but they returned two days later, pillaged and burned down the village, and left on the 12th July taking with them ten women who had been spared. These were never seen again.

At the trial it was argued by the defence that the villagers of Kalagon had been actively assisting British paratroopers and guerrillas operating in the area and that this justified the Japanese taking reprisals against them. It was contended that the annihilation of the inhabitants of Kalagon was not only a justifiable reprisal but also a military necessity[1] as part of the Japanese operations to clear the area of hostile forces. It was even suggested that there was no difference in the killing of women and children during the bombing of Japanese and other cities by Allied aircraft, and that in all operations of military necessity it was unavoidable that the deaths of women and children should ensue. Kalagon, as a

See Appendix, page 320.

village, was hostile to the Japanese in its entirety and, therefore, the whole of the village should be wiped out.

It is clear, however, that the massacre of the entire population of this village cannot be justified in international law,
and was a war crime. Taken at its best, the evidence in the
hands of the Japanese showed that less than 10 per cent of the
villagers had rendered assistance to the British in a minor
way, not by taking up arms against the common enemy, but
by helping the Allies by doing a certain amount of manual
labour and supplying certain provisions.

It cannot be maintained that the massacre of some six
hundred unarmed men, women and children was either a
legitimate reprisal for such opposition or a military necessity
for the protection of the Japanese troops. So far, at least, as
the women and children were concerned the order was manifestly illegal and the plea of obedience to superior orders,
which was also raised by the defence, cannot be accepted, nor
was it accepted by the Court.

Of all those who suffered under Japanese military occupation no people had better reason to remember its barbarism than the inhabitants of the Andaman Islands, where
many thousands met their death at the hands of the Japanese
forces.

Towards the end of July 1945 the food situation on the
islands was becoming serious. At a conference held at the
Naval headquarters on Andaman Island, it was decided to
transport to Havelock Island, an uninhabited jungle-covered
island off the north-east coast of South Andaman, a number
of 'useless mouths'. They were selected from those who,
owing to their not being employed by the Japanese, had no
ration cards. They included the aged and infirm, women and
children, and a number of malcontents and idlers whom the
Japanese classified as 'undesirables'.

Those selected were first deprived of their household and
private possessions, and then embarked on three ships. When
still some distance from the shore, as they approached

Havelock Island, the Japanese sailors forced many of the passengers into the sea to make their own way to the beaches, with the result that more than a hundred were drowned.

Those who managed to reach the shore were left there, without rations and without implements, to subsist as best they could on shellfish and jungle fruits.

By 21st September, six weeks after their arrival, only eleven out of the original three hundred who landed remained alive. They were collected and taken back to Andaman Island. The remainder had died of starvation or been drowned trying to get away. The Allied investigators who visited the island after the liberation of the Andamans, found the skulls and bones of a hundred and eight men, women and children and, on the beach below the high water mark, the bones of many others.

Eventually the Japanese commander and the Governor of the Andamans, together with seven members of the Naval staff, were brought to trial before a British Military Court after the Japanese surrender and accused of committing a war crime.

The Governor stated in his defence that the transportation of the 'useless mouths' to Havelock Island was part of an emigration plan. The Japanese authorities viewed with concern the food shortage on the Andamans, and had decided that non-workers could no longer be issued with rations since they would, in any event, die of starvation and they were considered 'a menace to the public peace'. Emergency measures became necessary and the emigration plan was put into operation.

It did not seem to have occurred to the Japanese Governor that if they wanted to lessen the number of mouths to be fed in the Andamans they could have sent them somewhere where they could find food. To leave them on an uninhabited island without the wherewithal to live, was plain murder and nothing else.

Another war crime, committed on the Andamans by the Japanese just before they left the islands, was ordered by the military commander on 13th August 1945. Seven hundred and fifty civilians were assembled and transported to Taimugli Island where, according to the order, they were to be shot and buried.

The Japanese officer detailed to carry out this massacre landed the victims on the island together with a firing squad of nineteen soldiers. Graves were dug and the execution then began. The men were shot first, followed by the women and then the children, who had just witnessed the killing of their parents and other relations. The bodies were then thrown into the graves and covered over. On his return to Army headquarters on Andaman Island the officer was told to return to Taimugli, exhume the bodies and burn them. He was also ordered to say, if subsequently questioned on the matter, that the civilians had been taken to Port Campbell and released.

The officer in command of the firing party was subsequently brought to trial before a British Military Court and put forward the usual plea of 'superior orders'. The Court quite rightly, in the circumstances, did not accept the plea as constituting a defence to the charge, but considered it as a mitigating factor when passing sentence.

Nevertheless, it is difficult to understand how they saw fit to pass such a light sentence as two years' imprisonment, for the accused officer executed the civilians, amongst whom were many women and children, in cold blood, and even if he did so in obedience to orders he should not have been dealt with so leniently for his share in such a revolting crime.

U

CHAPTER XIV

THE KEMPEI TAI

The practice of torturing prisoners of war and civilians prevailed wherever Japanese troops were in occupation and at many places, also, in Japan.

The Japanese indulged in the practice throughout the war, and there was so much uniformity in the methods used that there can be no doubt that it was the result of a definite policy adopted by the armed forces with the knowledge and approval of the Imperial Government.

Army and Navy units all used the same methods, but the torturers *par excellence* were the dreaded Kempei Tai, the Japanese counterpart of the Nazi Gestapo.

The Kempei Tai, however, unlike the Gestapo were the Army's Military Police administered by the War Ministry, and a Kempei Tai training school, where many of these methods of interrogation were learnt and practised, was maintained and operated in Japan by the same Ministry.

The Kempei Tai had full powers of arrest and investigation over both civilians and military, and in their particular brand of interrogation under torture they were past masters. Like the German Gestapo, they had obtained plenty of experience before World War II, for the Japanese Empire had been engaged in some kind of warfare since 1931 and the Kempei Tai had had plenty of time in which to perfect their technique.

The captured copy of a Japanese Army training manual also confirms other formidable evidence that torture was officially approved as a necessary aid to interrogation in certain circumstances.

This manual was entitled *Notes for the Interrogation of Prisoners of War*, and was issued by the Japanese Hayashi

Division in Burma on 6th August 1943. The following are a
few extracts from this illuminating treatise:

> Care must be exercised when making use of rebukes, invec-
> tives or torture as it will result in his telling falsehoods and
> making a fool of you.[1]
> The following are the methods normally to be adopted:
>
> (a) *Torture.* This includes kicking, beating and anything
> connected with physical suffering. *This method is only to
> be used when everything else has failed as it is the most clumsy.*[2]
> Change the interrogating officer after using violent tor-
> ture, and good results can be obtained if the new officer
> questions in a sympathetic manner.
>
> (b) *Threats.*
> (1) Hints of future physical discomforts, for example,
> torture, murder, starvation, solitary confinement,
> deprivation of sleep.
> (2) Hints of future mental discomforts, for example,
> not to be allowed to send letters, not to be given the
> same treatment as the other prisoners of war, to be
> kept back to the last in the event of an exchange of
> prisoners.

Among the more common kinds of torture practised by the
Kempei Tai were the following: the water treatment, burning, electric shocks, the knee spread, suspension, kneeling on
sharp instruments and flogging.

Thousands of Allied prisoners of war, and still more
civilians in the territories occupied by the Japanese, experienced excruciating torture at the hands of the Kempei Tai
and many hundreds died as a result of it. It is impossible to
appreciate what these unfortunate and innocent victims of

---

[1] This is known to all whose duty it is to get reliable information when
interrogating prisoners of war, as wise counsel. It was not, however, intended
that the Kempei Tai should always follow it. Their object was, often, to obtain
a confession of some sort during the interrogation of a victim and on such
occasions they cared not whether it was true or false.

[2] The words in italics were underlined in the captured copy.

Japanese brutality suffered unless a brief description is given of the principal methods employed.[1]

The Water Treatment

This was almost invariably applied. The victim was bound, or otherwise secured, in a prone position and water was forced through his mouth and nostrils into his lungs until he lost consciousness. Pressure was then applied, sometimes by jumping upon his abdomen, to force the water out. The usual practice was to revive the victim and repeat the process as required.

Burning

Torture by burning was practised extensively. This was generally inflicted by burning the victim's body with lighted cigarettes or cigars, but in some cases lighted candles, hot irons, burning oil and scalding water were used. The application of heat was usually made to sensitive parts of the body, such as the nostrils, the eardrums, the navel, the sexual organs, and, in the case of women, to the breasts.

Electric Shock

Electric current was applied generally to the most sensitive parts of the body, as in the burning torture.

The Knee Spread

This was a very frequent method of torture. The victim, with his hands tied behind his back, was forced to kneel with a pole, sometimes as much as three inches in diameter, inserted behind both knee joints so as to spread them as pressure was applied to his thighs, sometimes by jumping on them. The result of this torture was to separate the knee joints and so cause intense pain.

Suspension

Another very common form. The body of the victim was

[1] See also the section of illustrations by Leo Rawlings, following page 160.

suspended by the wrists, arms, legs or neck, and at times in such a manner as to strangle him or pull the joints from their sockets. This method was sometimes combined with flogging during suspension.

Kneeling on Sharp Instruments

A very painful form of torture. The edges of square blocks were mostly used as the sharp instruments. The victim was made to kneel on the sharp edges for hours at a time without relief. If he moved, he was flogged.

Removal of Nails

The removal of finger nails and toe nails, usually pulled out with pliers, was not uncommon, and the well known Chinese torture of driving small bamboo chips under the nails was also frequently practised.

Finger Bandaging

The fingers were bandaged together with a stick placed between each one. Extra pressure could then be applied by tightening the bandage by means of a piece of cord. This was extremely painful, and if it did not fracture the fingers they remained bruised and swollen for several days.

In addition to these standard methods of torture used by the armed forces and the Kempei Tai in every theatre of war and in all the occupied territories, Allied prisoners of war and civilians suffered many other forms of inhumane treatment and cruelty, the most common of which was flogging.

It was universally used at all prisoner of war and civilian internment camps, in all the prisons, in the labour camps, on board the prison ships and at all Kempei Tai headquarters. It was indulged in freely by the guards with the approval, and often under the direction, of the camp commandant. Special instruments were used in many of the camps, such as pieces of wood about the size of a baseball bat. Prisoners were sometimes forced to beat other prisoners, and they received internal injuries, broken bones and lacerations of the skin. Frequently they were beaten into unconsciousness, revived and then beaten again. Many were even flogged to death.

Among the Kempei Tai's torturers there were some individualists who invented variations of their own. One Malay Indian, who was a magistrate at Kuala Trengganu, was accused by the Kempei Tai of being a spy. He was left tied up to the leg of a table all night, and in the morning was nearly kicked to death. Later he was buried up to his neck and submerged in drums of dirty water. He described these last two incidents as follows:

> They brought me outside and buried me in the ground leaving just my head above ground. I was then made to close my eyes. When I did so one of the Kempei Tai men put his sword against my throat as if to cut it, and kept it there for some minutes. After that I was unburied and left out in the sun for the rest of the day. On the third day they put me in a benzine drum with forty gallons of oily water. They placed the lid on top of the drum and when I could not breathe any longer I tried to escape from the water. Using my full strength I managed to jerk the lid and it fell to the ground.

In Penang also the Kempei Tai used some unusual methods of torture on hundreds of innocent citizens with the object of forcing a confession from the victim that he was a Communist, or a spy, or in unlawful possession of a radio set. Two women were tied by a rope to a motor-cycle and towed naked round the prison yard.

Mental torture was commonly employed. A striking example of this was given in evidence before the Tokyo Tribunal, when witnesses testified about the ill-treatment which the Doolittle airmen received from the Kempei Tai after their capture.

After having been subjected to all the standard forms of torture they were taken, one at a time, marched blindfold for a considerable distance and then halted. The victim then heard voices and marching feet, the sound of a squad halting and loading their rifles as a firing party would.

A Japanese officer then approached the American pilot and said: 'We are the Knights of Bushido, of the Order of the Rising Sun. We do not execute at sunset but at sunrise.' The prisoner was then marched back to his cell and told that unless he talked before dawn he would be executed.

During 1943 and 1944 the Kempei Tai were busy throughout Malaya trying to break up the resistance movement against the Japanese military occupation, and hundreds of suspects were interrogated under torture.

Mrs Kathigasu helped many members of the Resistance by giving them supplies, clothing and money. In August 1943 she was arrested by the Kempei Tai, and taken to the Central Police Station in Ipoh, where she remained in custody for three and a half months.

She had been betrayed by one of the members of the underground organization to which she belonged, and every effort was made during her incarceration at the Central Police Station to get her to disclose the names of other members of the Resistance who were hiding in the Cameron Highlands on the borders of Perak and Piang.

This she steadfastly refused to do despite repeated torturing by Kempei Tai Sergeant Yoshimura, who was in charge of the local detachment. During those three months she was subjected to the water treatment and red hot irons were applied to her legs and back. Needles were pushed up under her finger nails, and she was continually beaten with bamboo canes. She was hung upside down by one leg for hours at a time and suffered many other indescribable tortures.

As none of these methods had yielded any results by the middle of November, she was taken from the Police Station to the Kempei Tai headquarters in the Gopang Road and there charged with listening to the radio news at Popan, the place where she had been arrested. After being charged she was again questioned regarding assistance which she had given to the 'anti-Japanese campaign'.

She still refused to give any information, and what then happened was told by her when giving evidence at the trial of Sergeant Yoshimura in Ipoh on 11th February 1946.

> My young daughter was hung from a tree about ten to twelve feet high, under which there was a blazing fire. She remained suspended there while I was tied to a post close by and beaten with a stick until it broke in two.
>
> Sergeant Yoshimura kept shouting to me to speak out, but speaking out, as I and my daughter well knew, meant death for hundreds of resistance people up in the hills. My child answered for me. 'Be very brave, Mummy, do not tell, we will both die and Jesus will wait for us in Heaven above.'
>
> On hearing those words I told the sergeant that he could cut the ropes and burn my child. I told him that my answer was 'No', and that I would never tell. All I can remember is that as they were about to cut the rope God answered my prayer. A Japanese officer who had arrived on the scene took pity, and ordered the sergeant to take down my child. She was sent home, and I was sent back to my cell.
>
> I stayed over a month at the MPHQ, when I was sent back to prison.

She was later tried by the Japanese and sentenced to death, but this sentence was commuted to one of penal servitude for life.

It is not proposed to give any further details of Kempei Tai brutality, or other examples of the reign of terror which accompanied them wherever they went. To describe one is to describe all.

In his opening speech for the prosecution in the 'Double Tenth' Trial, which opened at Singapore on 18th March 1946, Lieutenant-Colonel Colin Sleeman said this:

> It is with no little diffidence and misgiving that I approach my description of the facts and events in this case. To give an

accurate description of the misdeeds of these men it will be necessary for me to describe actions which plumb the very depths of human depravity and degradation. The keynote of the whole of this case can be epitomized by two words—unspeakable horror.

Horror, stark and naked, permeates every corner and angle of the case from beginning to end, devoid of relief or palliation. I have searched, I have searched diligently, amongst a vast mass of evidence to discover some redeeming feature, some mitigating factor in the conduct of these men which would elevate the story from the level of pure horror and bestiality, and ennoble it, at least, upon the plane of tragedy. I confess that I have failed.[1]

Those words describe, as no others could, the story of the Kempei Tai, a tale of unspeakable horror, and it is not surprising that the learned prosecutor could not find a single redeeming feature—for none exists.

---

[1] A full account of one of the Kempei Tai's most infamous exploits, the 'Double Tenth' investigation at Changi Gaol, Singapore, is given in 'The Double Tenth Trial', edited by C. Sleeman and S. C. Silkin, and published by William Hodge and Company, Ltd.

CHAPTER XV

RETRIBUTION

I. THE TRIAL OF JAPANESE MAJOR WAR CRIMINALS

On 7th October 1942 a Debate was initiated in the House of Lords by Lord Maugham, who raised the question of establishing an International Criminal Court for the trial of certain war crimes after the end of hostilities.

He reminded the House that both Great Britain and the United States of America were 'pledged to the principle that retribution for war crimes' was among the major purposes of the war, and urged that action should be taken at once to set up 'a channel of organized justice' by which the trial of those responsible for such crimes could be accomplished.

Lord Maugham emphasized the need for prompt action, as delay would mean the escape of the guilty. He reminded the House of the failure of the Allies to bring war criminals to justice after World War I, and of the futility of the Leipzig Trials. If the war criminals of World War II were not to go free, then machinery must be set up to apprehend them, and courts to try them.

When replying to the debate, Lord Simon, the Lord Chancellor, made the following announcement: 'It is proposed', he said, 'to set up with the least possible delay a United Nations Commission for the Investigation of War Crimes.'[1]

This Commission would investigate war crimes committed against nationals of the United Nations, directing its attention particularly to organized atrocities. The investigation would cover war criminals irrespective of rank, and its aim would

---

[1] Also known by the initials UNWCC.

be 'to collect material, supported wherever possible by depositions or by other documents, to establish such crimes, especially where they were systematically perpetrated, and to name and identify those responsible for their perpetration'.

A year elapsed, however, before a meeting of Allied and Dominion representatives assembled at the British Foreign Office to discuss the setting up of a War Crimes Commission. The functions and composition of the Commission were settled, and the War Crimes Commission came into being and began its regular sittings in 1944.

At the meeting in the Foreign Office it had been agreed that the War Crimes Commission should be empowered to set up panels which should enjoy the greatest possible degree of autonomy consistent with the central co-ordinating functions of the Commission. On 10th May 1944, the Commission adopted a proposal by the Chinese Ambassador establishing a Far Eastern Sub-Commission as a branch of UNWCC.

On 29th August 1945, the day after the Japanese capitulation, the Chinese Ambassador, as chairman of the Far-Eastern sub-committee at UNWCC, submitted a recommendation to the Commission for the formation of an International Military Tribunal for the trial of the Japanese responsible for 'criminal policies'. Also recommended were the establishment of a Central War Crimes Agency in Japan to collect evidence and to register war criminals, the setting up of a War Crimes Prosecuting Office, and the making of arrangements for the surrender of war criminals to the countries that had charged them.

These recommendations were approved and the International Military Tribunal for the Far East, on which eleven nations were represented, was established by virtue of a special Proclamation by General MacArthur on 19th January 1946.

Twenty-eight accused were brought before the Tribunal upon an Indictment containing fifty-five counts alleging crimes against peace, conventional war crimes, and crimes against humanity between 1st January 1928 and 2nd September 1945. With the opening of the trial in Tokyo on 3rd May 1946, the Declaration of Potsdam regarding Japanese war criminals was implemented. This Declaration had been made by the President of the United States of America, the President of the National Government of the Republic of China, and the Prime Minister of Great Britain, and it was later adhered to by the USSR.

It stated, amongst other things, that although the Allies did not intend that the Japanese should be enslaved as a race or destroyed as a nation, stern justice would be meted out to all war criminals including those who had visited cruelties upon Allied prisoners of war.

On 3rd and 4th May 1946 the lengthy Indictment was read in open court in the presence of all the accused, and the Tribunal then adjourned until 6th May to receive their pleas. All the accused pleaded 'Not guilty' and the Tribunal then fixed 3rd June for the opening of the case for the Prosecution.

The trial turned out to be a Marathon.

The Prosecution's case was duly opened on 3rd June 1946 and closed on 24th January 1947. The presentation of evidence for the Defence went on for eleven months and the trial did not finish until November 1948.

Two of the accused, Matsuoka and Nagano, who were brought before the Tribunal and charged on the opening day, died during the course of the trial. A third, the accused Okawa, was declared unfit to stand his trial and unable to defend himself.

As Article 12 of the Charter, which governed the Tribunal, required 'an expeditious hearing of the issues', and the taking of 'strict measures to prevent any action which would cause any unreasonable delay', the Tribunal thought it expedient to give in its judgment some explanation of the long duration of the trial.

Had it not been for the installation of a system, similar to that used at Nuremberg, by which simultaneous translations of the evidence into English, Chinese, Russian, French and

Japanese could be made, the duration of the trial would have been even longer.

Cross-examination and argument and other incidental proceedings had to be translated the slow way. The period covered by the charges, as the Tribunal explained, was one of intense activity in Japanese affairs both at home and abroad. The Japanese constitution became the subject of a violent struggle for power between the military and civilians who administered it.[1] As had often been the case in Germany, the military faction gained a predominance which enabled them to have their way not only in matters of peace and war but also in the conduct of foreign and internal affairs.

'The struggle between the military and the civil servants was a protracted one,' said the Tribunal. 'Many incidents marked the ebb and flow of the battle and there was seldom agreement between the Prosecution and Defence as to any incident which was the subject of controversy to which a wealth of evidence was directed.' The roles played by all the accused in those events had to be investigated, and every foot of the way was fought.

The Japanese language was also a great practical difficulty, for literal translation from Japanese into English, or vice versa, is seldom possible. Much could merely be paraphrased, and so great were the discrepancies that the Tribunal was forced to set up a Language Arbitration Board to settle matters of disputed interpretation.

The Tribunal also found that many of the Japanese witnesses were prolix and irrelevant, and much of the evidence tendered by the Defence was rejected because it had too little or no probative value. Many of the Prosecution witnesses were, necessarily, cross-examined by a large number of Counsel representing various accused, many of whom covered the same ground again and again.

In addition to all these delays the Tribunal experienced great difficulty with some of the documentary exhibits tendered, particularly because of the absence of many of the

[1] As summarized in Chapter I.

originals of important Japanese records of the Army, Navy, Foreign Office and Cabinet. Frequently what purported to be copies of these documents had to suffice.

The Tribunal commented in its judgment on the fact that the absence of the originals was attributed to burning during bombing raids, and to the deliberate destruction of all records by the Services after the surrender. It seemed strange that documents of such importance should not have been removed to places of safety when bombing commenced or was imminent.

Fortunately for the cause of justice much relevant information which could have been obtained from the missing documents was provided by the voluminous diary kept by the accused Kido. This diary covered all the most important events in Japanese political history from 1930–45, during which time Kido was successively Secretary to the Lord Keeper of the Privy Seal, a Minister of State and finally Lord Keeper of the Privy Seal himself, the permanent confidential adviser to the Emperor upon all matters of State.

All these difficulties, the Tribunal explained, more than doubled the length of the trial.

On 12th November 1948 the Tribunal gave its verdict on all the accused and then passed sentence. Below are set out, in respect of each accused, some particulars of his career, a précis of the Tribunal's verdict, and the sentence awarded.

Araki

At all material times, Araki was an Army officer of high rank. He became a lieutenant-general in 1927, was promoted to general in 1933 and, throughout that time, was prominent in the upper councils of the Army.

A protagonist of the Army's policy of political domination at home and military aggression abroad, he did much to stimulate the warlike spirit of Japanese youth, and as the Minister of War from 1931–4 played an active role in carrying out the campaigns in Manchuria and Jehol.

There was, however, no evidence that he had any responsibility for the war crimes committed by the Japanese forces, and the Tribunal acquitted him of all such charges. He was, nevertheless, convicted, amongst other things, of waging an aggressive war against China and was sentenced to imprisonment for life.

Dohihara

By April 1941 Dohihara had reached the rank of general in the Japanese Army, and had come to be regarded as a specialist on China. From April 1944 until April 1945 he commanded the forces in Malaya, Sumatra, Java, and Borneo. During that period the Allied prisoners of war, within the limits of his command, were treated no better than anywhere else, and many deaths occurred from starvation or malnutrition while the incidence of deficiency diseases was appalling.

It was urged on behalf of the accused that the worsening of Japan's war position in those areas and the breakdown of communications made it impossible to keep the prisoners of war supplied with even the most essential supplies. It is noteworthy, however, that the dreadful conditions in which the prisoners were living were not shared by their captors. Food and medicine, although available, were withheld from the prisoners, according to the evidence, in pursuance of orders for which Dohihara was responsible.

The Tribunal found him guilty of several counts in the Indictment and sentenced him to death by hanging.

Hashimoto

Hashimoto was both soldier and propagandist. After holding an appointment as military attaché abroad he retired temporarily from the Army in 1936 to write a book but reentered it in the following year.

He commanded an artillery regiment at the Rape of Nanking in December 1937, and was also in command of the Japanese forces which shelled the *Ladybird* and *Panay*.

From the beginning he advocated force for the attainment

of all Japan's aims and objectives, and no one was more outspoken in his views on aggression. He had, while in Europe, fallen for government by dictator, and did all in his power to eliminate the party system of parliamentary government in his country.

He was one of the leading conspirators in the plots of March and October 1931 designed to overthrow the existing Government and supplant it with one more favourable to the Army's policy.

He was a prolific pamphleteer, and an intrepid founder of secret societies devoted to the destruction of democratic government.

There was no evidence that he was in any way responsible for the commission of conventional war crimes, that is to say, contravention of the laws and customs of war, and he was acquitted of all the charges alleging such offences. The Tribunal sentenced Hashimoto to imprisonment for life.

Hata

In 1938, and from 1941 to 1944, when he was in command of the Japanese forces in China, atrocities were committed on a large scale by the troops under his command.

In some cases he knew what was going on and took no steps to stop it and, generally, he was indifferent to the sufferings of the Chinese civilians under Japanese occupation.

He took no steps to ascertain whether orders issued for the humane treatment of prisoners of war were being obeyed; indeed he had very good reason to know that they were not. The Tribunal sentenced him to imprisonment for life.

Hiranuma

As a member and one time President of the Privy Council he supported various measures which came before it involving the implementation of the aggressive plans of the military faction. At a meeting of the Jushin[1], held nine days before

[1] A body of senior statesmen called together to advise the Emperor on important policy.

Pearl Harbour to advise the Emperor whether there should be war or peace with the Western powers, he fell in with the majority view and 'advised the strengthening of public opinion against the possibility of a long war'. He was a consistent supporter of the domination policy of Japan in East Asia and the South Seas by warlike means.

The Tribunal found that there was no evidence directly connecting him with the perpetration of war crimes, but sentenced him to life imprisonment in respect of the charges of conspiracy and waging aggressive wars.

Hirota

As Foreign Minister, Prime Minister, and a member of the Council of Senior Statesmen, Hirota participated, from as far back as 1933, in the long-term conspiracy to wage aggressive wars. He consistently agreed to the use of force to obtain fulfilment of the Japanese demands although, in 1941, his advice to the Emperor as a member of the Jushin was against the opening of hostilities against the Western powers.

The Tribunal found that as Foreign Minister, between December 1937 and February 1938, he received reports of the Japanese atrocities after the fall of Nanking and took the matter up with the War Ministry. Assurances were given by the Minister of War that the atrocities would cease.

The Tribunal was of the opinion that Hirota was derelict in his duty in 'not insisting before the Cabinet that immediate action be taken to put an end to the atrocities. He was content to rely on assurances which (there was ample evidence to prove) he knew were not being implemented while hundreds of murders, violations of women, and other atrocities were being committed daily. His inaction amounted to criminal negligence'.

Hirota was sentenced to death by hanging.

Hoshino

There was no evidence to connect him with the commission of war crimes, so the Tribunal acquitted him of all such charges: He was, however, found guilty of conspiring to wage aggressive wars and taking an active part in waging them.

After Tojo became Prime Minister in October 1941, Hoshino was appointed Chief Secretary of the Cabinet, and a member of the War Planning Board. 'From this time he was in close association with all the preparations for the aggressive war . . . shortly to be waged against those countries attacked by Japan in December 1941.'

The Tribunal sentenced him to imprisonment for life.

Itagaki

This Army Officer was in the conspiracy from the beginning and up to the hilt.

In 1931, he was a colonel on the staff of the Kwantung Army and his part in the preparation and execution of the 'Mukden Incident' has already been described in Chapter I.

He was personally concerned in the movement which led to the establishment of the puppet state in Manchukuo and, after he became vice-chief-of-staff of the Kwantung Army, he actively participated in the formation of other puppet regimes in Inner Mongolia and North China. He was Minister of War in the Konoye Cabinet in May 1938, from which time the attacks on China continued and intensified.

Once again he took part in the preliminary moves which preceded the establishment of the puppet regime of Wang Ching-Wei.

It was he who tried to deceive his Emperor and obtain, by a trick,[1] his consent to the use of force against the Soviet Union at Lake Khassan.

A protagonist of Japan's 'New Order' in East Asia and the Pacific, he realized only too well that to bring it about would involve Japan in war with Russia, France and Great Britain, but he was fully prepared for that eventuality.

The Tribunal found that he was guilty of Count 54 of the Indictment which charged him, together with a number of other accused, with ordering, authorizing, and permitting

[1] See Chapter I.

those in charge of the camps and labour units for prisoners of war and civilian internees in Japan and territories under Japanese occupation, habitually to commit breaches of the Laws and Customs of War in respect of the many thousands of prisoners of war and civilian internees under their charge.

From April 1945 until the surrender, Itagaki was commanding the Japanese forces in Java, Sumatra, Malay, Borneo, and the Andaman and Nicobar Islands. As commander-in-chief he was responsible for the supply of food, medicine and hospital facilities for all those in the prisoner of war and civilian internment camps in his area. During that period conditions could hardly have been worse. Many died each day from malnutrition and deficiency diseases and those who survived took months to recover their normal health. Many today are permanent invalids.

Itagaki, in his defence, stated that Allied attacks on Japanese shipping had interfered with communications to such an extent that it was impossible to supply many of the areas. In fact, there were ample supplies available, but the accused argued in the witness box that the Japanese were expecting a long war and had to keep a big reserve.

The Tribunal, in its judgment, said that such an argument was tantamount to a contention that Itagaki was justified, in the circumstances, in treating the prisoners and internees with gross inhumanity.

The Tribunal rejected the defence and said 'by the policy which he adopted he is responsible for the deaths or sufferings of thousands of people whose adequate maintenance was his duty'.

Itagaki was sentenced to death by hanging.

Kaya

This civilian, who was in the Tojo Cabinet, was convicted of the charges which alleged active participation in the preparation for and the waging of aggressive wars in China and against the Western powers.

There was no evidence implicating him in war crimes but

he was sentenced to life imprisonment upon the other counts.

Kido

When Kido became Lord Keeper of the Privy Seal, whose principal duty was to advise the Emperor on political matters, he was able to use his influence to further the aims of the military faction who were bent on war.

Except for a short period, during which the Navy was trying to hold back because of doubts about the successful outcome of a Pacific War, Kido was a leading proponent of aggressive war and was largely responsible for the appointment, by the Emperor, of Tojo as Prime Minister in October 1941. He could have done much to prevent a war had he so desired, but he never advised his Emperor against it.

There was no evidence that he had any responsibility either directly or indirectly for atrocities or other war crimes, indeed his very position as confidential adviser to His Majesty made it impossible. He was, therefore, acquitted of the war crimes charges, but was sentenced by the Tribunal to imprisonment for life for his other activities.

Kimura

In April 1941 Kimura, an Army officer with considerable experience in the War Ministry, was made Vice-Minister of War.

During the early part of the Pacific War he was a member of the Planning Board and the Total War Research Institute, but in August 1944 he became commander-in-chief of the Japanese forces in the Burma area, and remained in command until the day of surrender.

While holding that appointment he allowed prisoners of war in his area to be employed on prohibited work in terrible conditions resulting in the deaths of many thousands. In particular he approved and circulated orders for the employment of such prisoners on the construction of the Burma–Siam Railway.

When he took over his command in August 1944 he had full knowledge of the atrocities which had been committed everywhere by the Japanese forces, and after his arrival such crimes continued unabated. From first to last he took no steps to prevent the commission of atrocities by the troops under his command nor was any disciplinary action ever taken against the offenders.

The Tribunal, in its judgment, dealt with Kimura's criminal responsibility in these words:

> It has been urged in Kimura's defence that when he arrived in Burma he issued orders to his troops to conduct themselves in a proper soldierly manner, and to refrain from ill-treating prisoners. In view of the nature and extent of the ill-treatment of prisoners, in many cases on a large scale within a few miles of his headquarters, the Tribunal finds that Kimura was negligent in his duty to enforce the rules of war.
>
> The duty of an army commander, in such circumstances, is not discharged by the mere issue of routine orders, if indeed such orders were issued. His duty is to take such steps and issue such orders as will prevent, thereafter, the commission of war crimes, and to satisfy himself that such orders are being carried out. This he did not do. Thus he deliberately disregarded his legal duty to take adequate steps to prevent breaches of the laws of war.

The accused was sentenced by the Tribunal to suffer death by hanging.

Koiso

When Koiso became Prime Minister it was known all over the world that the Japanese troops were committing every kind of war crime in all operational theatres.

It would have been impossible for Koiso not to have known of the prevalence and heinousness of such crimes. In any event, he cannot have been in ignorance of the state of affairs after a meeting of the Supreme Council for the Direction of War in October 1944, at which the Foreign Minister, in Koiso's presence, described the Japanese treatment of Allied prisoners of war as 'leaving much to be desired'.

Koiso remained in office as Prime Minister for a further six months, during which time the treatment of prisoners and internees never improved.

The Tribunal regarded Koiso's failure to take any action as 'a deliberate disregard of his duty' and sentenced him to imprisonment for life.

Matsui

By 1933 Matsui had reached the rank of general in the Japanese Army, and in 1935 was placed on the retired list.

In 1937 he was recalled to active duty and appointed to command the Shanghai Expeditionary Force.

Matsui had already considerable experience of military operations in China, for he had been a staff officer in the Kwantung Army, and it can have surprised nobody when he was subsequently made commander-in-chief of the Central China Area Army which included the Japanese Tenth Army and his former command, the Shanghai Expeditionary Force. It was this force which captured Nanking on 13th December 1937.

The long succession of horrible atrocities which followed the capture of the city has already been described in detail in Chapter II. The atrocities began on 13th December 1937, and went on until early in February 1938, during which time thousands of women were raped, about 200,000 people were killed and an enormous but unascertainable quantity of property looted or burned.

Of General Matsui's knowledge of the unspeakable conduct of his troops the Tribunal said this in its judgment:

At the height of these dreadful happenings, on 17th December, Matsui made a triumphal entry into the city and remained there from five to seven days.

From his own observations, and from the reports of his staff, he must have been aware of what was happening. He admits he was told of some degree of misbehaviour of his army by the

Kempei Tai and by consular officials. Daily reports of these atrocities were made to Japanese diplomatic representatives in Nanking who, in turn, reported them to Tokyo. The Tribunal is satisfied that Matsui knew what was happening. He did nothing, or nothing effective, to abate these horrors. He did issue orders before the capture of the city enjoining propriety of conduct upon his troops, and later issued further orders to the same purport.

These orders were of no effect, as is now known, and as he must have known. It was pleaded on his behalf that at this time he was ill. His illness was not sufficient to prevent his conducting the military operations of his command, nor to prevent his visiting the city for days while these atrocities were occurring. He was in command of the army responsible for these happenings. He knew of them. He had the power, as he had the duty, to control his troops and to protect the unfortunate citizens of Nanking. He must be held criminally responsible for his failure to discharge this duty.

The Tribunal sentenced Matsui to death by hanging.

Minami
There was no evidence implicating this accused in the commission of war crimes but the Tribunal found him guilty of conspiring to wage wars of aggression against China and the USSR and sentenced him to life imprisonment.

Muto
This officer in the Japanese Army held a number of important posts including Chief of the Military Affairs Bureau and later, in 1945, chief-of-staff in the Philippines.

He had also been on General Matsui's staff at the time of the Rape of Nanking. Although he knew, as did his commander-in-chief, that atrocities were being committed by the Japanese troops over a period of some seven weeks the Tribunal held that Muto, as a staff officer, was not in a position to take any steps to stop them, and could not be held criminally responsible.

From April 1942 to October 1944, when he became chief-of-staff to General Yamashita in the Philippines, Muto commanded the 2nd Imperial Guards Division in Northern Sumatra. The troops under his command there committed widespread atrocities for which, the Tribunal held, the accused as commander shared responsibility.

The Tribunal took the view that his position whilst holding the appointment of chief-of-staff in the Philippines differed considerably from that which he held under General Matsui; for as chief-of-staff he was in a position to influence policy.

> During his tenure of office a campaign of massacre, torture and other atrocities was waged by the Japanese troops on the civilian population, and prisoners of war and civilian internees were starved, tortured and murdered. Muto shares responsibility for these gross breaches of the Laws of War. We reject his defence that he knew nothing of these occurrences. It is wholly incredible.

Muto was sentenced to death by hanging.

Oka

Promoted to the rank of rear-admiral in the Japanese Navy, Oka became in October 1940 Chief of the Naval Affairs Bureau in the Navy Ministry and in that position actively participated in the formation and execution of the policy to wage aggressive war against China and the Western powers.

There was no satisfactory evidence that he was in any way responsible for the commission of war crimes, and the Tribunal acquitted him of all such charges.

Oka was sentenced to life imprisonment.

Oshima

Although he was an Army officer Oshima came into prominence as a diplomat when he was promoted from military attaché in Berlin to the post of ambassador.

He was a great admirer of Hitler and all his works, and from the commencement of his first appointment in Berlin did everything he could to further the plans of the military faction who were determined on a full military alliance with Germany.

Before he became ambassador, and was merely the senior military attaché, he even went to the lengths of short circuiting his own ambassador, dealing directly with von Ribbentrop.

He was one of the principal conspirators but took no active part in waging either the China or Pacific War, nor did his duties in any way involve him in responsibility for the ill-treatment of prisoners of war and civilian internees.

Oshima was, therefore, acquitted of all the war crimes charges, but was sentenced to imprisonment for life for his part in Japanese aggression.

Sato

The Tribunal found that whilst holding important posts in the Government, and as an army commander, Sato waged wars of aggression. He also knew all about the misbehaviour of the Japanese troops, for the many protests which were made by the Allies all came to the Military Affairs Bureau in which he was Chief of the Military Affairs Section. They were discussed at the meetings held twice a week, which Prime Minister Tojo attended, but the Tribunal held that Sato, who was in a subordinate position, 'could not initiate preventive action against the decision of his Chief'.

Sato was, therefore, acquitted of any responsibility for war crimes, but for his other activities he was sentenced by the Tribunal to life imprisonment.

Shigemitsu

This accused, Mamoru Shigemitsu, had a long and distinguished career in the Japanese diplomatic service, his first post of any importance being the occasion when he was a junior member of the Japanese delegation to the Versailles Peace Conference in 1919.

When war broke out between Great Britain and Germany

[297]

Shigemitsu was the Japanese Ambassador in London, and gained universal respect for his ability and his obvious friendship towards the British.

The Tribunal found that he had never conspired to wage any aggressive war. On the contrary, he had repeatedly tendered advice to his chiefs in Tokyo in direct opposition to their aggressive policies.

Because, subsequent to 1943 when he became Foreign Minister, Japan was engaged in an aggressive war in the Pacific the Tribunal found him guilty of 'waging a war of aggression'. He was also found guilty of 'deliberately and recklessly disregarding his legal duty to take adequate steps' to have the treatment of prisoners of war investigated. Because of its importance, and the fact that Shigemitsu was awarded a light sentence, that part of the Tribunal's judgment which dealt with his failure to press for the investigation of the conditions and treatment of prisoners of war is set out here in full.

During the period from April 1943 to April 1945, when Shigemitsu was Foreign Minister, the Protecting Powers transmitted to the Japanese Foreign Office protest after protest which they had received from the Allies. These were grave protests forwarded to the Protecting Powers by responsible agencies of state and in many cases accompanied by a wealth of detail. The matters of protest were, (1) inhumane treatment of prisoners, (2) refusal to permit the Protecting Powers to inspect all save a few prisoner of war camps, (3) refusal to permit the representatives of the Protecting Powers to interview prisoners without the presence of a Japanese witness, and (4) failure to provide information as to the names and location of prisoners.

The protests were dealt with in the Foreign Ministry in the first place. Where necessary they were passed to other ministries with requests for information to enable the Foreign Minister to reply to them.

One cannot read the long correspondence between the Japanese Foreign Office and the Protecting Powers without suspecting that there was a sinister reason for the failure of the Japanese Military to supply their Foreign Office with satisfactory answers to these protests, or at the least that there was a case for an independent inquiry by an agent other than the military, whose conduct was in question.

Protest after protest went unanswered, or was only answered after months of unexplained delay. Reminder after reminder by the Protecting Powers went unnoticed. Those protests which were answered were met, without exception, by a denial that there was anything to complain of.

Now it was in the highest degree unlikely that every one of the complaints made by responsible people and accompanied by circumstance and detail was completely unjustified. Moreover, the refusal of the military to permit inspection of camps, their refusal to permit representatives of the Protecting Powers to interview prisoners without the presence of a Japanese witness, and their failure to provide details of the prisoners in their hands gave rise to the suspicion that they had something to hide.

We do no injustice to Shigemitsu when we hold that the circumstances, as he knew them, made him suspicious that the treatment of the prisoners was not as it should have been. Indeed a witness gave evidence for him to that effect. Thereupon he took no adequate steps to have the matter investigated although he, as a member of the Government, bore overhead responsibility for the welfare of the prisoners. He should have pressed the matter, if necessary to the point of resigning, in order to quit himself of a responsibility which he suspected was not being discharged.

Such was the majority judgment of the Tribunal.

Its Indian member, Mr Justice Pal, delivered a very lengthy dissenting judgment holding 'that each and every one of the accused must be found not guilty of each and every one of the charges in the Indictment and should be acquitted of all those charges'.

His findings, however, were not based solely upon the evidence nor did they have any solid foundation upon the merits of the case. They appear to have been influenced by other considerations.

Mr Justice Pal's 'Recommendations', as they are designated in the written copy of his judgment, were given because, as he said, 'as a judicial tribunal, we cannot behave in any manner which may justify the feeling that the setting up of the Tribunal was only for the attainment of an objective which was essentially political, though cloaked by a judicial appearance'.

The opinion is widely held that the majority judgment in respect of Shigemitsu was unjust as he had demonstrated throughout his career that he was opposed to war and only entered the Japanese Cabinet to serve the cause of peace. But it is difficult to avoid the conclusion that if he had been a stronger character he could have done more than he did to disapprove of Japan's misdeeds.

It is evident from the light sentence which was awarded by the Tribunal that it did not regard his guilt as very grievous. In mitigation of sentence they took into account that he was in no way involved in the formulation of the conspiracy, that he took no part in waging a war of aggression before 1943, by which time his country had already been involved for some time in a war which vitally affected her future and in which 'the Military completely controlled Japan while he was Foreign Minister so that it would have required great resolution for any Japanese to condemn them'.

Furthermore the Tribunal, when sentencing Shigemitsu to seven years' imprisonment, stipulated that it should run from the date of arraignment, which was 3rd May 1946, so that by the time the sentence was passed two and a half years of it had already run.

Shimada

Until October 1941, when he became Navy Minister in Tojo's Cabinet, Shimada was an ordinary Naval officer and employed solely on Naval duties.

From then on, until the attack on Pearl Harbour and other places on 7th December 1941, he took part in all the major Governmental decisions on war policy.

The Tribunal held, however, that he had not been proved

to have any responsibility for the many 'disgraceful massacres and murders' of prisoners committed by members of the Japanese Navy in the islands of the Pacific Ocean, and on survivors of torpedoed ships, and acquitted him of all the charges alleging the commission of war crimes.

Nevertheless, for his participation in the planning and waging of an aggressive war between October 1941 and August 1944, the Tribunal sentenced him to life imprisonment.

Shiratori

This accused had been in the diplomatic service since 1914, and while ambassador in Rome from 1938 he collaborated with the accused Oshima, then ambassador in Berlin, to procure an atmosphere favourable for an all-out military alliance between his country and Nazi Germany. He even threatened to resign if the objectives of the military faction were not achieved.

He was an advocate of hostilities against China, an attack on Russia and, if necessary, war against the Western powers. Owing to illness he ceased to play any important part in national affairs after 1941, and it is somewhat surprising, therefore, that it was decided to bring him to trial.

The Tribunal sentenced him to life imprisonment.

Susuki

This accused was an Army officer and attained the rank of major-general in November 1937.

He was found not responsible for the commission of atrocities and other war crimes, but as President of the Planning Board he regularly attended the Liaison Conferences and actively supported the aggressive war policy.

For these activities the Tribunal sentenced him to be imprisoned for life.

Togo

There were only two comparatively short periods during

which Togo was in a position to play a leading role in the conspiracy to wage aggressive wars; from October 1941 to September 1942, and during the last few months before the Japanese surrender, when he was Foreign Minister.

Between September 1942 and 1945 he took no part in public life. The Tribunal found that he could not be held responsible in any way, even by neglect of duty, for the commission of war crimes.

He was found guilty, however, of conspiring to wage an aggressive war and sentenced to be imprisoned for twenty years with effect from 3rd May 1946, the date of arraignment.

Tojo

Perhaps the most prominent and the most blameworthy of all the Japanese major war criminals was Hideki Tojo.

From 1937, when he was the chief-of-staff of the Kwantung Army, he was in close association with those Japanese, and particularly the military faction, who were planning for the domination of China, East Asia and the Pacific.

He made plans for an attack on the Soviet Union and an extension of the military operations in China. Early in 1938 he vacated active command and became Vice-Minister of War, becoming Minister of War in July 1940.

In October 1941 he formed a Cabinet, and continued in office for almost three years. His part in the incidents which preceded the attack on Pearl Harbour has already been described in some detail in Chapter I.

The Tribunal found that he bore 'major responsibility for Japan's criminal attacks on her neighbours'. His responsibility for the ill-treatment of prisoners-of-war and civilian internees was grave indeed, and was summed up by the Tribunal in these words:

> The barbarous treatment of prisoners and internees was well known to Tojo. He took no adequate steps to punish offenders and to prevent the commission of similar offences in the future.
> His attitude towards the Bataan Death March gives the key to his conduct towards these captives. He knew in 1942 some-

thing of the conditions of that march and that many prisoners had died as a result of those conditions. He did not call for a report on the incident. When in the Philippines in 1943 he made perfunctory inquiries about the march but took no action. No one was punished.

His explanation is that the commander of a Japanese army in the field is given a mission in the performance of which he is not subject to specific orders from Tokyo.

Thus the head of the Government of Japan knowingly and wilfully refused to perform the duty which lay upon that Government of enforcing performance of the laws of war.

To cite another outstanding example. He advised that prisoners of war should be used in the construction of the Burma–Siam Railway, designed for strategic purposes. He made no proper arrangements for billeting and feeding the prisoners, or for caring for those who became sick in that trying climate. He learned of the poor condition of the prisoners employed on the project, and sent an officer to investigate. We know the dreadful conditions which that investigator must have found in the many camps along the railway. The only step taken as a result of the investigation was the trial of one company commander for the ill-treatment of prisoners.

Nothing was done to improve conditions. Deficiency diseases and starvation continued to kill off the prisoners until the end of the project. Statistics relative to the high death rate from malnutrition and other causes in prisoner of war camps were discussed at conferences over which Tojo presided.

The shocking condition of the prisoners in 1944, when Tojo's Cabinet fell, and the enormous number who had died from lack of food and medicines, is conclusive proof that Tojo took no proper steps to care for them.

We have referred to the attitude of the Japanese Army towards the Chinese prisoners of war. Since the Japanese Government did not recognize the 'Incident' as war, it was argued that the rules of war did not apply to the fighting and that Chinese captives were not entitled to the status and rights of prisoners of war. Tojo knew and did not disapprove of that shocking attitude.

He bears responsibility, also, for the instruction that prisoners who did not work should not eat. We have no doubt that his repeated insistence on this instruction conduced in large measure to the sick and wounded being driven to work, and to the suffering and deaths which resulted.

It was not surprising that after such a judgment the Tribunal sentenced Tojo to death.

Umezu

The last of the accused, in alphabetical order, was an Army officer named Umezu. There was overwhelming evidence to convict him of the conspiracy to wage aggressive war and of having taken a leading part in the waging of war against China and the Western powers, for he was commander-in-chief of the Kwantung Army from 1939 until July 1944 when he became Chief of the Army General Staff, an appointment which he held until the end of the war.

There was no evidence to implicate him in the commission of atrocities, or other war crimes, so he did not suffer the supreme penalty.

The Tribunal sentenced Umezu to be imprisoned for life.

II. THE TRIAL OF OTHER JAPANESE WAR CRIMINALS[1]

The task of identifying, locating and apprehending the many thousands of other suspected Japanese war criminals was a colossal undertaking, for which an elaborate Allied war crimes machinery had to be developed.

The main burden of this task fell upon the British and American military authorities and each country set up a special war crimes organization, the British in Singapore and the Americans in Tokyo.

Although their primary function was to deal with all cases in which war crimes had been committed against their own nationals, they co-operated with all the other nations concerned, and the information and evidence which they gathered together was made available to all.

[1] For the official account of the machinery set up to bring war criminals to trial see the *History of the United Nations War Crimes Commission*, HMSO, 1948.

BRITISH

The investigation and trial of those who had committed war crimes against British nationals became the responsibility of General Headquarters, Allied Land Forces, South-East Asia, which had to operate over a very large area: Singapore, Malaya, Siam, French Indo-China, Burma, Hong Kong, Tientsin, Shanghai, British North Borneo, the Netherlands East Indies, the Andaman and Nicobar Islands. A War Crimes Group was formed comprising a number of investigation teams, a registry section, a co-ordinating section and a legal section.

The entire organization was eventually brought under the control of the Judge Advocate General's Branch directly responsible to the Military Deputy of the Judge Advocate General in London.

The way in which these organizations functioned is described in the *History of the United Nations War Crimes Commission.*

When Japan surrendered, the Japanese forces in South-East Asia passed into the hands of the Allies, and with them the staff of prisoner of war camps, whose brutality was notorious. Photographs were taken of all these men, and the prints were circulated, particularly to Allied ex-prisoners of war at home, who then made affidavits concerning the treatment they had received. The person making the affidavit would be shown about six prints, one of which was of the person concerned in the charge, and from this photographic identification parade the individual photographs were identified. More than ten thousand of such photographs were taken and, when identified, were sent with the affidavits to the Registry at Singapore from where they were sent out to the investigation teams.

These teams operated throughout the whole area, sometimes in areas of comparative civilization and sometimes deep in the jungle. With the help of photographs, affidavits, local evidence and sometimes of voluntary statements made by the accused, they were able to build up cases which were sent to the Legal Section of the War Crimes Group.

Where a *prima facie* case was proved to exist the Legal Section

W

brought the accused to trial. Ex-prisoners from England attended the trial as witnesses but where their presence was not practicable, the affidavits made at home were used in evidence. All cases were not so simple and many suspects remained untraced owing to their having been transferred to another theatre prior to the capitulation, but efforts to trace them proceeded successfully.

By February 1948, nine hundred and thirty-one Japanese war criminals had been tried by British military courts.

UNITED STATES

A directive of the United States Joint Chiefs of Staff ordered the investigation, apprehension and detention of all persons suspected of war crimes, and made provision for handing over war criminals wanted by other nations. It also empowered General MacArthur, the Supreme Commander of the Allied Powers, to set up special international courts and prescribe rules of procedure for them.

By the same directive the military commanders of any nation taking part in the occupation of Japan were authorized to set up military courts for the trial of war criminals.

In pursuance of the directive two war crimes offices were established. The first, which was for the prosecution of Japanese major war criminals already dealt with in the first section of this Chapter, was called the 'International Prosecution Section'.

The other office was for the investigation of all other war crimes and the apprehension and prosecution of all those responsible for them.

The first branch of this office was opened as the War Crimes Branch of the United States GHQ Army Forces Pacific, and two regional branches were set up, one in Yokohama and the other in Manila.

In addition to these agencies, three more United States war crimes organizations were set up in China, India, and the Pacific Ocean islands.

[306]

This vast network covering an immense space performed outstanding achievements. It identified, located, apprehended and brought to trial thousands of Japanese war criminals. Thus, the Investigation Division investigated nearly three thousand cases. Its work made possible many trials, the most important of which was that concerning the Japanese General Yamashita.[1]

The investigations covered the following theatres of war: Burma, Siam, French Indo-China, Malaya, Singapore, Sumatra, Java, Borneo and the Celebes.

Another important case investigated was that of the Burma–Siam Railway on which some six hundred and forty United States Army, Navy and Marine prisoners of war were employed.

Many cases of the illegal execution of American airmen in Burma and French Indo-China were also investigated, and the perpetrators brought to trial, many of them before British military courts.

AUSTRALIA

The first information received by the Australian military authorities regarding the commission of war crimes by the Japanese forces against the Australian forces was after the Japanese invasion of New Britain in January 1942. The information came from survivors who escaped to the mainland.

Information of other atrocities committed by the Japanese in Amboina was also brought to Australia by soldiers who had managed to escape capture.

As a result of this information action was taken to obtain statements from all serving officers and men who were able to give information regarding breaches by the Japanese of the rules of warfare.

In June 1944 the Australian Government appointed a commissioner to enquire into war crimes perpetrated by the

[1] *History of the United Nations War Crimes Commission*, page 384.

Japanese against Australian military personnel. The commissioner appointed was Sir William Webb, Chief Justice of the Supreme Court of Queensland, who was subsequently appointed President of the International Military Tribunal for the Far East which tried the major Japanese war criminals at Tokyo.

After the Japanese surrender in 1945 much further evidence of the commission of war crimes by the Japanese was obtained from liberated prisoners of war and ex-internees, which resulted in the apprehension and identification of many alleged war criminals.

Shortly after the Japanese capitulation, a War Crimes Act was passed in the Commonwealth under which the power to convene military courts under the Act was delegated by the Governor-General in council to certain military commanders and senior staff officers in the field, and a special staff was set up at Australian Army Headquarters to deal with war crimes.

A number of 'War Crimes Sections' were set up by this Headquarters, two of which co-operated with the British in Singapore, and the Americans in Tokyo. The other section operated in New Guinea, and a number of other Pacific territories.

The Australian War Crimes Section in Singapore dealt mainly with cases in Malaya, on the Burma–Siam Railway, and the Netherlands East Indies, and worked in close co-operation with the British war crimes investigation authorities in Singapore, and with the Dutch military authorities in Java.

Many Australian military courts were set up for the trial of alleged war criminals and others were tried by British military courts upon which an Australian officer sat as a member. This network of investigation covered a very wide area, Malaya, Burma, Java, New Guinea, New Britain, the Celebes, Timor, the Ceram Islands, including Amboina, British and Dutch Borneo and a number of other territories.

Altogether over eight hundred Japanese war criminals were tried, of whom slightly less than one third were acquitted.

* * * *

At his interrogation in March 1946, the former Japanese Prime Minister and war leader, Tojo, made this statement.

> Since the end of the war I have read about the inhumane acts committed by the Japanese Army and Navy. These were certainly not the intention of those in authority, namely the General Staff, or the War or Navy Departments or myself. We did not even suspect that such things had happened. The Emperor especially, because of his benevolence, would have had a contrary feeling. Such acts are not permissible in Japan, the character of the Japanese people is such that they believe that neither Heaven nor Earth would permit such things. It will be too bad if people in the world believe that these inhumane acts are the result of Japanese character.

Regarding Tojo's statement that the Japanese war leaders did not even suspect that atrocities and other war crimes were being committed, the International Military Tribunal at Tokyo said this in its judgment:

> During a period of several months the Tribunal heard evidence from witnesses who testified in detail to atrocities committed in all theatres of war on a scale so vast, yet following so common a pattern that only one conclusion is possible. The atrocities were either secretly ordered or wilfully permitted by the Japanese Government or individual members thereof, and by the leaders of the armed forces.

Throughout the Sino–Japanese and Pacific wars, in every theatre of operations, unspeakable cruelties and merciless tortures were inflicted upon thousands of Allied prisoners of war and innocent civilians by all ranks of the Japanese

[309]

armed forces, without any compunction and, for the most part, without any feelings of compassion whatsoever.

We are the Knights of Bushido, of the Order of the Rising Sun. We do not execute at sunset, but at sunrise.

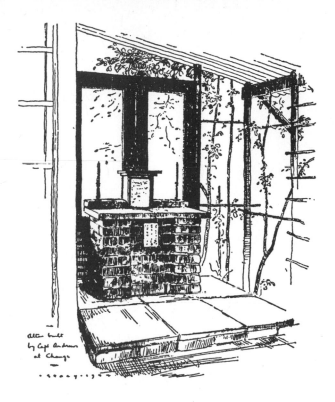

altar built
by Capt Andrews
at Changi

When the Selerang prisoner of war camp was evacuated in June 1944, and all Churches in that area were dismantled for removal to the Gaol area, a Memorial Altar was built by Rev. Captain E. L. Andrews, close to the old site of Holy Trinity.

He left a scroll with the following wording in Japanese:

THIS ALTAR HAS BEEN ERECTED AS A MEMORIAL TO THE FALLEN. OF YOUR CHARITY PLEASE RETAIN THIS BUILDING UNBROKEN, UNTIL THE END OF THE WAR.

This is the sole surviving landmark of the many churches built in the Changi area prior to the final move to the Gaol. As far as is known it is still standing.

APPENDIX

SOME LEGAL ASPECTS OF
WAR CRIMES TRIALS

I. THE PLEA OF 'SUPERIOR ORDERS'

THE plea of 'superior orders' has been raised by the defence in war crime trials more frequently than any other.

To understand the doctrine one must know something oɪ the history of its evolution. In 1919 an International Commission was appointed to consider and report to the Allied powers on the question of the immunity of heads of State in respect of the conduct of the war. This body was known as the '1919 Commission on Responsibilities', and when recommending the trial of heads of State and other high State administrators they made these reservations:

> We desire to say that civil and military authorities cannot be relieved from responsibility by the mere fact that a higher authority might have been convicted of the same offence. It will be for the Court to decide whether the plea of 'superior orders' is sufficient to acquit the person charged from responsibility.

Although there was not at that time any international judicial authority on the subject, there were few writers on international law who had not rejected the doctrine that the receipt of 'superior orders' was a complete justification of war crimes.

The German Code of Military Law provided that a soldier must execute all orders undeterred by the fear of legal consequences, but it added that this would not excuse him in cases where he must have known with certainty that the order was illegal.

[313]

This view was held and expressed by the German Supreme Court in Leipzig in 1921. The Court was trying two lieutenants, part of the ship's company of a German U-boat which, during the period of hostilities, had sunk the *Llandovery Castle*, a British hospital ship. In accordance with the orders of the submarine's commander to leave no trace, the two junior officers gave orders to fire on the hospital ship's lifeboats.

The judgment of this Court is of tremendous importance for this reason. Since the last war ended the impression has gained ground that the statements of the law on this subject which were inserted in the British and American manuals of military law in 1944 did not follow the accepted rule of many years' standing. Although this impression is mistaken there are reasons for its existence. In the British *Manual of Military Law* certain revisions and amplifications were made in 1914. In a chapter headed 'Laws and Usages of War on Land' the doctrine regarding 'superior orders' was declared to be as follows:

> Members of the armed forces who commit such violations of the recognized rules of warfare, as are ordered by their Government or their commander, are not war criminals and cannot, therefore, be punished by the enemy. He may punish the officials or commanders responsible for such orders if they fall into his hands, but otherwise he may only resort to other means of obtaining redress.

A similar statement appeared in the United States *Rules of Land Warfare*.

Under the heading, 'The Duty of a Soldier', an extensive correspondence on the plea of 'superior orders', in which I took part, was conducted in the columns of the *Daily Telegraph* in 1955. In one of these letters I had pointed out that the statement which appeared in the 1914 *Manual*, and remained without amendment until 1944, was based on the fifth edition of *Oppenheim's International Law*, which was corrected in the sixth edition, published in 1940; that it was not only inconsistent with the views of most writers upon the subject, but also with the decision of the German Supreme Court after World War I. The Court, applying the German Military Penal Code, which has already been referred to above, said in its judgment that the commander's order to leave no trace did not free the accused from guilt. A subordinate who obeyed the order of his superior officer was liable to punishment if it were known to him that such order involved a contravention of the law, in this case International Law. This applied to the two accused, the judgment continued, though it should be urged in favour of military subordinates that they are under no obligation to question the order of a superior officer, and they can count on its legality, but no such confidence can be held to exist if such an order is universally known to everybody, including the accused, to be, without any doubt whatever, against the law. This happens only in rare and exceptional cases but this case is precisely one of them, for in the present incident it was perfectly clear to the accused that killing defenceless people in the lifeboats could be nothing else but a breach of the law.

In estimating punishment it should be borne in mind that the principal guilt rests with the submarine's commander under whose orders the accused acted. They should certainly have refused to obey the order. This would require a specially high degree of resolution, and this fact, therefore, justifies the recommendation of mitigating circumstances in determining the punishment under the State Penal Code.

A severe sentence must, however, be passed.

In order to appreciate how mistaken is the claim that the statement in the 1914 *Manual of Military Law* had been the accepted rule for so many years, it is only necessary to remember the above judgment which showed that as early as 1921 it was not the accepted doctrine in Germany.

'It stood unchallenged for thirty years from 1912 to

1944,' wrote Brigadier-General Sir James Edmonds, the official historian of the 1914–18 War on the Western Front and the officer in charge of the military branch of the Historical Section of the Cabinet Office from 1919–45. It certainly stood unamended in the *Manual of Military Law* for all those years, though it is difficult to understand why. One explanation is that it related to a subject which between 1918 and 1940 was of no immediate concern to the Army, and its inadequacy only became apparent when renewed interest naturally arose during the last war. That it was not amended until the tide of war was flowing strongly in our favour is extremely unfortunate, for this has persuaded some people that it was the law which had been conveniently changed rather than its mis-statement corrected. Nevertheless it does not alter the fact that it was *not* a correct statement of the almost universally accepted International Law.

The German Supreme Court's judgment shows that German law is in line on this subject with International Law as accepted in other countries, and in itself is a refutation of the argument put forward by many German and Japanese counsel at the various war crime trials since the war, namely that British Military Courts who followed the amended version of Chapter XIV paragraph 443 in the *Manual of Military Law* were applying *ex post facto* legislation. The *Manual* is no legislative authority and the fact that for some reason a mis-statement of the law therein remained so long uncorrected is no justification for such argument.

Those who hold such strong views on the plea of 'superior orders', which are not supported by the facts, protest that to 'make a soldier in part responsible for the results of carrying out an order given to him by his lawful commander might prove harmful to military discipline'. One of them has said 'the essence of a soldier is that he should march, shoot and obey'. Theirs not to reason why.

No one would suggest that the Germans are blind to the necessity for unquestioning obedience; yet what do we find? That the German Federal Government in the Draft

Article IX of the Soldatengesetz (the law which lays down the rules of conduct for the new German Army) expounds the same doctrine as was established by the judgment of the German Supreme Court in the *Llandovery Castle* case thirty years ago. The soldier must not carry out any order that would lead him to commit war crimes, the Article states, but if he does not know, and the circumstances do not indicate to him, that by obedience to his orders he would commit a crime, no question of his guilt can arise. This does not reduce the status of the soldier to a mere automaton, it does not propound the doctrine that the 'essence of a soldier is that he should march, shoot and obey'; it states what I believe is the law, and has been the law for a great number of years.

There can be no dispute that it is the primary duty of a soldier to obey the orders of his officer, but if the order is obviously illegal on the face of it, the soldier has an equal duty to refuse to carry it out. This may not be easy, and it is for this reason that the soldier's difficult position should be taken into account as a mitigating factor when considering what the sentence should be.

If the soldier is to be regarded as nothing but an automaton, it follows that a young British platoon-commander fighting in enemy territory, who is ordered by his colonel to march all the women and children into the village church, fill it with straw, and then set it on fire, as the Germans did in 1944 at Oradour-sur-Glâne, has no alternative but to obey. I have yet to meet the officer in the British Army who would not unhesitatingly refuse to carry out such an order, and gladly face the consequences.

It is interesting and gratifying to know that those who are now raising Germany's new Army do not share so barbarous a view of the soldier's duties.

What was the amendment to the 1914 version of the *Manual of Military Law* which was so belatedly promulgated? It was as follows:

The fact that a rule of warfare has been violated in pursuance of an order of the belligerent Government or of an individual belligerent does not deprive the act in question of its character as a war crime, neither does it in principle confer upon the perpetrator immunity from punishment by the injured belligerent. Undoubtedly a Court confronted with the plea of 'superior orders' adduced in justification of a war crime is bound to take into consideration the fact that obedience to military orders *not obviously unlawful* is the duty of every member of the Armed Forces, and that the soldier cannot, in conditions of war discipline, be expected to weigh scrupulously the legal merits of the order received. The question, however, is governed by the main principle that members of the Armed Forces are bound to obey lawful orders only, and that they cannot escape liability if, in obedience to a command, they commit acts which both violate the unchallenged rules of warfare and outrage the general sentiments of humanity.

That passage, it is true, does not in so many words make ignorance of the legality of an order a complete legal defence. Nevertheless, it indicates to the Court that they should not convict the accused of a war crime committed in consequence of the order of his superior, unless well satisfied that he *well knew* he was committing an act which both violated the unchallenged rules of warfare and outraged the general sentiments of humanity. In a somewhat extensive experience of British war crime trials, I know of none in which the Judge Advocate, or if there was no Judge Advocate, then the Law Member, failed to remind the Court of their duty to satisfy themselves of the accused's knowledge of the illegality of the order before convicting him.

In practice, therefore, ignorance of the order's illegality did furnish a complete defence, and it is a pity that the amendment of 1944 to the *Manual of Military Law* did not state this categorically. The general upshot of the many judicial decisions on this plea of 'superior orders' is that if the order in question was, or must be presumed to have been, known to the accused as illegal, or was illegal on the face of it, the accused cannot then rely on the defence of 'superior orders'.

After the fall of Singapore in February 1942 over five thousand Chinese residents were massacred, in pursuance of an order issued by General Yamashita. The order stated that all the Chinese resident on Singapore Island who harboured anti-Japanese sentiments should be killed. These orders were carried out to the letter, and there cannot have been any doubt in the minds of the subordinate commanders who did so that General Yamashita's order would 'both violate the unchallenged rules of warfare and outrage the general sentiments of humanity'.

In my opinion a proper interpretation of the law regarding the acceptance of the plea of 'superior orders' is that ignorance of the illegality of the order should constitute a legal excuse, but the onus should be on the accused to satisfy the Court, having regard to all the circumstances, that he could not reasonably have known that it was illegal. This plea was raised in a great number of Japanese war crimes trials, and although the plea has rarely been successful, it has in many cases been accepted as raising mitigating factors.

At the trial of Gozawa Sadachi and others at Singapore, in 1946, a British Military Court in passing sentence addressed the following language to some of the accused.

Chiba Masami, your participation in the horrible scene which has been described in this Court is undoubted. But it would be unjust to deal with you on the same footing as your superior officers. The sentence of the Court, subject to confirmation, is that you be kept in prison for the term of seven years.

Tanno, Shozo, Yabi, Jinichiro, the Court considers that your brutality was carried out under the orders of your superior officers, but you were not unwilling brutes nor unversed in brutality. The sentence of the Court, therefore, subject to confirmation, is that you be kept in prison for the term of three years.

II. THE PLEA OF 'MILITARY NECESSITY'

This plea was frequently put forward at the trials of high-ranking German and Japanese officers. It was contested that as the purpose of war is to overpower the enemy, the achievement of that purpose justifies any means, including, in cases of necessity, the violation of the laws of war if such violations will afford either the means of escape from imminent danger or the overpowering of the enemy. This theory dates far back in the history of warfare. It originated and found recognition in those times when warfare was not regulated by the laws of war but by usages only. It is not without significance that it is of German origin, though by no means do all German writers on International Law endorse it. One of them, Strupp, disposed of it in these words: 'If this thing were justified no laws of warfare would exist, for every rule might be declared impracticable on the grounds that it was contrary to military necessity.'

In his summing up in the von Manstein trial, the Judge Advocate said, 'Once the usages of war have assumed the status of laws they cannot be overridden by necessity, except in those special cases where the law itself makes provision for that eventuality.'

When Lieutenant-General Baba was tried by an Australian Military Court at Rabaul, in 1947, he put forward the defence that the evacuation, by road, in December 1944 and May 1945, of about one thousand British and Australian prisoners of war from a camp at Sandakan was 'operationally necessary'.

The order for the first march had been given before Baba took over command in Borneo, but he admitted that he was aware of the poor physical condition of the prisoners, and that he ordered a reconnaissance of the country through which they were to march. During the march, which has already been described in Chapter VIII, a large number of prisoners died as a result of the hardships they had to suffer.

Baba received a report of this march early in 1945.

Nevertheless, he ordered the evacuation of the remaining five hundred and forty prisoners over the same route in May 1945. This second march proved even more disastrous than the first. The Court did not allow the plea.

In the preamble of the Hague Convention IV it is expressly stated that the rules of warfare were framed with regard to military necessities, 'the provisions of the Convention having been inspired by the desire to diminish the violations of war *as far as military requirements permit*'.[1]

The above defence has been constantly rejected by the accepted authorities on International Law, and by the tribunals before which it has been made, although the court which tried von Manstein accepted it in respect of the charges regarding his scorched earth policy and destruction of supplies.

III. GUERRILLA WARFARE

As a further instance of the plea of military necessity, it has often been argued by the Defence at war crimes trials that a commander is entitled to take any measures which are necessary for the protection of his troops against guerrilla bands, partisans, etc., provided he does not indulge in arbitrary methods. Furthermore, that only so long as they remain peaceful, are civilian inhabitants of the occupied territory entitled to protection, and if individual inhabitants commit hostile acts against the occupation the latter may call upon the former to help in preventing a re-occurrence. If the occupation does not receive such help, he is entitled to punish the inhabitants as a means of ensuring that further hostile acts are not committed.

The same submission has been made regarding *francs-tireurs*, namely that they are not entitled to any form of trial either by the laws or customs of war and may be shot on capture.

It is, therefore, necessary to consider the position of the irregular forces of belligerents. Sometimes the armed forces

[1] Author's italics.

x

of belligerents consisted throughout the war of their regular armies only, but frequently irregular forces took part. These irregular forces may be of two kinds:

(1) Those authorized by the belligerents, such as the Home Guard set up in 1940 in Great Britain, and constituted part of the armed forces of the Crown, and

(2) Those who act on their own initiative and on their own account without special authority.

Since the beginning of the present century even the latter category of armed forces has always been entitled to the privileges due to members of the armed forces of the belligerents provided it complied with certain conditions and fought in units, however small.

Such individuals as take up arms singly and severally (*francs-tireurs*) are still liable to be treated as war criminals and shot, but only after a proper trial.

It sometimes happens that on the approach of an invading enemy a belligerent calls the whole population to arms, in which event, provided they have some organization, and comply with the laws and usages of war, the combatants who take part in such a *levée-en-masse* enjoy the privileges due to members of the armed forces. The *levée-en-masse* may even be spontaneous as when the population of a territory not yet occupied takes up arms to resist the invading enemy without having time to organize themselves under responsible commanders or to comply with the conditions already mentioned. Such persons also enjoy the privileges due to the armed forces provided they carry arms openly and otherwise comply with the laws and usages of war.

The Prosecution in von Manstein's case argued that it was abundantly clear even from the evidence produced by the Defence that a *levée-en-masse* was organized by the USSR from the very commencement of the invasion, and that all those who took part in it consequently enjoyed the privileges due to the members of the armed forces, provided they complied with the requirements and that *whether they did so was a matter for investigation and consideration in respect of each individual concerned.*

The words I have placed in italics are of supreme importnace. In a case like von Manstein's, where all such persons were shot without trial it matters not whether the individual was entitled to be made a prisoner of war or could be treated as a war criminal and shot. The fact that such a person had been captured under circumstances which rendered him suspect of guerrilla warfare could not of itself justify his being treated on the basis of that suspicion having been proved correct. In its judgment in the Hostages Trial the Tribunal dealt with this question in these words.

> Suspicion is the state of mind of the accuser, and not the state of mind or an act of the one accused. It is a monstrous proposition that the state of mind of the accuser shall be the determining factor in the absence of evidence of guilt whether the accused shall, or shall not, be summarily executed.

There is also the decision in the important case of Rauter, an Obergruppenführer of the Waffen SS, who was charged with committing wholesale crimes against the Dutch population, including many Jews whom he sent to Germany as slave labour, and for conducting reprisals and murdering hostages. His case was reported in the *War Crime Law Reports*, Volume XIV. This case went to the Netherlands Court of Appeal, and according to their decision the relationship between the occupying power and the inhabitants of the occupied territory is guided by the following principle.

> The inhabitants of occupied territories are expected to maintain a peaceful attitude towards the occupation. This, however, is not in the nature of a legal obligation, and it does not in law prevent the inhabitants from resorting to hostile acts towards the occupation. The main legal consequence of this situation is that where the inhabitants commit hostile acts, the occupant is not relieved from his duty to abide by the laws and customs of war governing his conduct towards the inhabitants and, there-

fore, he may not commit acts of arbitrary revenge against them. . . .

It is required that the offender should be given a fair trial, full protection of his right to defence, and no excessive punishment may be imposed, having regard to the nature of the offence and the degree of the accused's guilt.

In Russia, for example, *franc-tireur*, terrorist, partisan and guerrilla, each was entitled to a trial which he never received. The Judge Advocate put it to the Court in these words:

That the Russians indulged in guerrilla warfare on a large scale is obvious. That it constituted a constant menace to the German forces is equally clear. No one who could be proved to have acted as a guerrilla could claim to be entitled to the status of a prisoner of war. This pre-supposes some form of trial, just as in the case of a spy, and it is no use a commanding general saying that he had no time for trials. The rules of war cannot be disregarded merely because it is inconvenient to obey them.

In Manila and the country round it hundreds of guerrillas were put to death without any form of trial. This action, without doubt, constituted a war crime.

IV. THE PLEA OF 'LEGITIMATE REPRISALS'

This plea has two aspects: it may be used to justify acts between belligerents which would not otherwise be legal, or it may be quoted as justifying measures taken by an occupying power against the population of an occupied territory which would otherwise be illegal. The taking of reprisals against prisoners of war is forbidden by Article II of the Geneva Prisoner of War Convention.

During the last war terrible reprisals were often taken by the German and Japanese armed forces indiscriminately against large numbers of the inhabitants of occupied territory. Perhaps the three most generally known are the massacre of almost all the inhabitants of Oradour-sur-Glâne, supposed to have been taken as a reprisal for the shooting of one German dispatch rider some fifty miles away, the killing of all the inhabitants of Lidice in Czechoslovakia as a reprisal for the murder of Heydrich, and the murder of over three hundred reprisal prisoners in the Ardeatine Caves near Rome upon the orders of Hitler, carried out by Field-Marshal Albert Kesselring, then the Supreme German Commander in Italy.

Many similar reprisals were carried out in Burma during the last few months of the late war against the inhabitants of villages who were supposed to have given assistance to British paratroopers and Burmese guerrillas.

There is a distinction, though of no interest to the victim, between hostages and reprisal prisoners. The former are taken into custody in order to guarantee with their lives the future good conduct of the community to which they belong; the latter are arrested if some incident has taken place and are put to death by way of retaliation or reprisal. In either event innocent victims forfeit their lives for offences committed by others.

Although in certain circumstances the taking of hostages was, before the Geneva Convention of 1949, permitted under International Law, their subsequent execution, except for capital offences of which they had been properly convicted, was clearly forbidden by Article 50 of the Hague Convention of 1907 which reads, 'No collective penalty, pecuniary or otherwise, can be decreed against populations for individual acts for which they cannot be held jointly responsible'.

The international law regarding reprisals as it existed during the last war, and before the Geneva Convention of 1949, can be stated as follows: Reprisals should not be undertaken before there has been an inquiry, and a genuine effort made to apprehend those responsible for the incidents which justify reprisals being taken. They must never be excessive, and should not exceed the degree of violation committed by the enemy.

The Germans frequently issued orders that for every German soldier or civilian killed, one hundred men taken from the place where the incident occurred would be shot. Should several soldiers or civilians be killed or wounded all the men of the place would be shot, the place set on fire and the women and children interned in concentration camps.

When a Japanese force was dispatched to carry out a reprisal on the inhabitants of the village of Kalagon its commanding officer was authorized, if necessary, 'to kill all the inhabitants'.

Such orders were clearly in breach of accepted International Law. They were undertaken arbitrarily, without any adequate steps being taken to discover the offenders, and far exceeded in their severity what was either proper or necessary. They were not real reprisals as the term is understood by international jurists. They were nothing more nor less than brutal acts of indiscriminate vengeance which both violated the unchallenged rules of warfare and outraged the general sentiments of humanity.

INDEX

INDEX